FALLING FOR ANOTHER DARCY

LOVE MANOR ROMANTIC COMEDY

KATE O'KEEFFE

WILD LIME BOOKS

Edited by Wendi Baker
Cover design by Sue Traynor
Copyright © 2021 Kate O'Keeffe

Wild Lime
Books

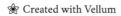 Created with Vellum

ABOUT THIS BOOK

First comes love, then comes marriage, then comes baby in the baby carriage. Right?

That's the way the song goes, anyway. For Emma Brady, marrying her Mr. Darcy was a road to happiness that is about to take a sharp turn to trouble. Creating a tiny Mr. Darcy isn't exactly proving to be easy. Sure, being newly-weds mean they're more than happy to give it a good shot, but as time ticks along, Emma and Sebastian's efforts come to nothing.

It's time to call in the big guns.

For Emma, that means mood swings, hot flashes, ovulation kits, and more needles than a haystack. Add that to an increasingly disapproving Granny, and Sebastian and Emma's love is being put to the test in a way they never saw coming.

Will they get the family they so desperately want? And will their love survive? Or will Emma's fairy tale ending with her Mr. Darcy slip between her fingers?

ALSO BY KATE O'KEEFFE

It's Complicated Series:
Never Fall for Your Back-Up Guy
Never Fall for Your Enemy
Never Fall for Your Fake Fiancé
Never Fall for Your One that Got Away

Love Manor Romantic Comedy Series:
Dating Mr. Darcy
Marrying Mr. Darcy
Falling for Another Darcy
Falling for Mr. Bingley (spin-off novella)

High Tea Series:
No More Bad Dates
No More Terrible Dates
No More Horrible Dates

Cozy Cottage Café Series:
One Last First Date
Two Last First Dates
Three Last First Dates
Four Last First Dates

Wellywood Romantic Comedy Series:
Styling Wellywood
Miss Perfect Meets Her Match

Falling for Grace

Standalone title:
One Way Ticket

Writing as Lacey Sinclair:
Manhattan Cinderella
The Right Guy

CHAPTER 1

One year. One blissful year. That's twelve months of utter, unrivaled, delirious happiness. Twelve months of being married to Sebastian Huntington-Ross, my Mr. Darcy. And it has been nothing short of perfect. Everything I could have ever dreamed it to be, and so much more.

It's love, pure and simple. And I tell you, when you find it, hold onto to it *tight*. It's the best feeling in the world.

Sure, there are people out there who were praying we'd fail (I'm looking at you, Granny-slash-Geraldine-slash-Evil Plotter Woman), but for us it's been smooth sailing. A year of harmonious matrimony.

Ugh. That makes me sound freaking *ancient*.

Which I'm not yet. Thirty is the new twenty, right? Or something like that, anyway.

After our beautiful wedding at the picture-perfect chapel of my dreams back home in Houston, Texas, I moved permanently into Martinston, Sebastian's ancestral home. It is the most stunning manor house in all of England, bar none. Not that I'm biased, you understand. With its ridiculously high ceilings, exquisite antique furniture, and gorgeous gardens, fields, and woods for as far as the eye can see, the place is fairy tale castle-level amazing. The Emma I was before I went on the *Dating Mr. Darcy* reality TV show would never have imagined she could live in a place like this. The Emma whose entire apartment could fit into Martinston's kitchen.

Yet still, here I am. Mrs. Huntington-Ross, Lady Martinston.

Yup, after a year, I'm still not used to that one.

"Come on, Brady. It's about to start." Sebastian pats the seat next to him on the sofa, remote control in hand, his warm brown eyes speckled with the chunks of gold smiling up at me. The TV is on pause, the wine is ready to be drunk, and my super hot, super amazing husband of one whole year is waiting for me to snuggle up to him on the sofa for an idyllic evening together. He looks like a cross between the smooth James Bond and Hollywood hunk Henry Cavill. I mean, seriously. What's a girl to do?

I drag my attention from him. "I'm trying to find Frank," I say as I make tsking noises. "He hasn't been out in ages, and the last thing I want is for him to leave a kitty deposit some-where for your granny to find. Again."

"That did not go down well. She turned so pale, I thought she was going to faint."

I think of Sebastian's elderly granny with her alabaster skin that quite possibly has never seen the sun. She's told me with a sense of pride that she's as pale as the day she was born, thanks to never having had to "toil in the fields" or "sell posies on the busy streets." Geraldine Huntington-Ross thinks she lives in a Dickens novel.

"Honey, she always looks like that," I say with a wry smile.

"That is fair to say. But the point is she wasn't happy. And an unhappy Granny is not a good thing."

My mind darts to the way in which she only grudgingly accepts me as Sebastian's wife. Oh, and the plot she devised with Sebastian's childhood friend, Jilly Fotherington, to cut me out of the picture and take my place. You could say I'm reading too much into things, but I'm pretty sure the woman doesn't like me.

I get down on all fours, scanning under each of the chairs in the room for my cat. "For some reason Frank has decided to play a game of cat and mouse with me right now, and I don't like my chances."

"Well, it's pouring rain out there tonight, and he *is* a cat. They're not exactly known for their love of water."

I lift the fringed skirt on a high-backed reading chair. His golden eyes glint at me. "Aha! There you are." I reach under the chair and rub my fingers together. "Come on, Frank," I coo in my best nonthreatening *I'm not going to make you go out in the rain to do your kitty business* voice.

When he doesn't respond, I reach into my pocket and pull out his favorite fishy treats. "I've got some of these. I know how much you love them."

Frank, it would seem, is not a cat to be asked twice. He snatches the first of the treats from my fingers and makes short work of it, his purr telling me he'd like some more. He follows the trail out, and soon enough I've got him wrapped up in my arms as I nuzzle his soft, warm fur. "Okay, mister. Do you think it's time to go outside and do your thing?"

He shoots me a look that says, "Can't you see it's raining out there, human?"—I'm fluent in Frank—and I think better of it, plunking myself down next to my husband to feed Frank some more treats as he snuggles into my lap.

Sebastian raises a questioning brow in my direction.

"What? He can use the litter box."

The edges of his mouth pull into a smile as he shakes his head at me. "Shall we watch the show?"

I wrap my arm around his and lace our fingers together. "The first ever episode of *Saving Pemberley*, starring the incredibly cute and relatable lord and lady of the manor? Heck, yes."

He chuckles and presses "play," and the frozen image on the screen bursts into life as orchestral music fills the room.

I let out a squeal as the show title appears on the screen and then pans to an image of Sebastian and I dressed as Mr. Darcy and Miss Elizabeth Bennet. Or Mrs. Darcy, more accurately. We started filming a few weeks after we got married, and there was something very romantic about dressing up in our Regency finery once more.

Johnathan's handsome, smiling face fills the screen. Not only is Johnathan Sebastian's best friend, but he's also the presenter on *Saving Pemberley* and *Dating Mr. Darcy*.

"Hello, and welcome to a very special show. Tonight, we embark on a new adventure, starring Sebastian Huntington-Ross, your Mr. Darcy."

I give Sebastian's arm an excited squeeze.

"You fell in love with him on Dating Mr. Darcy *as he searched for his Miss Elizabeth Bennet. Now, you can watch him and Emma, his new bride, work to save the beautiful manor house they call home. Will they be able to preserve this priceless home for future generations? Or will it need to be sold to be used as a shelter for stray dogs, or worse yet, demolished to allow for new housing, its priceless artefacts donated to museums or sold off for a few measly quid."*

It's my turn to raise my eyebrows. "That's a bit dramatic, isn't it?"

"Drama sells, apparently."

"Were we ever considering housing stray dogs at Martinston?"

He presses the *pause* button. "As Heather likes to put it," he begins, referring to Heather McCabe, the head of the production company behind *Saving Pemberley*, "the truth is always a rainbow of gray."

"Fifty shades?" I waggle my eyebrows at Sebastian, and he laughs.

"Something like that. Let's keep watching." He presses *play* once more.

"Over the course of the coming weeks, you'll go on a journey with Mr. Darcy and his bride to answer these questions. Ladies and gentlemen," Johnathan says with an expansive arm gesture, *"I give you* Saving Pemberley." The camera pans out to take in an aerial shot of Martinston in all its aristocratic splendor.

"The house looks good," Sebastian comments.

"Who are you kidding? It looks phenomenal."

We settle in to watch the episode, Frank, his tummy full of treats, now curled up in my lap sleeping soundly. There are lots of recaps of Sebastian on *Dating Mr. Darcy*, and a cheesy segment with the two of us sitting side by side in the great hall, grinning at one another like we'd just won the lottery. Which is exactly what it felt like to me when I married my gorgeous husband.

And it still does today.

The camera focusses mainly on Sebastian, although they do show a clip of me with my long dark hair tied up in a sensible ponytail, wearing a khaki green puffer jacket as I water some plants in a pair of rubber boots—called "wellies" here for reasons unknown to me—which is something I've never done at Martinston. The garden sits firmly within Sebastian's mother, Jemima's domain. But the production crew told me to do it, and so I did it happily.

The show wraps up with Johnathan asking whether us opening the house up to the paying public will be enough to save "Pemberley" from having to be sold off.

Spoiler alert: it's not enough, but they won't find that out until the next episode when we open the now wildly successful café we named "Elizabeth's" in memory of my reality show alter ego. That combined with ticket sales has kept us in the black, and any concern that we and Sebastian's family won't have a roof over our heads has been tucked up snugly in bed.

Sebastian switches the TV off and turns to me. "That wasn't so bad, was it?"

"Other than the part when they showed those dogs, who aren't even ours, growling and barking at the gate, it was pretty good."

"That's what they call 'artistic license.'"

"Or outright lies?" I tease.

He laughs as he reaches for me. "Come here, you." He lifts me onto his lap, and Frank darts from my lap in protest. My legs straddling him, he pulls me into a kiss that leaves me tingling.

"You looked so sexy in those wellies. Do you think I could get a private viewing of you in those and...let's say nothing else?"

"Nothing else? Sebastian Huntington-Ross, I am deeply outraged."

"Are you now?" he asks with a laugh that rumbles through me.

"I didn't know you've got a thing for gardeners."

"Actually," he says with another kiss that has my head spinning, "I've got a thing for my hot Texan wife."

"I'm guessing you'll want me to team a ten-gallon hat with those wellies, huh?"

"Now we're talking."

As he reaches under my top and slides his hands up my bare back, sending a jolt of anticipation through me, I hear the creak of the door and look up in surprise to see not only Sebastian's mom, but his granny with a disapproving look on her lined face.

Not that this is anything new. The day that woman gives

me a look that's *not* disapproving I think I might faint from shock.

I instantly dismount Sebastian and readjust my top in an attempt not to appear as though we were about to engage in, well, *marital activity*. We might be a newly married couple who do what newly married couples do, but getting caught out by my mother-in-law and judgmental grandmother-in-law still puts a halt to proceedings pretty quick. As you would expect.

"Mother, Granny," Sebastian says in a surprisingly steady voice as he rises to his feet. I've had to get used to that here. Sebastian always stands whenever his mom or grandmother enter a room. It's super formal and weird to me. Where I'm from, you only got up to go fetch another Coke.

"Don't let us interrupt, you two," Jemima trills in an unnaturally high voice. She must be feeling about as comfortable as I am right now. "Come, Geraldine. Let's, err… go for a stroll in the garden."

Geraldine scoffs. "Jemima, it's after nine at night and it's raining cats and dogs out there. Have you gone completely mad?" She clunks her way across the room with the aid of her cane and sits down carefully on one of the seats facing us. "It's fortuitous that we found you in such a position."

I blink at her in disbelief. It is?

Jemima is still hovering by the door, clearly uncomfortable. "What about the library, Geraldine? There's a book collection I thought you might be interested in. I only came across it a few weeks ago, and I think you'll find it quite fascinating. It's about the history of bridges in the British Isles, which is a thoroughly enthralling topic—"

"Oh, Jemima," she scolds. "I haven't got the least interest in bridges. Take a seat, will you?"

"But—"

"Now."

Defeated, Jemima replies, "All right." She slinks into another one of the armchairs and shoots us an apologetic smile.

"We thought you were both out for the evening," Sebastian begins.

"We're back," Geraldine replies, pointing out the obvious.

"How are you this evening, ma'am?" I say to Geraldine as she steadily lowers herself into a seat by the fire with the aid of her cane. It has a brass handle in the shape of a wolf, which appropriately casts her as a Bond villain. All that's missing is the hairless cat.

"I've told you before, Emma. In England 'ma'am' is what we call the Queen. Please remember to call me 'Granny' now that you're family. You're no longer on your Texas ranch here."

I open my mouth to reply and shut it again. Having grown up in a modest house in inner-city Houston, the only time I've been on a Texas ranch was when I was filming *Dating Mr. Darcy*. "I forgot...Granny. Habit, I guess. You can take the girl out of Texas, as they say."

Geraldine purses her lips in obvious distaste. "Quite. Now. I have something I must say to you both."

Must she?

"It's gratifying to see you're still engaging in what is characteristically considered the honeymoon phase of a marriage."

Sebastian's eyes find mine briefly before he replies, "Thank you?" Because what do you say to that? *Yes, we're at it whenever we get the chance. Can't get enough of it, actually. We're at it like the proverbial rabbits. Our room, the living room, the garden, even your room when you're out at the opera* (okay, we've never actually done it in Geraldine's room, and nor do we plan to, but you get the picture).

She steeples her fingers, fixing us with her glare. "An heir. That's what we need."

"An heir?" I swallow. She's already made it abundantly clear that as Lady Martinston, it's my duty to provide the family with the next generation. The first time she mentioned it, in fact, we'd literally been married less than three minutes. You've got to admire the old girl's tenacity, I guess.

"Yes," she snaps, "an heir. How often are you engaging in marital relations?"

"Mummy, I hardly think—" Jemima protests as Sebastian's eyes widen at me.

"Let them answer, Jemima," she quips. "It's been a year and still not even a sign. You're not getting any younger, you know, Emma. I'm certain your fertility has already begun to wane. When I was your age, I'd finished having my children."

I offer her a weak smile. *That was because it was the 1800s and there was no TV.*

"Granny, we haven't even had that conversation yet," Sebastian says. "Give us a chance, please."

"What's the delay? You're clearly raring to go if that little display earlier is anything to go by. Make it *mean* something, my dear boy."

I suck in air, every part of me cringing. The mood has gone from sexy rubber boot fun to creating an "heir" in two minutes flat.

Could this get any more awkward?

"Thank you for your concern, Granny, but when Emma and I decide we're ready to start a family, we will be sure *not* to tell you until we actually have something to tell you."

"Does that mean you're already trying?" Jemima asks, a healthy dollop of hope in her voice. "Because we can leave right now and let you get on with it if you like."

Oh, no. *Awkward!*

Jemima rises to her feet. "Can't we, Geraldine?"

"I suppose," Geraldine grumps.

I squeeze my eyes shut, fantasizing that I'm *not* in the living room with my mother- and grandmother-in-law, my clothes and hair disheveled next to my husband as they discuss our sex life.

"Good-bye, you two," Sebastian says with a tone of finality in his voice.

Jemima bustles over to the door, clearly keen to get far away from this whole thing as quickly as possible, while Geraldine rises from her seat onto her creaky bones as though she's an arthritic sloth in no hurry to get anywhere.

It takes for*ever*, stretching the awkwardness out to a breaking point.

Eventually, she reaches the door and turns back to us. "Missionary position. That's the best for procreation. That's all your grandfather and I ever did, and we had all the children we wanted."

Why did she have to put that image into my head. Why?

"Good-bye, Granny," Sebastian says firmly, and thankfully, she leaves the room, closing the door after her.

Alone once more in the cavernous room, we catch one another's eyes and instantly dissolve into peals of embarrassed laughter. Catching his breath, Sebastian says, "I'm so sorry about that, Brady. The word awkward doesn't even begin to describe that exchange."

"Missionary position?"

Sebastian's shoulders shake as he laughs. "Granny can be very direct when she wants to be."

I think of the way in which she announced that I wasn't good enough for her grandson and that I would be doing everyone a big favor if I just simply disappeared. "Ah, yes. That's very true."

He laces his fingers in mine and claims my lips with a

kiss. "Brady, I have an idea. How about we grab those wellies of yours and head up to our bedroom away from any prying eyes."

"And lock the door?" I ask.

His eyes sparkle as his face pulls into his sexy grin. "Lock it, bolt it, and hide the key."

CHAPTER 2

"*D*id you watch the show, Mom?" I ask as I sit in the weak winter sun in the garden, wrapped up in a puffer jacket, with a scarf and wooly hat, my earbuds in place. I should probably be in the warmth inside, but being from Texas, the whole getting properly cold in winter thing is still exciting to me.

"Of course I watched it, honey. It was wonderful, and Pemberley looked just as incredible as it is in real life. So pretty!"

"You know the house is called Martinston, right, Mom? Pemberley is just for the show."

"Of course I do. I just like the idea of my only daughter living in a place called Pemberley, dressed up like you're in a Jane Austen book. You looked like Keira Knightley in *Pride and Prejudice,* only you've already got your Mr. Darcy."

"Aw, thanks, Mom." We might have similar coloring, but with my non-ballerina build, I'm sure I looked nothing like Keira Knightley in *Pride and Prejudice.* But I'm taking the compliment all the same.

"Have people reacted nicely to it? I so hope they'll begin

12

to see how special my daughter is."

The media has still not exactly warmed to me as Sebastian's wife. It's old news that they wanted him to choose Phoebe on *Dating Mr. Darcy*. They weren't exactly thrilled he chose the contestant who embarrassed herself by falling out of the limo onto the red carpet and who he fell in love with off camera. They wanted to see our love story unfold before their eyes, which I totally get. I want to see that when I watch a show, too, but things sure feel different when you're on the other side of the camera.

"I've been avoiding reading what they're saying. I don't want to know about how much they still *don't* want me to be with Seb."

"Well, I'm sure this show will fix any of their misgivings. You mark my words, honey, they will love you before the season is over."

I smile. My mom is my biggest fan.

"How's the family?"

"Everyone's good. Zara is coming for a visit this weekend. She's been in London since last month, and I've been missing her."

I liked Sebastian's kid sister, Zara, from the moment I laid eyes on her. She's funny and smart and incredibly cheeky to her big brother, who can get a bit serious from time to time. When she's in London at her interior design store, things are definitely a lot quieter around here.

"Zara is a sweetheart. You'll have fun. Did Jemima ever get that chicken coop she was talking about when I was there last summer? I always say a house isn't complete until you've got a coop full of chickens laying their eggs."

"Mom, you've never had chickens in your life."

"I would if I had as much land as the Huntington-Rosses. Land as far as the eye can see. Tell her to get chickens. Lots o' them."

I laugh. "I'll be sure to mention it to her. Hey, you'll never guess what Geraldine said to us last night." I love to tell Mom about all the outrageous things my grandmother-in-law says to me, mainly because I know she'll be as surprised as me. If I'm honest, it's also because I know she'll be in my corner.

"What did she say?"

"She told us to get started making babies because I'm not getting any younger and the family needs an heir. Can you believe it?" I wait for her reaction, expecting her to be just as amazed as I was by it.

"She's right, honey."

I can barely believe my ears. "Wait, what? Are you saying you agree with her?"

"I know you don't want to hear it, and Geraldine is hardly the best person to deliver the message, but she's got a point. If you want to have a family, it's better to start earlier rather than later."

"Mom, I've just turned thirty, not forty-five."

"But thirty isn't twenty-five, honey."

"You're kinda pointing out the obvious right now, Mom."

"Did you know a woman's fertility declines by something like eighty percent every year after you turn thirty? That's a scientific fact."

"Eighty percent a year?" I ask with a chortle. "I don't think so."

"It might not be exactly eighty percent, but it's something like that. It's a dramatic decline, whatever the actual number is."

"I'm not sure we're in that space yet. We've only ever had a general chat about how we both want a family someday. Never any actual planning or anything."

"Maybe it's time?"

I open my mouth to reply and then close it again. Not Mom too?

"Look. We've only been married a year. Is there a rush? Because I don't think there needs to be a rush. Besides, we're both super busy with the house and all the activities around it, plus Seb has his job at the bank, and Timothy has been selling super well in Body Sports," I say, referring to mine and my BFF, Penny's activewear line we named for our dads. "Did you know we've had a three hundred percent rise in orders in the England stores alone in the last quarter? Three *hundred* percent."

There's a long pause, prompting me to add, "Mom? Are you still there?"

"Honey? Did you ever wonder why you never had any brothers or sisters?"

Random question.

"I figured you only ever wanted one kid."

"Your dad and I wanted more, but it wasn't possible for us."

I get a heavy feeling in my stomach. What happened to talking about Timothy's awesome sales? "Oh. I-I didn't know," I mutter.

"We wanted a whole tribe of kids with a bunch of siblings for you, just like we both had when we were growing up. But you know what? We tried and tried. Believe me, we did everything. I changed my diet, I worked out more. Remember those Jane Fonda workouts?"

"Sure," I reply, not wanting to have this conversation at all. I did some of those work outs with her.

"They were all to help me get pregnant. We tried doing it at different times of the month, in different positions. Sometimes I would lie with my legs up the wall afterwards to, you know, stop it all from sliding on out."

"Mom!" I yell, and my insides decide to curl up and die from the overshare. As close as I am to my mom, I can't say I'm exactly loving this conversation right now. In fact, I'd say it's the opposite of loving this conversation. Hating it. Every word.

Thankfully she pulls back from sharing more details. "It was hard, honey. That's what I'm trying to tell you."

"Well, you ended up with me, I guess, so it was all worth it in the end," I say lightly, hoping to wrap this TMI chat up *pronto*.

"Oh, this was all after you were born. I'd tuck you into your crib for a nap, then if the time of the month was right, I'd call your dad and tell him he needed to get himself home to—"

"Mom!" I shout, more forcefully this time. I so don't want to know where she's going with this, although I can totally guess where. I metaphorically stick my fingers in my ears and sing *la la la la la* to block it all out.

I miss the good old days of two minutes ago when we were talking about *anything* but this.

What is it with the senior women in this family wanting to talk about sex all of a sudden? I much prefer it when we all knew we did it but no one would ever dream of mentioning it. A far simpler—and so much less traumatizing—time.

"Emma, listen to me. I was twenty-six when I had you, and then I could not get pregnant again."

"What are you saying? I've missed my window already?" I say with a laugh, because of course she's not saying that.

Is she?

"If you and Sebastian want a family, start trying."

"Okay, Mom. I'll talk to Seb about it," I reply to placate her.

"You're gonna have to do a whole lot more than just 'talk' about it, honey," she replies with a chortle.

Stop. Just stop.

I plug my metaphorical ears with my metaphorical fingers. *La la la la la.*

16

"Sure, Mom."

"Do you remember me telling you about the condition I have? Endometriosis can be the cause of fertility issues in women, and you may have it."

"But you said you had pain with it. I don't have any pain."

"You can have Endo without pain, honey. You should read up on it. I'll send you an article. There are a lot of good resources out there these days, not like when I was young and no one seemed to want to talk about it at all."

"You don't have to send me the info. I'm pretty sure I'd know if I had it."

"Honey, it's better to be forewarned and forearmed. If you've got a problem, it's better that y'all deal with it now rather than getting right down the track and realizing it's too late. I don't want that for my baby girl."

"Okay. Send me the link," I concede.

"You're probably fine."

"Oh, I'm sure I am."

"Oh, and one other thing before I go. Do you and Seb do it in the missionary position? Because that is the best position to conceive. It's nice and deep and—"

"Mom, stop!" I say forcefully, putting a sudden—and much needed stop—to any further description she would care to add. I thank her hurriedly for her advice, say a quick good-bye, and hang up.

I stay seated on the old stone bench, my breath visible in the cold air as I mentally chew over what Mom has said. Suddenly everyone wants to offer advice on Sebastian and me starting a family. And what's more, that advice seems to be unilaterally *do it now!*

I rise to my feet and stretch my arms above my head. It's gotten cold out here, and the chill has begun to seep through my layers. I make my way through the gardens, deep in thought. Mom was four years younger than I am when she

17

had me and couldn't have any more kids. Four years. That's a lot younger in the fertility stakes—not the eighty percent decline year on year Mom claims, I'm sure, but a lot all the same. I'd never thought thirty was old, especially not when only a couple of my friends back home have begun to have kids already and the few friends I've made here aren't even in that space.

Should we be trying? I mean, we've only been married a year, and it's not like we're pushing forty or anything. Surely, we've got time?

Reaching the kitchen, I pull open the heavy door, clomp across the stone floor, and head up the stairs into the main part of the house. I'm due to meet Sebastian in the City of London for his work Christmas party tonight, and I've got to figure out which outfit says *I'm the wife of a senior investment banker, but I'm super approachable and fun too*. It's a lot of pressure for one dress.

A couple of hours later, with my choice of the ever-useful Little Black Dress and a pair of heels, I step out of the Tube station in the City and walk down the busy street to the restaurant where tonight's event is taking place. Sebastian works for a wealthy bank, so I know it's going to be a pretty swanky affair full of expensively dressed people sipping expensive drinks in opulent surroundings. I'm not disappointed. It's one of those classic London places with black trimmed windows and an unassuming sign in lower case above the door.

It's a different story inside. The ceilings are high with black chandeliers hanging over tables and the walls are covered in gilded mirrors. As I walk through the door I'm immediately struck by the warmth of the room and the lively chatter emanating from the large crowd standing in the bar area.

"Madam. How can I help you?" a woman asks as the door swings closed behind me, taking the cool evening air with it.

"I'm here for a Christmas party. It's for Integra. In fact, I think it's all the departments here tonight, so they might have booked the whole place." A quick scan of the room, and I spot a few familiar faces.

"Your name?" she asks me without cracking a smile.

"Emma Brady. I mean Huntington-Ross. I'm Emma Huntington-Ross. I forget sometimes." She shoots me a quizzical look, so I add, "I only got married last year. Changed my name, even though I knew I had the choice not to, of course. I mean, I've been Brady all my life, so it felt kinda weird, but I figured, why not?"

Why am I sharing this with her? It's like I've caught a case of the TMIs from my mom.

"I see," she replies with cool disdain for this babbling over-sharing American standing on the other side of her podium. She consults her list. Landing on my name, she looks back up at me and says, "Can I take your coat, Mrs. Huntington-Ross?"

"Sure, thanks." I unbutton my London-weight winter coat (read: super warm for this thin-blooded former Texan) and hand it to her.

As she steps out from behind the podium, my eyes drift to her dress. It's the same as mine. As in exactly the same. High boat neck, sleeveless, hitting just above the knee. The classic LBD. I glance around the room and notice all the female servers are wearing the same dress.

Terrific. I've arrived at my husband's work party, dressed like the hired help.

"Feel free to join your party," she says to me, and I offer her a weak smile as I leave to go search for my husband among the throngs of Christmas revelers.

I say a couple of hellos to people I recognize as I make my

way through the hordes, aiming for the bar. A few of them are already pretty tipsy, the men slapping one another on the back and laughing loudly, the women giggling and chatting and flirting with the guys.

All pretty typical office Christmas party stuff.

Sebastian's assistant greets me like her BFF. "Emmmmmmmaaaaaah! How are you, girl?" she says as she plants a bright red lipsticked kiss on each of my cheeks.

"I'm great, Susie. Happy holidays."

"Oh, my gosh, you are *so* American? We say, 'Merry Christmas,' not 'Happy Holidays?'"

"Got it. Merry Christmas, then."

Susie poses every sentence as a question, and it's taken me months of knowing her to work out that she doesn't expect an answer to each and every one. It has something to do with her being an Aussie from a small town humorously called Humpty Doo apparently—seriously, it's a place. Or at least that's what Sebastian told me.

"You are such a Doris," she replies with a broad grin.

A Doris? Is that like a Karen?

"But in a good way? I mean, you are Seb's wife and he's totally schmick-o, you know? Schmick-o."

I've also learned that "schmick-o" is a good thing, although I'm not exactly sure what it means. Susie has provided me with quite the education.

"That's so true. Seb is totally schmick-o. You've got that right."

Another girl arrives, ambitiously balancing four glasses of white wine in her hands. "Take it, take it, take it!" she demands of Susie, who promptly relieves her of two of the glasses.

"Beauty," Susie says before she takes a sip from one of the glasses and then from the other.

I raise a questioning eyebrow.

"It's so we don't have to keep going back to the bar?" she explains.

"Got it." I smile at the other girl. "Hey. I'm Emma, Sebastian's wife."

"Hi! I'm Carolyn," she replies. "I work for Jeremy in Corporate Broking. He's such a creep. Isn't he a creep, Suze?" She slings an arm around Susie's shoulders, managing not to spill a drop of her wine. It's impressive.

"Total creep," Susie confirms as she clinks one of her glasses against Carolyn's, wine sloshing over the top.

"Susie's my work bestie," Carolyn explains to me. She tucks one of the wine glasses under her chin and holds up her crossed fingers, which is quite a feat. "We're like this."

"Bloody oath," Susie confirms.

I've no clue what a bloody oath is, but it sounds kinda grisly, so I change the subject. "Have either of you seen Seb?"

"Oh, he's at the bar with Odette," Carolyn says. "They've been talking for ages."

I scroll through the database of *Seb's Work Colleague's Names I Need to Remember* but can't locate anyone with that name. "I don't think I know anyone named Odette."

"She's the new analyst we poached from Riley's," Carolyn replies. "She's on the telly and everything."

Susie gives an enthusiastic nod. "She is *so* amazing? So inspirational? She's a mum and has a successful career? She makes it all look so easy. You've got to meet her?"

"I'm sure I will. I'll go find them now. Enjoy your, err, drinks," I say.

"It's a Christmas party? You're meant to get blotto?" Susie says.

"Of course," I reply with a head nod. *Blotto?* That has to mean "drunk."

"See you later?" she adds.

Was that an actual question?

I throw them both a grin. "Sure thing."

As I turn away from Carolyn and Susie from Humpty Doo—I mean, how cute is that name?—I meet a wall of expensive suits and enough cologne to give me asthma. Which I don't suffer from, but the scent is so overwhelming it's like these guys took a bath in cologne.

"Excuse me," I say to the men in an attempt to get past them.

One of them turns to me, gives me a quick onceover, and says, "Brilliant. I'm to'ally parched. You take these, and we'll 'ave another round." He thrusts a set of stacked glasses into my hands. "Same as before, lads?"

"Oh, I'm not a server," I protest with a smile, but he's already turned his back on me as he gets the list of drinks from his besuited friends.

Stupid dress.

"We'll 'ave two pints of Newky, a pint of Guinness, and a lager with a lime top for Poofter Patrick 'ere, thanks, love."

The group of men laugh rowdily as someone slaps the one who's clearly "Poofter Patrick" on the back.

He gives a half-smile to the group, clearly not appreciating the label. "What's wrong with a lager with a lime top, mate? It's just a beer, innit?" he protests.

"It's a beer with cordial, mate. It's a frickin' toddler's drink."

Because *so* many toddlers drink beer?

"Poofter Patrick the Frickin' Toddler!" one of the other guys taunts to uproarious laughter from the group.

I roll my eyes. Traders. That's what these guys are. A loud, flashy boys' club, full to the brim with testosterone, and a competitive streak that makes Olympian athletes look like hobbyists.

The guy who handed me the glasses turns back to look at me, and his face falls. "I'm not payin' you, love. It's an open bar. So go on, then. Run along. Go get the beers in for the menfolk. We're about to die of dehydration here."

I narrow my eyes at him. Patronizing, much? What a jerk.

"Actually," I reply with the sweetest smile I can muster for a group of besuited cavemen and their condescending leader, "as I said, I'm not a server here. So you can take *these* back," I thrust the stack of glasses at him and add, "and, if you'll excuse me, I'm trying to get to the bar to get my own drink *as a guest*."

Probably from sheer surprise that the "server" had the gall to talk back, the cavemen part, and I waltz past them with my head held high.

Why hadn't I worn another outfit tonight? I mean, what are the odds I would be wearing the same dress as the staff? It's not like I bought it at *Waitress Dresses Are Us* or anything.

I reach the bar and wait for one of the staff to place my order as I scan the room. I spot Sebastian a few people down from me, his back to me, leaning in as he listens to a slim woman speaking. She's got gorgeously thick, straight dark hair and a fine-featured, pretty face, which her smile lights up as she talks. She must be the inspirational Odette, poached from Riley's. Well, she's definitely pretty, that's for sure.

With no hope of getting his attention in the noisy, busy room, I order my bottle of Budweiser and make my way over to him.

"Brady," he says with a broad smile when I tap him on the shoulder. He places a quick and chaste kiss on my lips and introduces me to his companion. "Odette Rojas, this is my wife, Emma. Odette's a new analyst at the bank."

She reaches out and shakes my hand, offering me a smile. "It's so lovely to meet you, Emma." She runs her eyes over my dress. "I didn't know your wife worked here," she says to

Sebastian. "How lovely for you both to have the Christmas party here."

I shake my head. "Oh, no. I don't work here. I just made a very poor decision to wear a dress I don't think I'll ever wear again," I reply with a laugh. "I've been given empty glasses by a bunch of traders who tried to order some drinks from me just now. Apparently, there's a drink that involves beer with lime cordial."

"Ah, yes. That's a drink for people who don't like the taste of beer," Sebastian says as someone taps me on the shoulder.

I swing around to see a woman in a sexy black sequin dress. "Can I order from you? We've been waiting at the bar. The service in this place is terrible. You need to tell your boss to sort it out fast."

I open my mouth to reply as Sebastian says, "Emma is not a waitress, Monique."

Monique has the good sense to look embarrassed. "Oh, I'm so sorry. Are you off duty? Because you should change, or this sort of thing will simply keep on happening."

"She's Sebastian's wife," Odette explains.

Monique's eyes bulge. "Why are you a waitress, then? Surely Sebastian earns enough to keep you?"

I blink at her in shock. *Keep me?* What is this, Regency England where ladies had no choice but to be "kept" with no way of earning their living?

"I chose the wrong dress tonight, that's all. A mistake I won't be making again in a hurry."

Monique's lips twitch in amusement as she looks down her ski jump nose at me. "Quite."

"And I run my own super successful business, you know," I add, knowing I'm acting defensive and trying to prove something to this woman. But I'm running with it. "It's an activewear line called Timothy. You might have heard of it?"

"I watched *Dating Mr. Darcy*. We all did. I know all about

your 'activewear line,'" she replies with more than a dash of condescension as she does air quotes with her elegant hands and perfectly manicured nails.

Sebastian wraps his arm around my shoulder. "I'm not one to boast, but my wife *is* pretty amazing."

Monique's eyes wander from Sebastian to me and then back again. "I'm sure she is," she simpers. "Now, if you'll excuse me…" She trails off as she turns her back to us and begins to talk with someone else.

"Who's Monique?" I ask him quietly. "She seems super nice."

Sebastian chuckles. "She's a corporate broker, too. Works in the ICT division. Don't worry about her. She thinks she's better than most people."

"Well, she's not," I sulk with my bottom lip protruding. I know I sound like a petulant child.

I feel a warm hand on my arm. "Emma, would you like this? I thought it might help differentiate you from the waitresses, which is an issue for you right now." Odette holds out a beautiful pink and red scarf. I recognize it as a design from the new collection by the fancy French label, Hermès. Being in the industry, I know my fashion.

I take it in my hand and feel it's silky texture. "Are you sure?"

"Of course. We can't have you accosted for drink orders by every Tom, Dick, or Harry."

"Or Monique," Sebastian adds.

Odette pulls her full lips into a smile that lights up the room. "Or Monique."

I take the scarf gratefully from her, warming to her immediately. "Thanks, Odette."

"It's my pleasure. Us girls need to stick together. Here, let me help." She arranges it into one of those effortless ties French women perfect and I've never gotten a handle on. A moment later, her handiwork completed, she adds, "Gorgeous."

"You are so sweet. Thank you," I gush. She might be intimidatingly beautiful and she might have half the Integra's employees in awe of her, but she's super sweet.

"It suits you," Sebastian says. "Odette, you're very kind."

"It's my pleasure," she simpers, her ridiculously pretty face glowing. "In fact, why don't you keep it, Emma?"

"But it's brand new."

She lifts a shoulder. "It suits you better than me."

"I can't, but thank you."

"Please, take it as a gift. Between you and me, I get Hermès products at wholesale rates. My sister runs a string of high-end fashion shops. I've literally got stacks of them back at my flat."

An image of Odette's stunning home pops into my mind. It would be filled with a stack of Hermès scarfs and other exquisite things, high ceilings, hardwood floors, and gently billowing sheer white curtains surrounding open French doors. I'm not sure why the sheer white curtains would be billowing, but they definitely are.

"Only if you're sure?" I ask uncertainly, and she replies with an incline of her head. "You're total a lifesaver," I tell her.

"Since my wife is no longer likely to be mistaken as the hired help, let's get another round of drinks in from the actual bar staff, shall we?"

Sebastian is right, the scarf does do the trick. I don't get asked for snacks or drinks or even called "love" for the rest of the evening. By the time we're on the train, whizzing through the city back to Martinston, Sebastian declares the evening a success, I'm tipsy, and Odette and I have become firm friends.

CHAPTER 3

*I*t's a cold, brisk morning a few days later, the weak winter sun fighting to be seen through the mist as Sebastian and I run through Martinston's woods.

"Race you to the top," he says and immediately takes off, his feet pounding the dirt.

"Not fair!" I call out as I push myself to catch up. It's a losing battle, and by the time I reach the felled tree beside which we kissed while on Dating Mr. Darcy, he's already stretching out his quads, grinning at me.

"About time you turned up, Brady," he says.

"I was three seconds behind you," I protest. I catch my breath before I tackle the topic that's been simmering in my mind for days. "Seb? Can I ask you something?"

With one leg now stretched out on the tree, he replies, "Of course. What is it?"

"It's probably kinda silly, but I was talking with Mom earlier in the week."

"How is she? She's not had a relapse, has she?"

"Nope. No more cancer. She did say something though, and it's kinda got me thinking."

"That can't be good." He shoots me a cheeky grin as he changes legs to stretch out the other one.

"I'm trying to be serious here. What she said has been playing on my mind."

He cocks his head at me. "What did she say?

"You know how I'm an only child? Apparently, that wasn't by choice. Mom and Dad wanted more kids, but they couldn't have them."

His stretching finished, he moves closer to me. "Was that hard to hear?"

"Not really. I mean, like any only child, I had fantasies about having brothers and sisters. It wasn't that, though. It was the fact they couldn't have any more that got me thinking. She reminded me she has something called endometriosis, which meant she suffered with pain and ultimately couldn't have any more kids."

"Your poor mum. That's awful."

"She said something else, too. She told me we should start trying now, rather than waiting."

"Trying for a baby?" he asks, and I nod, suddenly nervous.

What if he says he doesn't want to start a family now—or ever? I mean, I know we've talked about wanting a family in the future, but we've never actually made any firm plans, and the future is always that distant land where anything is possible. Talking about it now makes it feel real.

"Look, I know we both said we wanted to have kids someday, and I for one didn't even consider when that day would be. But she got me thinking."

He leans up against the felled tree. "Do you want to start a family now?"

"And there it is, the million-dollar question," I reply with a light laugh. "I do love the idea of us having our own little baby, but it also scares the living daylights out of me."

"Why?"

28

"Because of all the responsibility. We both work hard with our careers and with running this place, and having a new, little person running around, needing our attention could be…" I trail off.

He smiles down at me and finishes my sentence for me. "It could be incredible."

I grin up at him, my heart fluttering as people dance the salsa in my tummy. "Are you saying what I think you're saying?"

"I don't know. What do you think I'm saying?"

I swallow down a lump rising in my throat. "Do you want to start a family?"

His lips stretch into a smile, his eyes full of love. "I think I do."

My happiness bubbles up like an erupting volcano. "I think I do, too."

He lets out a laugh, and before I know it, he's wrapped me up in a hug, lifting my feet off the ground and is spinning me around. I let out an excited giggle. I feel closer to him than I've ever felt.

"I love you, Seb," I mutter into his ear.

"I love you, too, Brady." He places me back on the woodland floor, leans down, and kisses me like he means it. And he means it, because it's one of those knock-your-socks-off kisses that leaves me in absolutely no doubt how he feels about me.

"I can't believe we've decided to start a family," I say when we come up for air.

His hands trail down my back. "If only it were warm, we could start some *en plein air* baby making right here and now."

"On plan what?"

"*En plein air*. It's French for outside."

It takes me a moment to work out what he means. "You

29

mean getting it on out here in the woods?" I ask with a laugh, and he nods, his eyebrows waggling. "Seb, it's winter!"

He brushes his lips against mine, and I close my eyes as it sends a shiver across my skin. "Race you back to the house," he says, and he turns and dashes away from me, down the rise toward the house.

"You are not playing fair, Lord Martinston!" I yell as I dart after him.

He throws a cheeky grin over his shoulder at me. "I promise to make it up to you in our bedroom."

I chase after him, giddy. I'm married to the hottest, best guy in the country, and he wants to have a family with me.

I've got to be the luckiest Texas gal this side of the Atlantic.

* * *

"BODY SPORTS WANTS *how many* crop tops?" I guffaw, barely believing my ears.

Penny's grin reaches from ear to ear on my laptop screen. "I know, right? And to think they didn't even want to stock our line only a year ago."

"How are we going to keep up with that kind of demand?"

"By working super hard, babe."

We've come a long way since Penny once sewed up all our designs in the early days of Timothy when we ran the operation from her garage. Now, we've got a factory that does all the sewing for us, and although Penny is still designing all the pieces, she and I can spend most of our time focusing on running the business.

I push out a puff of air, my heart fluttering with excitement—and a healthy dollop of trepidation, too. "Penn, this is what we've been working towards. This is the big break we needed to take the British market by storm."

"I know, right? You have done such a great job getting them on board. I'm sending you a crown and sash that reads *Persistence Queen* for sure."

I think back to all the sales pitches and phone calls and chasing I've done to get Timothy Activewear in front of Body Sports. They'd agreed to stock our label in some of their stores some months ago, and now we've broken through with this huge order.

"It's all been worth it. We need to celebrate!" I say.

"Especially if Body Sports expands into Europe, which is what they told you, right?"

"Right. They're opening stores in Paris, Milan, Madrid, and Berlin in the next six months, and if they all stock our line—"

"We'll have it made."

A mixture of panic and excitement rolls around my belly. "Yup."

"Let's not get ahead of ourselves, 'kay?"

"Penn, we already have."

She laughs. "True. You know, the other channel we should consider is fashion outlets. A lot of them carry activewear now, and it could be a real opportunity for us."

"Totally. Imagine if we could get into GSS? They're huge in Europe."

"I know, right? Millionaire Alley here we come. Well, you already live in a mansion."

"This is different. This is you and me. Two girls from the wrong side of the tracks making it big. And it's a manor house, not a mansion."

"Potato potah-to."

"Literally no one says potah-to."

"Hey, Em? I need to tell you something."

"What is it? More orders from super big sports stores?"

"Something different. You know how Trey and I wanted a

31

big family? Well, we're gonna be adding to that in about five and half months. Jacob's getting a little sister or brother."

"You're pregnant?" I squeak as excitement for my friend mounts.

"Yes ma'am, and oh my gosh, have I been sick with this one."

"Oh, Penn. That's amazing news! Not the sickness part, of course, but the baby part. Are you super excited?"

"Yes and no. I mean, don't get me wrong, we are over the moon that Jacob's gonna have a new baby brother or sister, but I'm overwhelmed with all the work we've got right now. Plus I know what it's like to have a newborn. Let's just say you'll need to step up when my time comes."

"Girl, I have got your back."

"I know you have, Em, and I love you for it."

"Speaking of babies and the like, have you ever thought we could do a maternity line?"

"Workout clothes for pregnant women?" She lifts her shoulders in a shrug. "Sure I have."

"Well, I've been doing some research, and I think there's a gap in the market that we could fill quite nicely."

Ever since my conversation with Sebastian about starting our own family, I've had a heightened awareness of all things pregnancy and baby. Some may say I'm *#obsessed*, but all I am is curious. Any pregnant celebrity catches my eye and I want to read all about them and their pregnancy, I'm seeing baby photos through significantly softer eyes, and I've been known to watch toddlers in the village playground as they bumble around on unsteady feet, melting my heart with every step.

"Okay. It's worth investigating. Send me your research, and we can talk more about it."

"Perfect." I chew on my lip for a moment before I add, "Penn? Maybe we will both be expecting soon."

"What do you mean? Are you pregnant?" Her voice rises to the level only dogs can hear.

"No, not yet but we have decided to start trying."

"Oh, Em! That is so exciting. I bet you'll get pregnant just like that. That's how it worked for me and Trey. First time trying and *boom!* pregnant. I got whiplash by how fast it all happened."

"I hope you're right."

"Why wouldn't I be? You're newlyweds. You'll be putting the rabbits to shame right now."

"Mom said something to me about not being able to get pregnant after they had me. She said they tried, but it didn't work out. Obviously."

"You're not your mom, so don't even think about it. You need to think positive thoughts and let nature take its course. Oh, you two are gonna make such beautiful babies!"

"Let nature take its course. Exactly." My grin stretches from ear to ear. "And thanks, Penn. You're the best."

"You know it's true, babe."

A reminder pops up on my screen with a *ding*.

"I've gotta go. I'm meeting Kennedy and Phoebe for dinner in London tonight. Kennedy's started her new job, and I am so excited to see her, and I haven't seen Phoebe for weeks."

"It's a *Dating Mr. Darcy* contestant reunion, huh?"

Phoebe and Kennedy were contestants on the show with me way back when I first met Sebastian. Phoebe has since gone on to fall in love with and marry Johnathan, now living here permanently, and Kennedy has recently moved to London from her native San Diego. Having two friends from the States who get what we all went through on *Dating Mr. Darcy* helps me keep my sanity.

"I guess it's a reunion, although we've left odious Camille out of the mix. For obvious reasons."

"Ah, the contestant who tried to blackmail Sebastian into marrying her."

"That's our Camille."

"You know, I love the way you just drop it into conversation that you're having dinner in London. You've come a long way, girl."

"We both have, Penn. Love you!"

I get dressed up in a cute new gray woolen dress and boots and take the train into London with the Great British commuters, all bundled up in their winter coats and scarves.

Kennedy, Phoebe, and I have agreed to meet at a pub off Marylebone High Street, near Kennedy's new job as a journalist for a trendy magazine. Phoebe has been in the West End for the day, attending a matinee of the Royal Ballet with a group of fellow ballet teachers over in England for a vacation.

I reach the pub, and my phone rings. It's Heather McCabe from the production company responsible for both *Saving Pemberley* and *Dating Mr. Darcy*. Not exactly my favorite person. But she does like to check in every week or so now that *Saving Pemberley* is on air, usually to tell me how hot my husband is.

"Emma. I'm checking in. How are you?" Heather asks in her brisk, no nonsense tone.

"Other than the media's persistent dislike of me, I'm great," I reply as I pause at the entrance to the pub. And yes, my voice is definitely coated in a healthy layer of sarcasm right now.

"Yes, I did see the latest comments about you in the garden. I thought you looked rather fetching in those wellies."

"If they're not still going on about how they would have preferred Seb to have married Phoebes, they're laughing at how much time I spend in my rubber boots in the garden, doing nothing with the same plant."

"But Emma, darling, you are the one they love to hate. You're ratings *gold*," she says, as though this was somehow meant to give me comfort.

"Sure. Great."

"Everyone still adores Sebastian, of course, which is fantastic. I knew he'd be the perfect Mr. Darcy."

I roll my eyes. "He does a great job."

"Are women still demanding the pond scene from him at Martinston?"

"Yup."

"Good, good. One of these days he might just oblige."

"I'm thinking not."

"You never know," she replies, clearly holding out hope. "Now, I must dash. Love to Seb."

She hangs up before I get the chance to reply, which I don't need to do. It's a classic Heather phone call: *everyone loves to hate you and Seb's amazing, keep up the good work, rah rah rah.*

I push Heather and the whole TV show from my mind as I walk through the doors into the pub. It's one of those gorgeously traditional English establishments, with a large, curved mahogany bar, black and white tiled floor, and chandeliers hanging from a dark ceiling. The effect is moody and romantic, and I can just imagine the likes of Lord Byron and his cronies discussing the finer points of poetry over a pint here back in the day.

"Emma! Over here!"

I spot Phoebe waving at me from one of the tables by a leadlight window. She's sitting with Kennedy, and I rush over to greet my wonderful friends. I am so grateful to have them as friends here in my new English life—particularly with a false start with Jilly who was plotting to have Sebastian dump me behind my back throughout our entire friendship. But we don't need to go into that whole ordeal right now.

Moving on dot com.

"It is so good to see you two." I give each of my friends a hug and take my seat. I notice a half pint of beer on the table in front of me. "Is that mine?"

"It sure is. It's called Pudding Beer. Johnny thinks you'll like it."

I eye it dubiously. "You got me a beer called 'pudding?' As in American pudding or British pudding?"

"Does it matter?" she asks with a shrug.

"My British beer education continues, huh?"

"Johnny has taken it upon himself to get Emma away from American beer and instead try the many, many beers they have here in Britain," Phoebe explains to Kennedy.

"Why?" she asks, and I laugh to myself. That's precisely what I asked, too.

I eye the beer. "Okay, I'll give it a shot." I take a sip and am immediately struck by how much the beer reminds me of a combination of danish pastry combined with hops and...dirt. Definitely dirt. It's straight up weird. "It's interesting," I say.

"That is one glowing endorsement," Kennedy says with a laugh.

I snort-giggle. "It tastes just plain weird. Here, try it." I push the half pint glass over toward her, and she shakes her head.

"I'm not gonna drink something that put that look on your face."

"I think I'll go get myself a bottle of Bud," I say as I leave the table to head to the bar.

A few moments later, I'm back at the table, my cold beer in hand. "Wow, Kennedy. You actually *live* in London now. I am so excited for you. How's the new job?"

"Amazing, scary, exciting, and I feel like I'm totally out of my depth," she replies.

"I bet you're not. You're a great writer," Phoebe says.

"I don't feel like one right now, having left my friends and family and everything I've ever known because I'm avoiding having to see my ex and his new *wife*. I've moved to another country on the other side of a massive ocean, I've started a new job at one of the most famous magazines on the planet, and I'm renting a room in someone's house that's the size of my car back home."

I raise my eyebrows. "That's a lot."

She widens her eyes at me. "Right? But you know what? I'm up for it, and I am stoked to be here with you two."

"I think you're so incredibly brave to do all that," Phoebe says. "Isn't she brave, Emma?"

"Phoebes is right. You've totally changed your life, but it's gonna work out just great. I know it is."

Kennedy smiles, and her beautiful face lights up. "I have a feeling it will. Or I'll die trying."

"But wait. Your ex got *married*? The ex your sister signed you up for *Dating Mr. Darcy* to get over?" I ask.

She presses her lips together and gives a grim nod. "Yup. Any hopes we could rekindle what we had have well and truly been exterminated by a chick in a big white dress."

Phoebe waves her hand in the air. "You're better off without him. Any guy who would choose another woman over you is insane, in my mind. I mean, just look at you."

She leans back in her chair. "Literally *both* your husbands did exactly that."

"I guess that's kinda true," I concede, uneasy. Being a contestant on the show meant Kennedy "dated" Sebastian just as Phoebe and I did.

#Awkward.

"Other than our husbands is what Phoebe means. Right,

37

Phoebes?" I say, trying to salvage the situation here—and doubtlessly failing.

"Absolutely. And now that you're here, we can introduce you to all the amazing single guys we know. Right, Em?"

"Right," I confirm resolutely.

"Uh-huh." Kennedy does not sound impressed as she takes a sip of her drink.

"Johnny's got this one friend who is super nice. His name is Stuart, and he's smart, totally put together, good-looking, and has a great job here in London. He's one of those guys who's so well put together, you feel like a sloth next to him, you know? And I've never seen him with a woman, just different guys. He sure knows a lot of guys." She pauses for a moment, pensive, and adds, "Although now that I think about it, he's probably not the right guy for you."

"Why? He sounds great," Kennedy says.

Phoebe scrunches up her face. "Because I'm pretty sure he's gay."

A giggle has me spurting my beer out of my mouth. I wipe my face dry with my hand. "Oops. That was gross."

"It was totally gross," Phoebe agrees.

Kennedy laughs. "So let me see if I've got this straight. No pun intended. This Stuart guy is probably gay, and you thought you would set me up with him?"

"Oh, he's not out or anything like that. He might not be gay. In fact, I'd say it's a fifty-fifty chance."

Kennedy cocks an eyebrow. "I think that's a hard pass, girl. Call me crazy, but I'm not exactly excited about being set up with a guy who might or might not be gay. Dating is tough enough without that whole thing thrown into the mix."

Phoebe gives a shrug. "I guess I'll try to think of someone else."

"You don't have to," Kennedy protests. "Getting set up never works."

"It does. Sebastian's got some single friends. One of them might do?" I speculate.

"Are they fifty-fifty on heterosexuality, too?" Kennedy asks with a smirk. "Because what's dating without a major challenge?"

I return her smile. "I'll get back to you on that one." I turn to Phoebe. "How's it going setting up your ballet school? Last time I saw you, you'd found a location."

"Oh, it's going fine," she replies and begins to concentrate on mixing the ice cubes around her drink with a straw.

Strange.

"Fine?" I question. Phoebe is usually so excited to talk about the school it's hard to get a word in edgewise. I eye her across the table. "Phoebes, are you blushing?" I ask.

Her face turns from pale pink to a bright fuchsia that Ru Paul would be proud of. She gives a self-conscious shrug and murmurs, "It's hot in here, that's all. Lots of bright lights."

I glance around the dimly lit pub. "Uh, no it's not."

"Are you okay?" Kennedy asks.

She swallows and lifts her eyes. "I haven't been working on the school much lately. I've been, uh, not feeling well."

My mind immediately turns to cancer and fear grips me. Having a mom diagnosed with breast cancer totally out of the blue has put me on high alert. "What's wrong? Have you been to the doctor? You need to get in there quick so they can catch anything going on super early."

"Don't worry, it's not cancer."

I let out a relieved sigh. "That's good news. What is it then?"

"Well," she begins, and slowly, the cogs in my brain begin to turn over. I eye her drink on the table. It's an orange juice.

She says she's been feeling sick. She and Johnny got married before us.

Bam! it hits me. I know what she's going to tell us.

"Phoebes, can I ask if you've been sick because of something good?"

Phoebe's eyes dart between us, her pretty face lighting up. "Johnny and I are expecting."

"Oh, my gosh, Phoebes!" I collect her in a hug, and Kennedy follows suit. "A new little Bentley baby. That's amazing news."

"Congratulations, girl," Kennedy gushes.

"It all happened so fast. I mean, we decided to start trying for a family, and the next thing we knew, I was pregnant. The whole thing has been kind of amazing."

"All it takes is one eager egg and one willing sperm," Kennedy says with a laugh.

"Nice detail," I comment. "Exactly how pregnant are you?"

"Are there degrees of pregnancy? I'm just about three months now. I was gonna tell you both in a couple weeks once we got past the three-month threshold."

"Hold on a sec." I do some mental math. "Didn't you and Johnny go to Prague to celebrate your birthday about two and a half months ago?"

Phoebes cheeks glow. "What can I say? It was a very romantic trip."

"It clearly was," Kennedy says. "So can you tell us anything else? When are you due? Do you know if it's a boy or a girl? All that stuff."

"June and no, we're leaving the sex as a wonderful surprise."

I grin at her, so happy for my friend. "I bet Johnny is over the moon."

Her face tells us she's utterly content. "He is. He jumped on the sofa and did a dance when I got the test result."

I arch an eyebrow. "He pulled a Tom Cruise?"

"Oh, yeah, only not on Oprah. You two are the first to know. We haven't breathed a word of it yet to our families."

"Well, we are honored you chose to tell us. Aren't we Kennedy?" I ask, and she agrees.

We spend the rest of our first drink and part way into our second discussing this wonderful news. Eventually, Kennedy raises the question of whether Sebastian and I are "in that space" yet, and all eyes are on me.

"What would you say if I told you we're thinking about it?"

"Are you saying you might want to try?" Phoebe asks, her eyes widening.

"I'm saying…we've talked about it."

"Oh, Em! We could be new moms together," Phoebe says and immediately adds, "As long as you don't feel left out, Kennedy."

Kennedy raises her hands in the "stop" sign. "Don't make major life decisions based on not wanting me to feel left out. That would be beyond insane."

"Totally insane," I confirm. "And just to let you know, we're nowhere near pregnant. We only started trying a couple weeks ago. I'm sure it'll take some time."

Phoebe pats her totally flat belly. "That's what I thought."

I lean my elbows on the table and say, "The thing is, my mom told me that she and Dad had trouble conceiving. She thought I might have issues, too."

"What kind of trouble?"

"She has something called endometriosis which apparently meant they couldn't give me a brother or sister."

"But they had you, so you're bound to be fine," Phoebe says. "That's proven fertility."

I grin at her. "I bet you're right."

Kennedy raises her glass of wine, and we clink. "To reality TV show babies."

I give a snort-giggle. "That cannot be a thing."

"You've done *Dating Mr. Darcy* and *Saving Pemberley*, Em. What's to stop you doing a show like *Baby Darcy*?" Kennedy suggests.

"Or *Making Darcys*," Phoebe adds.

"Or I know. How about *Darcy: The Next Generation*. It could be Jane Austen meets *Star Trek* in modern day England." Kennedy laughs at her own joke.

"These are all amazing ideas, girls, but it's a hard no from me. Call me crazy, but I don't think I want to be filmed going through a pregnancy."

"Ooh, I know! How about *Keeping Up with The Darcys*?" Kennedy suggests, completely ignoring my protest.

"That might have to wait until they've got a brood," Phoebe says. "How about *Married to Darcy: The Baby Files*? That would be super cute."

"Okay, you two," I say, shaking my head as I laugh. "I'm gonna nip this in the bud right now. There will be no reality TV show about us having a family. We are done on that front."

"With a combination of yours and Sebastian's genes, what gorgeous babies you will have," Kennedy says.

"I know, right? Totally gorgeous," Phoebe confirms.

"Thanks, girls." I beam at my friends. They might enjoy ribbing me every now and then, but they are the sweetest and most supportive friends ever. And knowing they've got my back as we embark on this new adventure only makes our friendship all the sweeter.

CHAPTER 4

*T*rying for a baby is fun. Really, *really* fun. I don't get why people find it all so stressful. I mean, you're doing something you want to do with the man you're in love with, right? And your chances of conceiving are so much higher if you do it a lot, so you've got to do it all the time. Like *all* the time. And what's more, the result is going to be *the* most incredible thing you could ever imagine. A baby. *Your* baby. It's the miracle of life, people!

What's not to love?

Of course normal life has got to carry on, too. Sebastian has his job in the City, which is getting busier and busier, Timothy is booming with our designs flying off the shelves, and we're continuing to manage Martinston being open to the public, too. And that's not even taking into account the Huntington-Ross family events. Dinners, parties, charity events, the opera. There hardly ever seems to be a time in the family calendar to Netflix and chill.

And what's more, we can't simply slink off and hope our absence won't be noticed. We found that one out the hard way. I'm not going to go into it, but let's just say I've learned

KATE O'KEEFFE

that hiding under your bed, hoping not to get discovered does not work. Those Huntington-Rosses are like bloodhounds on a scent. Particularly Geraldine.

In the Huntington-Ross family you've got to do your duty. Turn up to events. Suffer through the opera. Stay for all eight courses of the meal.

It's exhausting.

Today is Sunday, and that means the family is all at the large mahogany table in the dining room with its high, vaulted ceilings and red walls covered in portraits of the family over the generations. I tell you, it's more than a little off-putting to have to eat with an audience of dead relatives watching your every move.

Zara is back from London for the weekend, which always lightens the mood—mostly because I adore her, but also because she's not afraid to call Geraldine out—and today we've got Sebastian's uncle, Hector, and his Amal Clooney-lookalike wife, Serafina, a beautiful woman from Italy, joining us. It's fair to say Uncle Hector is Geraldine's least favorite relative, so the atmosphere is tense. But then everything is tense when it comes to Geraldine, so it's pretty much the status quo.

"How's the new business, Hector?" Jemima asks as we sit down to our first course.

"Oh, don't ask him that, Jemima," Geraldine scolds. "We don't want to hear about what dreadful and quite probably illegal dealings your brother is involved in these days. Why lower the tone when we have such appetizing food to ingest?"

Uncle Hector erupts into uproarious laughter. "Oh, Geraldine. You are absolutely charming with your hilarious comments. Always such a hoot!" he replies with a loud, barking laugh.

"I was certainly not trying to be a 'hoot' as you put it," she

44

replies curtly, her pinched expression completely hoot-less. "I was merely stating the facts."

"Of course you were!" Uncle Hector replies with a fresh laugh as he wipes his eyes with his cloth napkin. "Oh, such a hoot."

"Come on, Hector. Tell us about it?" Jemima insists. "Your life is so interesting. You always have such wonderful stories to tell."

Hector is a man who loves the sound of his own voice, so he needs no further encouragement. "Well, as some of you know, my last enterprise didn't work out quite as I'd planned," he begins.

Geraldine harrumphs. "Is that how they're referring to a business going belly-up these days, is it?"

Hector chortles. "See, pookie?" he says to his wife. "She's a hoot."

"What iz da hoot?" she asks in her heavily accented English.

Uncle Hector doesn't miss a beat. "A hoot, pookie, is a person who makes fun of someone who is extremely debonair and quite often deadly handsome." He winks at me across the table as though I'm some sort of accomplice in this outright fabrication.

"I never knew that," I reply sweetly.

Serafina nods along as though what he's saying is not only accurate but makes perfect sense. "My-a huz-band is da handsomest," she says proudly as she pats his chubby cheek, which is glowing from the wine he virtually inhaled on his arrival.

"Aw, love you so much, pookie," he coos. "Now, where was I? That's right. My last business taught me that just because you've got the most outstanding idea anyone has ever had, not everyone will be able to appreciate it. Which is their loss, I'm afraid. Their loss indeed."

Jemima cocks her head to the side. "Was this idea the gold equestrian helmets? Because I did wonder if they might be a tad too heavy. Or was it those butler robots? I did think they were an awfully good idea, despite the fact ours caught fire and nearly burned the great hall down."

"The fires weren't our fault. It was an unseasonably warm autumn this year," he rebukes. "They simply overheated in the soaring temperatures."

"*That's* why you're saying the robots caught fire, Uncle Hector? The heat?" Zara asks incredulously. "Wasn't it so cold it snowed this autumn?"

I suppress a smile.

"I think it did snow, yes," Sebastian replies, and we all watch Uncle Hector for his reply.

"Well, anyway, my point is as one of this country's leading entrepreneurs, I need to take risks. Some of them pay off, some of them don't. It's a mindset I'm blessed with. Really, in my mind you're either born with an entrepreneurial flair or you're not. Not many of us have got ancestral manor houses to suck dry, you know." He gives Sebastian a pointed look.

"Oh, Hector. You are so terribly gauche," Granny complains, the look on her face like she's sucked a lemon dry.

"What is da gauche?" Serafina asks Uncle Hector.

"It means successful," he fibs, and once again she beams as she pats him on his cheek, and I roll my eyes. Can you believe this guy?

It's enough to make me vomit into my salad.

"My gauche huz-band," she coos, and he purrs at her as though he were a cat.

Sebastian manages to ignore the display and instead says, "We've been working very hard on making this house turn a profit. Thanks to opening it to the public and the publicity we've had from the television show, I'm happy to report we're moving from the red into the black."

"Isn't Sebastian wonderful?" Geraldine coos as she gazes at her favorite grandchild.

Uncle Hector ignores her. "Now, this reality television malarkey. How did you get into that? Pretty lucrative, I imagine, eh?" He turns his attention on me. "Although they don't like you awfully much, do they, Emma?"

I open my mouth to reply and then shut it again. He's right. The media still hasn't exactly warmed to me, despite the fact I've appeared in the last three episodes doing things like slotting those velvet rope hooks into poles to stop the public from touching the priceless antiques and of course standing around, tending to the same freaking plant in my rubber boots.

"They'll learn to love you, Em, just you wait and see," Zara says, and I shoot her a grateful smile. "An American married to an English aristocrat is very *Downton Abbey*, you know. People love that show."

"Didn't the woman he married have a sizeable family fortune? Our Emma came with nothing but the clothes on her back," Geraldine says. "Oh, and her cat."

I smile benevolently at her, ignoring her jibe. "I didn't know you've seen *Downton*, Granny."

She may have showed a dash of contrition for trying to break up Sebastian and me while we were engaged, but what small kindness she once showed me has well and truly shriveled up and died. The difference now is that I'm no longer interested in jumping through endless hoops I have no hope of managing just to please her. I know that in her eyes I will never be good enough for her grandson, and the way I see it, that's her problem. Not mine. I'm pleasant to her, of course— not only is she my grandmother-in-law, but we live in the same house, albeit a freaking huge one—but I'll never again try to please her as I once did.

I *know* I'm good enough, just as Sebastian is good enough

for me.

"Jemima made me watch it," Geraldine sniffs.

"And you loved it," Jemima adds with a smile.

"It felt very familiar, that's all," she replies. "There is one other difference between Cora and Emma, however, and that's the fact that Emma has yet to produce an heir." Geraldine raises her eyebrows at me, as though I might reach under the table and pull an heir out of my purse at any moment.

"Oh, I'm sure that'll happen at some point," Jemima comments. "Isn't that right, you two?"

Sebastian and I share a look but remain silent.

"It is the duty of any Huntington-Ross to procreate," Geraldine says. "We must keep the line going, and we must keep it as pure as possible. Although I imagine that particular ship has well and truly sailed."

Oh, good grief! I'm now making the Huntington-Ross family line *impure*?

"Wow, Granny. You're acting as though Emma's sole purpose in life is to give birth to the next generation," Zara says.

"It is," Geraldine states simply. "And the sooner she gets on with it the better."

"You're making babies, are you?" Uncle Hector asks. "Jolly good to hear it."

"Za baby? You have za bun in da oven?" Serafina asks me.

"No. No baby in any oven here," I reply.

Geraldine pulls her lemon-sucking face. "Pity."

Zara rolls her eyes. "You are *so* old-fashioned, Granny. This is the twenty-first century, you know, not Victorian England. Women have choices these days. We can have careers and travel the world and choose not to have children if we don't want to."

Geraldine and Jemima take in a collective breath, their

eyes darting to me.

"Is that true? Have you decided *not* to have children?" Jemima asks as she looks between Sebastian and me.

Sebastian's eyes find mine, and we share a small smile. "I'll take this one, shall I?" he asks, and I nod. "We'd may as well tell you all now that we're all together. Emma and I have talked about it, and we have agreed we would like to start a family."

"Oh, darling. That's wonderful news!" Jemima says, her hand flying to her chest.

"Seriously? I'm going to be an aunt?" Zara asks excitedly. "You know, at some time in the future, that is. Not now, obviously," she adds.

"No. Not now," Sebastian says firmly. "But we'll let you all know when we have any news."

Uncle Hector leers at Sebastian. "You're in the fun phase now, my boy. You'll have to have as much rumpy pumpy as you can manage, eh?"

"Rumpy pumpy?" I mouth to Sebastian, and he grins at me as he waggles his eyebrows suggestively.

Uncle Hector raises his glass. "Here's to making babies, eh wot!"

"I'm not going to drink to that," Geraldine sniffs. "It's unseemly."

For once, I agree with her.

"How about we toast something else?" I suggest as I raise my own glass. "Here's to family."

"To family," everyone echoes, and even Geraldine looks happy—or maybe it's just indigestion? I've only ever seen her genuinely happy a handful of times, so it's hard to tell.

"And here's to the next generation," Jemima adds, and I beam at Sebastian.

We're going to make everyone so happy when we have a child, and I for one cannot wait until it happens.

CHAPTER 5

J've been in London all morning, having met with two potential new stockists when I make the snap decision to surprise Sebastian at his work. His office is only three Tube stops from my last meeting, so I'm there in a flash, right at lunchtime. Standing on the sidewalk outside his glass high-rise, proud of myself for doing this, I'm about to call his cellphone when my eyes land on him walking toward me. He's with another man and Odette—of the Hermès scarf fame. The three of them appear to be deep in conversation.

So deep in fact he doesn't even notice me, and all three of them walk through the rotating door and straight past me.

"Sebastian!" I call out, and he swings around.

"Brady Bunch." He reaches my side and pulls me in for a quick kiss. "I thought you had meetings. What are you doing here?"

"I thought I'd surprise you."

"We were just going to grab a bite to eat." He gestures at Odette, who's wearing a camel coat and looking just as chic as when I met her, and another man in a suit. "You remember Odette from the Christmas party, and this is Rakesh."

Odette beams at me as she presses her cheek against mine. "Emma. How lovely to see you again."

I breathe in her perfume, her hair tickling my nose. "Hey, Odette."

"No need to hug or kiss me. Not unless you want to," Rakesh says with a self-deprecating laugh.

"Would you like to join us for lunch, Brady? We're heading to Eduardo's for some pasta."

"Sure." Although my plan was to have lunch with my husband alone, I'm more than happy to tag along with the work threesome.

"Why do you call her Brady?" Rakesh asks as we make our way down the busy street.

"My last name was Brady before I changed it when we got married," I explain.

"I wish I hadn't changed mine when I got married," Odette says.

"I bet," Rakesh says. He catches my eye and adds, "Odette is recently divorced, you see."

"Oh, I'm sorry."

"Don't be. I'm now that highly prized female: single, over thirty, with children." Her laugh tinkles, like a spoon against a crystal glass.

The men walk ahead of us down the street.

"I don't think you'll find it hard to meet another guy," I comment as we round the corner. The woman is gorgeous. Tall, slim, with a porcelain pale complexion and blue eyes. "If you want another guy, that is," I add hurriedly.

"Someday. Right now I'm focusing on my darling children and my career."

"How many kids do you have?"

"Two darling little treasures, five and seven. Joaquin and Antonella."

"Beautiful names."

"Their father is Chilean, and he wanted them to have Spanish names, despite the fact we agreed to bring them up here," she says by way of explanation.

We reach the restaurant, and Sebastian holds the door open for us to walk through. "After you, ladies."

"Your husband is such a gentleman, Emma," Odette comments.

"Literally," I reply with a giggle. When she looks at me blankly, I add, "He's Lord Martinston."

"I didn't know. I've only been at Integra for a couple of months. Does that make you Lady Martinston?"

"It does, although no one calls me that. Plain old Emma works just fine for me."

"I'm not sure there's much plain about you, darling," she says, and I smile at the compliment coming from her.

"Ditto," I reply because, well, she's Odette.

Our mutual admiration society off to a flying start, we are ushered to a table near the back of the restaurant and chat about a variety of things as we order our meals.

"Tell me how you balance a high-flying career and two young children," I ask her.

"Oh, I wouldn't say I'm a highflyer," Odette replies modestly.

"Because no one in their right mind would consider someone with a regular spot on Bloomberg TV talking expertly about the health sector as a highflyer. Does the term 'industry expert' mean anything to you?" Sebastian asks her, tongue firmly in cheek.

"That doesn't make me a highflyer. It just makes me a hard worker," she protests.

"Sure. If you say so," Sebastian replies, smiling broadly at her. "You should watch her on TV, Emma. She does a great job."

"I'll be sure to do that," I reply.

I'll admit, I'm beginning to feel a little intimidated by this woman. Not only is she stunningly gorgeous with two children, a successful career, and a stack of Hermès scarves at her doubtlessly gorgeous home—billowing sheer white curtains, remember?—but she's nice as well. And that, people, is a rare combination.

"Do you know what I just realized? I'm the only one at this table who's not been on television," Rakesh says.

Sebastian slaps him on the back. "You need to lift your game."

"I'll apply to a dating show, shall I? Although I don't have a stately home or have your good looks, Sebastian, which might be a problem."

Sebastian shakes his head in amusement. "Semantics, Rakesh. Semantics."

"I don't know, Rakesh. I think you'd make a very dashing Mr. Darcy," Odette says.

A server arrives, and we order our lunches. As the men talk, Odette tells me, "I've only been at the bank for a short while, but your husband does seem to get rather a lot of stick for the TV shows."

"I'm sure it's nothing he can't handle," I reply.

She places her hand briefly on my forearm. "I do wish the media was kinder to you, though, Emma. So what if the audience didn't get to watch your love affair develop on screen. It's no one's business but your own, and I think you're a simply darling couple."

"Thank you," I reply, feeling exonerated and affirmed by her. "Now, if you could just get the rest of the British population to agree with you on that, I'd be super happy."

"They wanted Sebastian to marry that blonde contestant,"

Rakesh says as though this is new information to us all and not something the media has gone on and on about since *Dating Mr. Darcy* aired.

"Phoebe," I say. "Shame she was in love with the presenter then, wasn't it?"

Sebastian changes the subject. "How's the Spindex research looking?"

"Very promising," Rakesh replies, and I'm grateful to Sebastian. A girl can only take so much of the incessant *he should have married another contestant* baloney.

Seriously, people, it's been two years. Get over it. Please.

"Look." Odette holds her phone out, and I see a photo of two adorable children. The girl has her dark hair in braids tied with pale blue ribbons, and the boy has a cheeky grin on his chubby-cheeked face.

"Are these your kids? They are totally adorable."

"Thank you. Joaquin loves all things football, just like his father, and Antonella told me last night that she wants to be a mermaid when she grows up."

"A solid career choice."

"That's what I told her."

"Was your ex a football player?" I ask, and she nods. "As in American football or soccer?"

"He played soccer. He's retired now, but he did quite well with it all."

Rakesh interrupts with, "*Quite well?* He represented his country and he played in the premier league here in Britain."

"So he was a professional soccer player?" I ask her.

"Yes, with the ego to match," Odette replies with a dismissive flick of her wrist. "All I care about is that he's a good father to my children. That's all that matters at the end of the day."

I share a small smile with Sebastian across the table. My husband will always be a good provider, but I know that will pale in comparison to what an amazing dad he'll be to our kids when they come along.

"His ego is well deserved. There's the small fact he scored more points in a single game against Germany ever," Rakesh adds, clearly a fan.

"He was another lifetime for me," Odette replies, and the tension in her features makes me wonder whether all this talk of her ex-husband is beginning to get to her. He is her *ex*, after all.

"When are you on TV? I'll make sure to watch it," I say to move the subject to something less contentious.

Odette offers me a grateful smile. "It's probably pretty dry for people not in the industry, but if you want to, you can stream it anytime. It's live Tuesdays at nine."

We finish up our lunch, and I walk with the others as they return to the office. Once Rakesh and Odette have left us, Sebastian gives me a kiss on the lips.

"Thank you for being so nice to Odette. She's been through a hard time what with changing jobs and the divorce."

"Of course. She's nice."

"Oh, she is, and I'm certain she'd appreciate your friendship."

"How about I invite her out sometime? We could go get our nails done or watch a movie. Something totally girly."

"That sounds wonderful." He kisses me once more. "I've got to dash. See you at home later tonight. Love you."

"Love you, too."

I wait and watch as he makes his way through the revolving door and disappears into the cavernous building before I make my way back to the Tube stop. Although it wasn't the romantic meal for two I was hoping for, it was still nice to get to know Odette better and see that beyond the surface perfection, she's as human as the rest of us.

CHAPTER 6

*Y*ou know how I said trying for a baby is fun? Well, I've come to learn that it is and it isn't. Don't get me wrong, the actual trying is fun, but the getting pregnant part? Well, it's not exactly working out the way I'd expected.

We've been officially trying for several months, and so far, there's been a lot of sexy time action but no miracle of life happy-ending. I've tried not to let it get to me. I've told myself it's perfectly normal for it not to work right away. It's rare for couples to get pregnant in the first few months. I've even told myself it's a blessing in disguise that I'm not pregnant yet because I get to focus on developing the new Timothy maternity line with Penny. What's more—as she rightfully pointed out—I get to enjoy lazy Sunday mornings in bed, as many evenings out as I like, and all the things she had to give up when her first little one came along.

So, I spend a lot of time telling Sebastian, and pretty much anyone who'll listen, that I'm enjoying this time before our world gets turned upside-down by a baby and how lucky we are to be a young married couple in a magical English spring.

Sometimes I even believe it myself.

But the longer we try with no result, the more worried I become. Mom's words ring in my head. Have I left it too long? Everything I've read says thirty isn't too old, but is it too old? Rationally, I know it's not, that plenty of women have babies after thirty.

But maybe it's too late for *me*.

Eventually, after Sebastian tells me that my relentless pursuit of pregnancy is becoming borderline obsessive, he suggests we need a vacation to, and I quote, "focus on other things."

That isn't going to cut it for me. *I'm on a mission here, people!* So instead, I suggest we go get ourselves checked out by a doctor, just to be sure everything's in proper working order.

"Seb, it's just to make sure, that's all. You remember what my mom said."

"Brady, it's only been a few weeks."

"Months," I correct.

"It's been *months*?"

"Mm-hm. Three and a half months, to be precise, and so far, zero, zilch, nada."

"Well, not zero, zilch, nada exactly," he says as he wraps his arms around my waist, pulling me against his firm body. "It has been a lot of fun."

A smile bursts across my face. "That's true." I push myself up on tippy-toes and press a kiss to his lips. "I've loved every minute of it."

"Me too."

"But, Seb? We can't be doing it just for fun anymore. We need to get serious about this now."

He brushes his lips against mine. "You certainly know how to sweet talk a man."

I let out a giggle. "Can we go get checked out? Just for peace of mind, if nothing else."

"For you, Brady, anything," he replies with a smile.

And that is how we find ourselves walking hand in hand down the street toward the medical center in the nearby village, bundled up in our winter warmers despite the fact it's early spring, feeling a mixture of excitement and trepidation for what the doctor is about to find.

"What's your doctor like?" I ask. I may have been living in England as Sebastian's wife for over a year now, but I haven't needed a doctor for anything.

"Dr. Sheffield is old school, that's for sure. No fuss, says it like it is. He's been my doctor all my life, and he was Father's doctor before me. In fact, I'm pretty sure he delivered him. He knows the Huntington-Rosses pretty well."

"How old *is* this guy exactly?"

Sebastian laughs as he pulls the door open for me to walk through. "Well, he was around for the Spanish flu pandemic of 1918, I believe."

"Seriously?" I guffaw.

"Oh, yes. And the Black Death in Medieval Europe, of course. Oh, and the big cholera outbreak, too."

I nudge him with my elbow. "Cholera? The Black Death? That would make him at least seven hundred years old."

"Well, he *is* very old."

I giggle, and it ends in a snort.

"But seriously, you'll like him. He's a nice man, and he's very experienced. I'm sure he'll be able to set your mind at ease and tell us to keep on doing what we've been doing."

I give his hand in mine a squeeze. "I hope you're right."

"I will be. Just wait and see."

We enter an old building that looks like it's a good few

hundred years old, cross the wide hall, and enter the medical center. We're greeted by an older woman with reading glasses balanced on the end of her nose, her hair cropped in a short, sensible style.

"Lord Martinston. How wonderful to see you!" she exclaims when her eyes land on Sebastian. "I saw you were in the calendar for today, and I thought to myself, 'Meredith, you are one lucky woman getting to see that young Lord Martinston again.' I did, I said that to myself, I did."

Sebastian's lip quirks. "Good morning, Meredith. I must say, you look younger and younger every time I see you."

Meredith's blush rises up her face to her graying hairline. "Oh, stop it. You are such a charmer. A charmer, I tell you!"

"I do try," Sebastian replies with a smile. "This is my wife, Emma."

She inclines her head. "Lady Martinston. It is such an honor to meet you, it is."

I beam at her. Being called Lady Martinston happens infrequently enough that although we've been married for over a year now, it's strange to hear it. Me, a Texas girl from the wrong side of the tracks who grew up in a house the size of Martinston's kitchen is a freakin' English aristocrat.

"Please, call me Emma," I reply, embarrassed.

"Emma it is." Her face creases into a broad smile. "Lovely, lovely."

"Yes, it is...lovely," I reply.

"Shall we wait over here?" Sebastian suggests.

"Oh, yes. Why don't you both take a seat. Dr. Sheffield will be with you soon."

We sit down on a couple of wooden chairs, and I immediately notice the *ticktock* of a wall clock in an otherwise silent room.

"It's so quiet in here," I whisper to Sebastian.

"Dr. Sheffield is one of only two doctors at this practice,

so they probably don't have many patients, not one of those big practices you get in London. And it's probably for the best we're here on our own. This village loves to gossip. The local lord and lady of the manor visiting the GP is bound to set tongues wagging."

I attempt a smile. That clock is doing nothing for my nerves. "True."

As we wait, those nerves grow until they start a dance party in my belly. I begin to tap my feet on the patterned rug to given them an outlet. Thoughts bounce around my head, thoughts that have barely occurred to me since we started this journey. Thoughts, now that we're sitting here waiting to discuss our lack of pregnancy status with an official *health professional*, are taking up the entire real estate of my brain.

What if he runs some tests and finds there's an issue?

What if that issue is with me and I can't do anything about it?

What if it's a *big* issue? Like I've got no eggs left or my tubes point in the wrong direction or I don't have any tubes at all? Oh, my gosh! What if I don't have any tubes? I need tubes! No tubes means my eggs will have nowhere to slide down to get into my uterus, which means Sebastian's swimmers won't be able to find them, which means no babies! I need tubes. Without them I—

Sebastian's warm hand on my arm interrupts my train of thought. "Are you okay, Brady?" he asks quietly.

I force an exhalation of air. "I'm kinda nervous and thinking the worst, I guess."

"It'll be okay. We're only here to have a chat. That's all."

I nod my head like a bobblehead character. "A chat. Right. Just a chat."

"Just a chat," he confirms. "Why don't you read a magazine or something?" He collects a magazine from the side table. "How about a *Tatler* from twelve years ago? I'm sure it will have invaluable information in it. See?" He points at a statement on the cover and reads it aloud. *"What the It Girls are wearing NOW.* Brady, you need to read this."

I take the magazine from him, grateful for the distraction. "I need to know what the It Girls were wearing twelve years ago?"

"I believe it may change your life," he deadpans. "And if it doesn't, I'm sure there are several other articles that will."

"Well, first up I'll need to know what an It Girl is."

He chortles. "No one knows, Brady. No one knows."

I flick through the magazine and land on an article about the "young royals," who these days are approaching middle age. They look young, happy, privileged, and in love—all of which is totally true.

"Sebastian Huntington-Ross!" A deep, booming voice startles me, and I look up to see a stooped, elderly man with thinning hair in a white coat and neat collar and tie, with a pair of thick horn-rimmed glasses.

Sebastian leaps to his feet, and I do the same. "Dr. Sheffield. How do you do. This is my wife, Emma." He shakes the doctor's hand vigorously, who looks genuinely happy to see his patient.

"Marvelous, marvelous, Sebastian. Just marvelous. And Emma Huntington-Ross!" Dr. Sheffield booms as though announcing me to the room at a posh Regency ball.

"That's me," I reply with a smile pasted on as my nerves come swooping back. Thoughts of formerly young royals and It Girls evaporate from my mind.

We're here to find out if something's wrong.

"Come, come. Let's sit down and have a chinwag, shall we?"

"A chinwag?" I mouth to Sebastian. It sounds like something a dog might do.

"He means a chat."

Ah, another quaint British expression. The list is ever-growing. "Got it."

"You're looking absolutely spiffing, old chap," Dr. Sheffield says to Sebastian as he slaps him on the back, and I have to stifle a giggle. He's calling *Seb* "old"? This guy might not have been alive for the Medieval Black Death, but he only missed it by a decade or two.

"Thank you, Doctor. You're looking extremely well yourself," Sebastian replies.

The doctor sits down behind a large oak desk. "It's all down to the lard."

"The lard?" I ask, wondering if I heard right.

"You know, lard. Animal fat. It's great stuff. People are getting on board with these low carb, high fat diets these days, what with your Ketogenics and whatnot. But we've been eating that bloody good stuff all along. Never stopped, and I'm still ticking."

My eyes dart to Sebastian. "Actual lard, huh? Who knew?"

"We did, Emma. That's my point." Dr. Sheffield gives me a look that questions my mental ability to follow the conversation.

"Okay. Good to know."

"Right. Let's get down to business, shall we? What can I do for you fine folks today?" He raises his gray bushy eyebrows at us in expectation. There are three prominent, thick hairs poking out of the tip of his nose.

"We've decided to start a family," Sebastian announces.

"A family, eh? Good-oh. That's a fine idea for you young folk."

Sebastian shoots me a small smile. "We thought so."

"What do you want from me, then? A checkup? Make sure all the equipment is in tip-top working order?"

"Perhaps, although we thought we could have a general talk with you about it first. You see, we've been trying for a

FALLING FOR ANOTHER DARCY

few months now, and we've not had any success," Sebastian explains.

"There's more to it, actually," I add. "My mom said she and my dad had a hard time conceiving after me. I wondered if it was something to be concerned about?"

"Was it a geriatric first-time pregnancy?"

"Excuse me?" I say in surprise. "She's fifty-seven next summer, so she's getting older, but she's not geriatric exactly."

"Women who give birth to their first child over the age thirty-five are considered geriatric mothers," he explains.

"Right. I did not know that. And no, she was twenty-six when she had me."

"Right-o." He scribbles something on a notepad. I imagine it says *not the product of a geriatric first-time pregnancy*, but it could be something else. "Do you know if there was any medical reason for her infertility?"

"She wasn't *infertile*," I say. That word strikes me as shocking and so very, very final.

"Ah, yes, old girl, but she *became* infertile."

"I guess," I reply doubtfully. As he continues to scribble on his notepad, I tell him, "She told me she had endometriosis."

He jerks his head up and peers at me over his horn-rimmed glasses. "Endometriosis, you say. Well, that could be something that needs further investigation, eh wot?"

"I've never had any symptoms, so I don't think I have it," I reply hurriedly. Because I haven't and I don't.

"No lower abdominal pain during menstruation? No gastrointestinal concerns? No pain during sexual relations?" he asks me.

A hot blush creeps up my cheeks. "Come on, Dr. Sheffield. You've gotta let a girl retain some air of mystery in her marriage," I reply.

Sebastian places his hand on my back. "Don't worry. I'll

still fancy you, no matter what," he whispers in my ear, and I shoot him a quick, nervous smile.

I clear my throat. "None of those," I reply.

"Good-oh. Do either of you smoke?" he asks, thankfully changing the subject.

We shake our heads.

"Drink? What am I saying, I bet you still enjoy a decent red, eh, Sebastian? Châteauneuf-du-Pape, if I recall from your family Christmas party a few years ago. Splendid evening. Splendid."

"I do enjoy a glass, that's true. We both drink but not to excess."

"Good-oh, good-oh. Let's get you both on the scales, shall we?"

After we've both been weighed, we sit back down and Dr. Sheffield leans his elbows on his desk and fixes us with his stare. "Have you tried having sexual intercourse? You know, a bit of rumpy-pumpy? Hanky-panky? Having it *ooooff*?"

He pronounces the last word as "owwwwfff" in that very British way, and it catches me totally off guard.

I shoot Sebastian a concerned look. What the...?

The doctor leans back in his chair and roars with laughter, which promptly turns into a wheezing cough that goes on for an uncomfortably long time.

It's worse than the ticking clock for my nerves.

Once he's regained his composure, he tells us, "I do like a good old joke from time to time. Helps lighten things up, eh wot. Of course you've tried sex."

"Well, yes," Sebastian replies with a touch of embarrassment in his voice.

"You'll be at it like rabbits, I imagine. Of course you are. You're newlyweds. You'll be hiding the old sausage any chance you get. Eh?"

Hiding the sausage? A giggle builds, and I divert my eyes from my husband to avoid letting it out.

Sebastian never mentioned his doctor was a raving lunatic.

"Something like that, Dr. Sheffield," Sebastian replies.

"Good-oh. Splendid news. The important thing to remember is that you've got to do it at the right time. It's not enough to simply turn up and make a jolly good show of it. If the train isn't at the station, the coal can't be loaded, no matter the quality of that coal. So make sure your train is fully parked up, Emma."

Ugh. No!

"Could we maybe talk in actual medical terms?" I ask. "I'm finding it hard to follow what you're saying about trains and coal and...things."

"Naturally. You're an American," he says to me. "Do you have trains and coal where you're from?"

"Ah, yup."

"Yes. Well. I'll try to use global language, shall I?"

"Sure. That'd be great."

"What you want is for Sebastian's soldiers to hit their target and ram their message home." He pumps his fist against his palm.

I cross my legs, tight. "Excuse me?" I guffaw, my eyes wide.

"Picture this. The soldiers are Sebastian's sperm, and your egg, Emma, is the enemy fortress that must be penetrated for the good old fellows to win the battle."

My jaw drops open. There is so much wrong with that statement, I don't even know where to begin. I land on the most perplexing. "By your definition, my eggs are the bad guys. Right?" I squeak.

"Well, yes," he replies, as though I've pointed out some-thing that's completely obvious to everyone in the room.

My eyes dart to Sebastian, who offers me a sympathetic look.

"R*iiii*ght," I reply.

"Have I lost you? I thought a war metaphor would work quite nicely."

"I'm not sure this is all that helpful," Sebastian says, taking in the appalled look on my face.

"I do find my patients need a picture in their minds. It brings it to light, as it were. But if you'd prefer, I can get a little less dramatic?"

I let out a relieved breath. "That would be great, thank you."

"All right. What we want is those sperm to burrow deep down into that egg of yours, Emma. If just one of those millions of sperm manages that, we've got a zygote situation on our hands. And that, my dear people, is precisely what we want."

"A zygote situation?" Sebastian questions.

Dr. Sheffield leans back in his chair, satisfied with his little speech. "Exactly."

"What's a zygote?" I ask. I glance at Sebastian. "Do you know?"

He shakes his head.

"A zygote occurs in the fallopian tube or ampulla."

When we both just gawp at him in confusion, he adds, "It's a fertilized egg."

"Oh. Got it," I say as Sebastian says, "That's what we want."

"How old are you?" he asks me.

"I'm thirty."

"Ah."

Ah? What does *Ah* mean?

"Is that a bad thing?" I ask.

"It's fine," he replies with a flick of his wrist, sounding totally like it's not fine in the least.

My hands begin to sweat. *Fine* does not sound like what we want right now. *Fine* isn't great. *Fine* is...only fine.

"But I thought my fertility was still strong and that it won't begin to lower until I'm older. A lot older."

"It's tapering off, old girl. But it's nothing to be alarmed about right this moment. Well, maybe a little."

I blink at him.

"What I want you to do is start tracking your cycle by taking your temperature every day." He begins to scribble on a notepad. "It rises when you are at your most fertile, so you'll be looking for a pattern to know when you're most likely to conceive."

"When I'm ovulating," I say, relieved he's dropped the soldiers and fortress metaphors in favor of actual medical terminology—despite referring to my alarming "tapering" fertility.

"Do you have a thermometer?"

"We do," Sebastian replies.

"Take your temperature before you even think of getting out of bed each and every morning. You're looking for a pattern, Emma. Women's temperatures rise immediately before ovulation."

"I did not know that," Sebastian comments.

"Me neither."

"You could also go and buy one of those test kits they've got at the chemist to measure the luteinizing hormone, which pushes the egg down the fallopian tube. Pamela down the road at Smith's Chemist can help you with one of those." He rips a page off his pad and hands it to me. "Here you go."

"Thanks." I glance at the scrawl but can't work out a single word. Doctors and their handwriting.

"Sex twice a day when you're ovulating. More if you can manage it," he instructs.

I blink at him once more. "More than twice a day?"

"When it comes to making the next generation, you can't go firing into the wind. It's got to be targeted. Let's get those soldiers working for us, shall we?"

And we're back to soldiers. Awesome.

He rises in his seat, indicating our appointment is now over. "Let's see if we can't make you the next Lord or Lady Martinson."

"I think we can manage that, Dr. Sheffield," Sebastian says with a sideways glance at me, a smile playing on his lips.

"That often?" I whisper.

"We can give it a jolly good try, anyway," he whispers back, and I suppress a giggle because let's face it, there are worse things than being told to have lots of sex with the man you love, who also happens to be a handsome Mr. Darcy doppelgänger.

"Good-oh, old man. Give it a few months, and if you're still not sprogged up, we'll have another chinwag."

I beam at the doctor. This might have been one of the weirder conversations I've had in my life, but we've got a plan now and I'm a million percent more positive. "No problem."

"Give my best to your mother and granny, Sebastian. Cheerio. Pip pip."

We say good-bye to Dr. Sheffield and leave the practice. Sebastian wraps his arm around my shoulder as we wander down the quiet village street toward the village green.

"Do you think you're game for up to two or more times a day?" Sebastian asks.

"Are you?"

"If I have to," he says with a cheeky grin. "It'll be hard work, but I'm sure we're the couple for the job."

I snort-laugh. "We are pretty good at it."

He stops and pulls me into his arms. "The best," he murmurs before he kisses me so well, it takes my breath away.

"Do you think it'll work?"

"We can but try, Brady. We can but try."

CHAPTER 7

$\mathcal{I}$n theory, doing it two or three times a day sounds fun. In practice? Let's just say it puts the pressure on in a big way.

Don't get me wrong here. I've got the hottest husband to walk the face of the Earth, and I am certainly not complaining about that. But when you know you've got only a matter of a few days in a month in which you can conceive, things get a little more...routine. Less spontaneous. Almost like a chore.

I've been doing exactly as Dr. Sheffield told me, taking my temperature every morning before I get out of bed. All Sebastian's family had was one of those ancient glass thermometers filled with toxic mercury—I mean who has those these days? Other than the Huntington-Rosses, that is—so I went out and bought an up to date, state-of-the-art version you simply pop in your ear and, hey presto, you've got your temperature read.

And then I visited Smith's Chemist, as Dr. Sheffield suggested, and got myself an ovulation predictor test kit, and my life was transformed. It's so easy. All you have to do is pee on a stick and wait for a few moments to see if you're ovulating. No tracking your temperature and predicting when you're ovulating. Just a simple message: ready to go or hold off for now.

When I wake up one fine Saturday morning in late spring, I stretch out to hug Sebastian only to find his side of the bed is empty. I roll over to check the clock and see that I've slept way in. It's coming up on ten o'clock! I *never* sleep in that long. I must have been super tired from working so hard on the new Timothy maternity line.

I can hear the sound of people talking outside and furniture being moved. Sebastian will be up organizing last minute things for the reopening of the house today.

I throw the covers off and pad across the floor to collect my robe from the back of the door. Grabbing an ovulation test stick from the top drawer, I make my way down the hallway to the bathroom where I sit down and let nature take its course.

As I'm washing up, the little display on the stick changes, which means one thing: I'm ovulating. We've got only a short window of time to capitalize on this, and with a family dinner tonight, there's not a lot of time.

Last month, Sebastian was away in Europe on business when I ovulated, and so we missed our window entirely. This time, we're both here at Martinston, so I'm not going to let anything come between us and making that baby.

I glance out the window and notice a small collection of paying visitors already milling around in the gardens. If we're quick, we could get the deed done and get back out there before anyone notices.

All I need is my husband.

I rush down the hallway back to our room, swing the door to the walk-in wardrobe open, and grab the first dress I see. I pull it on hurriedly, thrust my feet into a pair of tennis shoes, collect the ovulation test stick from the bathroom, and trip lightly down the grand staircase to find Sebastian. A few steps down, I spy visitors eyeing up the antiques, the red velvet ropes already in place to tell them which areas they are allowed to visit. A booming voice is telling a group when the staircase was built and where the wood was sourced.

My exit is blocked.

I slink back up the stairs and out of sight.

Since *Saving Pemberley* went on air, the house is always heaving with visitors on open days. The show has been a runaway success on that front, which is precisely what we wanted it to be—only not today when I'm on an important mission.

With the stairway exit blocked, the only other way out is the servants' stairs.

I race down the long corridor to the hidden door covered in wallpaper. I pull it open and dash down the stairs, only to come to a crashing halt as I come face-to-face with another group of visitors. Too late, they spot me, and they all go quiet as they peer up the stairs at this strange woman in a mismatched outfit, holding an ovulation stick in her hand.

"Hi," I say, giving them all a small, awkward wave. "I hope you're enjoying your tour of Martinston today."

"It's brilliant, love, thanks so much for asking," a member of a group of four or five elderly ladies says.

"What are you doing up there?" someone asks.

"Do you live 'ere?" a man at the back asks. "Only, you sound American."

"Oh, I know who she is. She's the lady of the manor. That's Lady Martinston," a woman in a bright pink sweatshirt and matching pants replies. "Aren't you? You're the one from the telly what married the lord."

"Is she the girl who fell out of the limo on *Dating Mr. Darcy*?" someone else asks.

72

"That's right. I forgot about that part. That was, like, so funny," a woman who must be in her mid-twenties says. "But then she went on to marry Mr. Darcy, and now she gets to live here."

"That's right," I reply with a smile all the while thinking *MOVE!* Don't they know I've got to go have baby-making sex with my husband right this minute?

Don't answer that. If they knew, it would be just plain weird.

"Can you answer some questions?" one of the older ladies asks, and she looks so hopeful, I can't help but agree to do so.

"Of course. What would you like to know?"

They begin to pepper their questions at me, and there are a *lot.*

"When were these kitchens last used?"

"Is that the original fireplace?"

"What's it like to be a lady?"

"Do you have a portrait of yourself in the house somewhere, or is it just some crummy old photo?"

"Do you have servants, like on *Downton Abbey*, and are any of them Irish chauffeurs because I like the idea of having an Irish chauffeur?"

"Oooh, or a gay footman. Do you have a gay footman?"

The last question comes from the woman in the bright pink ensemble. "Why's your dress on backwards?"

They gaze up at me in expectation.

"Excuse me?" I ask, thrown by the last question.

"Your dress, love. It's on backwards. I can see the label here." She places her fingers at her neck.

My fingers fumble over the label at my throat. Dang it! It is on backwards—and inside out. In my hurry to reach Sebastian, I didn't even look in the mirror. I just grabbed that ovulation stick and ran.

"And what's that in your hand?" Pink Woman asks.

Uh oh.

My eyes dart to the ovulation stick before I hastily thrust it behind my back, embarrassment creeping up my body from my toes like a bathtub filling to the brim with piping hot water. I've got to do some quick thinking, stat! "It's, ah, it's a tool used to measure the depth of the floorboards upstairs."

Where the heck did *that* come from?

"Really?" a woman asks with a disbelieving frown. "Why would you need to measure the depth of the floorboards?"

"It sounds off to me, too, pet," a man at her side says.

"Oh, it's a very common problem in these older houses," I say, making it all up on the spot. "You see floorboards get worn down from all the foot traffic over time." I gesture at everyone's feet as though they are personally responsible for the imaginary floorboards wearing out. "We need to measure them regularly to make sure they're a certain height. It's so that people don't fall through and hurt themselves."

Where am I getting this stuff?

There's a murmur among the crowd.

"It's a health and safety issue. It is in fact a very serious job," I say to add some gravitas to my little made-up speech.

"Are you saying it's not safe for us to go upstairs?" a man asks, his brows knitted in concern.

"Yes, are you? Is it not safe up there?" someone else asks.

"We've paid good money to visit this house. We should be allowed to walk on the floorboards."

"Not if they're not safe, we won't."

"But there are a lot of good things to see up there. My sister Mildred said it was the best part."

I wave their concerns away with my hand—the one not holding the ovulation stick. "Oh, it's all fine. I measured them myself, and you're totally safe. Nothing to worry about at all."

I try to sound confident—and not like I'm making this crap up on the spot as I hold an ovulation testing stick behind my back, wearing a dress that's both inside out and on backwards.

Just your standard Saturday morning at Martinston.

"Well, that's a relief," the man gushes. "Isn't it a relief, Marion?"

"I daresay it is," Marion replies. "I'd hate to miss out on the reception room. I heard it's quite magnificent."

"Oh, it is for sure," I reply with a smile. "Now, if you'll excuse me, I'm going to slip past you and get on with measuring the, ah, bushes out in the garden."

"You've got to measure the bushes?" the man asks.

"Oh, yes. We take the height of our bushes at Martinston very seriously," I say as I make my way through the crowd, aiming for the back door—and my freedom. "It's all part of creating the most wonderful visitor experience possible for you all."

"Well, we appreciate your work," the man says. "Don't we, Marion?"

"We do," she announces, and others agree.

As I back away from them, a smile pasted on my face, I feel for the door handle behind me. "Thank you so much. I sure hope you enjoy your visit here at Martinston today!"

I pull the door open, turn, and dash through it.

"That's a jolly useful tool, that stick," I hear someone say as the door slams behind me.

I race across the gravel, making a beeline for the ladies' room in the café. I need to fix this dress situation before anyone else notices.

I rush by people who are wandering through the gardens, some listening to tour guides, some enjoying the weak English sun. I slip past a group of elderly women chatting at the entrance to the café. I'm beginning to weave through a cluster of tables to get to the ladies' restroom, when I feel a warm hand on my arm.

"Emma?" a voice says.

I blink at the immaculately dressed woman before me. She's in a cream cable-knit sweater with puff sleeves tucked into a pair of camel high-waisted belted pants, her long, dark hair pulled back by a pair of sunglasses balanced on her head.

"Odette," I murmur in surprise. "What are you doing here?" I offer her an easy smile. Well, it's not easy, exactly, let's face facts here. I'm in a dress that's both on backwards and inside out, I'm holding an ovulation test stick that now feels like it's screaming at me to get on with the business at hand, and I've not even run a brush through my hair. There's nothing easy about this situation at all.

"I came with my children to do a tour of the house and gardens," she replies. "They're having a hot chocolate with marshmallows at the table over there with my friend and her child." She indicates a table against the wallpaper-covered wall where three well dressed children are sipping their drinks. An equally well-dressed woman smiles and waves at me, and I wave back.

"I hope it's okay that we're here," Odette says, her brows pulled together as her eyes glide over me. "Sebastian insisted we come as his guests, but we wanted to do our bit to support your *Saving Pemberley* efforts."

"Right. Yes. Got it. I just didn't expect to see you."

She smiles kindly at me. "Of course you didn't. I'm very much looking forward to meeting the rest of the family at our dinner next month."

"I'm sorry, what?"

"Sebastian invited me to come here for dinner." She puts her hand over her chest. "I'm so sorry. Didn't he mention it to you?"

Uh, no.

"I'm sure he did and it slipped my mind. I've got a lot going on right now."

She eyes my dress as the ovulation test stick burns a hole in my hand. "Quite."

Deeply uncomfortable, I say, "Look, Odette, I'm running late for...a thing. I've gotta go."

"Did you know your dress is on backwards and inside out?" She asks it quietly so no one else can hear, but humiliation still prickles my skin.

"Is it?" I say, my voice unnaturally high. "Oh, goodness me. I'll need to handle that quickly, then." I edge away from her.

"Sorry to hold you up. I'll let you go."

Suddenly feeling bad that I'm so obviously brushing her off, I add, "I'll come find you once I've dealt with my, ah, thing. Okay?"

Her face breaks into a pretty smile. "That would be lovely. And don't forget the dress situation."

"I'm on it." I turn on my tennis shoed heel and dash into the ladies' restroom. Once inside one of the stalls, I jam the stick into the side of my underwear and whip my dress off. Once I pull it back on, I step out of the stall to do my final adjustments as I regard myself in the mirror. With my unkempt hair and makeup-less face, I don't look like I could win a Miss America competition any day soon, but I'm presentable enough for the task at hand.

Maybe I should have brushed my teeth?

But there's no time to second-guess myself. I need to find my husband, and I need to find him now.

As I exit the restroom, I scan the café, but there's no sign of him here. Odette catches my eye from the table and offers me a smile and a thumbs-up. I give her a quick wave and make my way outside. There are people everywhere, their numbers swelling in the last ten minutes. I rush around looking at every tall, broad man I can find, but there's no sign of my husband.

I stop by the garden wall and wrack my brain. Where could he be? He's not in the kitchen, he's not in the café, he's not in the formal gardens, he wasn't upstairs...

And then I've got it. The pond! He'll be at the pond.

You see, ever since *Dating Mr. Darcy* aired, people have bemoaned the fact there was no "pond scene" on the show. It's the famous scene from the BBC's '90s version of *Pride and Prejudice* starring Colin Firth, in which Mr. Darcy, wracked with unrequited love for Miss Elizabeth Bennet, strips down to what must have been a scandalous state of undress in 1813 —his tantalizingly wet white shirt and a pair of tight breeches—and dives into Pemberley's pond.

Unsurprisingly, Colin Firth's Mr. Darcy has had women's hearts aflutter ever since.

Back when we were engaged, Sebastian performed an inadvertent pond scene in front of a crowd of people when he dove into the pond, in a fit of gentlemanliness, to save my hat. Heather McCabe from the company that produced *Dating Mr. Darcy* put serious pressure on him to repeat the performance in *Saving Pemberley*. Of course he refused, not wanting to fuel the media's fires. But that hasn't stopped women from luring my poor husband down to the pond in the hopes the mood will take him and he'll strip down and dive into it.

So far, no banana. But it doesn't stop them from trying, and Sebastian is far too sweet not to allow himself to get dragged down there.

I dodge visitors on the limestone path and finally reach the pond. My hunch was right. I spot him in a gaggle of women by the water's edge.

"Would you ever consider chasing after my hat if it accidently blew into the pond, Mr. Darcy?" a brunette woman in a plaid jacket asks.

"His name is Lord Martinston, Prue," hisses another woman in a yellow fluffy sweater that makes her look like Big Bird.

"Would you ever consider chasing after my hat if it accidently blew into the pond, *Lord Martinston*?" Plaid Jacket says as she bats her eyelashes at Sebastian. "Or could I call you Sebastian?"

"Sebastian is fine with me," he replies with that dazzling smile of his, "but I don't see a hat on your head in order to chase after it."

"Details," Plaid Jacket replies with a wave of her hand. "I could take my jacket off? Or my shirt? It's very thin material. I bet it could get blown away at any moment."

Wow. Just wow.

"*I've* got a hat," Big Bird says as she produces a beat-up old cap from her purse. "You could swim out to get this one for me." Without waiting for his response, she flings the hat like a Frisbee out into the pond. Everyone watches as it lands with a plop onto the water.

"Oh, no. I appear to have dropped my hat," Big Bird says in a monotone. "Is there anyone here who can help me?"

The women turn to look at Sebastian in expectation.

Shocker.

My husband needs rescuing.

"Excuse me, ladies!" I say loudly as I push through the group. I come to a stop at Sebastian's side. "Sebastian, you are needed back up at the house for an urgent matter," I say in an efficient and authoritarian tone of voice. "A super urgent matter, in fact."

"A super urgent matter?" he questions, although I can tell by the sparkle in his eyes that he knows what I'm doing—just not why yet. "Well, in that case, ladies, I'm so sorry to have to leave, but duty calls."

There's a collective "Awww!" from the group.

"Come back, okay?" Big Bird says. "My hat isn't going to save itself." She nods in the direction of her beat-up old cap, floating in the middle of the pond.

"Of course," he replies with a small bow, looking every inch like a modern-day Mr. Darcy. "Now, if you'll please excuse me."

We leave the group and walk up the limestone path together toward the house.

"Thank you, Brady. That was getting awkward."

"It's nothing you haven't dealt with before. But there really is an urgent matter I need you to attend to."

His brow creases in concern. "Oh? What is it?"

"I'm ovulating."

He looks around the property at all the people. "Now?" he asks, and I nod.

"As Dr. Sheffield said, we've got a short window each month. I think you have to ravish me, Mr. Darcy, and ravish me good."

He lets out a low laugh. "It's tough making the next generation."

I take his hand in mine. "But for me, you're the *only* man for the job."

A certain period of time later—and I'm not saying how long exactly as that is no one's business but our own—Sebastian and I reemerge from our bedroom ready to deal with the visitors. This time, I've left the ovulation test stick behind, run a brush through my hair, and even applied some makeup befitting a lady of the manor.

"Ready to face the world again?" Sebastian asks.

"Absolutely," I reply with a firm nod of my head as he

pulls the door open. "Seb? What if we've made a baby just now?"

He places his hand lightly on my belly. "That would be incredible."

I grin up at him. "This could be it, you know. This could be the one that does the trick."

He raises his eyebrows at me. "I hope so. Although I think we'd better keep working at it, just in case it's not."

I let out a contented giggle, and it ends in a snort. "If we have to," I mock.

As we step outside into the late-morning sun, a voice asks, "Was the bush the right height, love?"

"I'm sorry, was what the right height?" Sebastian asks her, confused.

"The bush. She was measuring them with a little contraption thing-y before."

Sebastian raises his eyebrows at me, and my cheeks begin to warm. "Oh, yes. They were just perfect, thank you," I reply.

"I'm glad to hear it," she says before she wanders off.

"You were measuring a bush?" he asks me.

"It's a long story," I reply with a chuckle. "Let's just say I had to come up with a legit reason for holding an ovulation stick in my hand."

"Next time, maybe leave the stick behind."

"Good plan."

He cups my face in his hands and brushes his lips against mine. "We might have made our baby today."

"We might have." I gaze up at him, my heart full of love and hope. Because maybe, just maybe he's right. Maybe we did make our baby today.

CHAPTER 8

"*I*sn't it awesome to get told by your doctor that you've got to have loads of sex with your hot husband?" Kennedy asks over her dim sum one Sunday morning the following month in London's Chinatown.

"When you put it that way," I concede as I take a sip of my jasmine tea.

"When I go to the doctor, I get told things like 'take these antibiotics for seven days' and 'use this anti-fungal medication on your big toe.' Fun stuff like that."

"She's right," Phoebe confirms, her swollen belly now fully noticeable. "There are definitely worse things."

"Don't get me wrong. I'm not complaining about that side of things. I just wish it'd actually work."

"No news?" Kennedy questions.

"Nope. No news," I confirm with a grim shake of my head. "Even after I had to drag Seb away from a bunch of women trying to get him to do the Mr. Darcy pond scene a few weeks back."

"Are they *still* trying to get him to do that?" Phoebe questions.

"Voraciously."

"It's a totally hot scene, that's why," Kennedy explains with a mouthful of shrimp dumpling.

"Oh, I get it. Seb's a bit over it, though." I push a pork puff around my plate with my chopsticks. "He says Colin Firth has a lot to answer for, and I said he was only doing what the script told him to do."

Kennedy sighs. "But oh, did Colin Firth do it well."

"I think we can all agree on that," Phoebe says.

Kennedy plucks another dumpling off the shared plate. "Girl, it'll happen for you when it's your time. The baby thing, I mean, not the pond scene."

I offer her a weak smile. "Sure."

"Loads of couples take time to conceive," Phoebe says.

"You got pregnant when Johnny just looked at you." I try my best not to sound resentful but probably fail spectacularly. "It's taking forever!"

"It did happen quickly for us, but I'm not sure that's all that common," she replies, her hand placed protectively over the top of her growing belly. "It'll happen when it's meant to happen, Em. I'm a firm believer in that."

"Well, can you please consult your crystal ball and let me know when? That way I can chill the heck out about this. It's totally gotten into my head. It's all I can think about, and I've got a business to run."

Phoebe reaches across the table and places her hand on my arm. "Oh, honey. I'm sorry. That has to be so hard for you."

Tears prick my eyes. She's right, it has been hard. Really hard. I went into this thing thinking we should start trying now so that we could get pregnant easily, like Penny and Phoebe have. Sure, Mom's problems were in the back of my mind, but I've always been the type of person who sets a goal for herself and does her best to achieve it. With no family money behind me, I worked my butt off to put myself through college. Then I threw my heart and soul into making Timothy a success. Heck, I even embarrassed myself on a reality TV show to help get the label out there. If I could do the same for having a baby, believe me, I *so* would.

But this Type A achiever is finding it increasingly hard to achieve the baby goal.

I paste on a brave smile for my friends. "You know what? You're right, Phoebes. It will happen when it's meant to, and I just need to let it be. I'll leave it up to the universe or whatever."

She smiles at me. "Atta girl."

"The crystal ball thing might not be a bad idea," Kennedy says as she loads her plate up with more tasty morsels. "My sister had issues conceiving, and she went to see this psychic who told her that she'd have a baby boy by the time the sun reached Taurus. Or was it Gemini? Oh, I always get those two mixed up. Anyway, my point is that this psychic was right on the money. My sister had twin boys the following May."

Phoebe says, "That could have been a coincidence."

"Yeah, I'm not gonna go start seeing psychics or anything like that. Imagine if they told me I'd never have kids?" I shudder. "Nope. Not happening."

"I'm totally with you, girl, but I remember she did a bunch of other stuff, too," Kennedy says.

"Like what?"

"I'll ask." She picks her phone up off the table and begins to tap at the screen.

With Kennedy occupied, I ask, "How are you, Phoebe? Are you over the morning sickness?"

"Yes, thank goodness," she replies with a smile. "Now it's mood swings, fatigue, a sore lower back, and popping out of my pants." I must have an appalled look on my face because she adds, "But it is the most wonderful time of my life. Truly it is."

"Convincing, Phoebes."

She giggles. "It's not easy, but I'm not complaining."

"Veronica has messaged me back, saying she tried the following things," Kennedy announces as she reads the screen. "Seeing a psychic—we already know about that one—doing it in the missionary position, lying perfectly still for twenty minutes after sex with her legs up the wall, and eating an all-meat diet."

I eye the pork rib on my plate. "All meat? Sure." I pick it up and nibble on it. It's delicious. "I could get on board with that."

"She also said eating a pineapple immediately after sex might help."

"What? Why?"

Kennedy shrugs. "I dunno. Google it. I'm only relaying this stuff." Her phone beeps again. "She said acupuncture can help, too."

I shake my head. "I'm not sure I want to have someone poke a whole load of needles into me voluntarily. I'm not some sort of masochist."

"But if it helps?" Phoebe asks.

"Not a fan," I say resolutely. "Anything else?"

Kennedy's phone beeps, and she consults it once more. "It says here she's pretty certain she conceived when they did it outside." She looks up at me. "Can you get it on in the garden?"

"That does not sound the least bit scientific to me. Besides, this is spring in England, not Texas."

"Less chance of getting bitten on the butt by a snake while you're doing it, though," Kennedy says with a wink. Her phone beeps again, and she reads it aloud. "If nothing works, tell her to go see her doctor."

I drop my shoulders as I exhale. "I've already done that, and I didn't love the experience."

Kennedy makes a face. "I feel so bad for you."

I force out a breath, my shoulders tense. "You have no idea how frustrating this is. I don't know why it can't just happen for us."

"You're pretty stressed, huh?" Kennedy says.

"I guess I am."

"Maybe you need to just chill out and let it happen?" she suggests.

"That might be it, Em. You might have wound yourself up so tight you've started to get in your own way," Phoebe says.

I bite my lip, deep in thought. I know they've got a point. I've been so focused on trying to get pregnant, of doing it at the right time each month, of waiting and waiting for any signs I'm pregnant. Perhaps chilling out is the key?

"I've got an idea. How about you plan a romantic dinner and scatter rose petals on the bed and dress up all sexy," Kennedy says. "You know, make it *fun*. Forget the ovulation stick things and just enjoy it."

"I guess," I reply unconvincingly.

"I think it'd be good for you to just let it happen," Kennedy says, her eyes flicking to Phoebe's.

"It would, babe. It'll take the pressure off." She focuses on something over my shoulder and exclaims, "What are the guys doing here?"

I look up to see Sebastian and Johnathan make their way through the busy restaurant. Handsome in their Sunday morning casuals, several women's heads turn as they reach us.

"Cool. I get to be the dateless and desperate one again," Kennedy says with a laugh, although I know she half means it. Love has so far evaded my dear friend here in England, and I want nothing more than for her to find someone.

"I hope you've saved me some pork ribs," Sebastian says as he plants a kiss on my lips and greets my friends.

"No can do, dude," I reply with a shake of my head. "I'm on an all-meat diet from here on out."

"You are?" he questions.

"I'll explain later."

"Is it okay if we join you?" Johnathan asks.

"We finished our blokes' coffee get-together early, and we're famished," Sebastian says.

"Of course," Phoebe says.

We make room at the table as the guys take their seats and set about collecting their dim sum from the passing carts.

"This all looks so good!" Johnathan announces.

"How was the Cambridge boys' club?" I tease, referring to the group of "blokes" he and Johnathan have just been hanging out with.

"You two are in a boys' club?" Kennedy questions.

"That's what my dear wife likes to call it," Sebastian replies. "It's just a group of men who happened to attend the same university getting together periodically."

"Exactly. It's a Cambridge boys' club," I repeat, and Sebastian laughs as he shakes his head at me.

"How is the old school tie today?" Phoebe asks with a smirk, referring to the social network that's such a big part of this new world we've both married into. If you go to the *right* school and the *right* college, you're set up for life. Funny how I went to a school with metal detectors and a community college and still ended up here.

"The old school tie is alive and well, my darling," Johnathan replies with a grin.

The guys begin to eat, and Johnathan tells us about how he's surprised Phoebe with a redecorated nursery.

"Johnny, you are the cutest husband ever," I say to him, and he gives a self-deprecating shrug.

"Phoebe's worth every drop of yellow paint," he replies, and they share a loving look. "And besides, the last time the nursery at the house was used was for me, so it's well overdue a refresh."

"It was a little out of date," Phoebe tells us, "like a few things in Johnny's family home. He thinks it's run down, but I think all that family history stretching back generation upon generation is absolutely charming."

"If charming is another word for ramshackle, then you're right," he replies with a gentle laugh. "My family's house might not have Martinston's grandeur, but it's still a whopping big house that needs updating."

"But the nursery *was* charming," Phoebe protests, "even if I love it so much more the way it is now."

"Darling, I'd peeled a huge chunk of the wallpaper off, and my sister destroyed the carpet with all her tea parties for her doll collection. Not to mention Poppy used to sleep in there with me all the time, so there was a distinct dog odor in the room."

Sebastian chuckles. "It sounds like it was more of a biohazard than a nursery."

"Oh, definitely." Phoebe giggles. "I do love the idea of our baby being in the same nursery Johnny was in as a child, though. It's got a certain circularity to it."

"The circle of life. It's a *Lion King* thing," Kennedy says. "What does it look like now? Any pictures, guys?"

As the others discuss the finer points of nursery interior design while perusing a bunch of photos, I feel Sebastian's hand on my shoulder.

"Are you okay, Brady? You've gone awfully quiet."

"I'm just lost in my thoughts, I guess. We were talking about 'you know what' before you got here."

"Which team is most likely to win the F.A. Cup this year?" he teases.

"Yup. A group of girls meet for dim sum to discuss men's soccer. A group of *American* girls at that," I deadpan.

"It has been known to happen." He leans in closer and says, "What's going on?"

"I was telling them how I'm just bummed about the whole baby thing, that's all."

He gives my shoulder a squeeze. "I know you are, and I wish I could say something to make it feel better. Between you and me, I love you so very much, you know."

My gaze locks with his and contentment spreads through my chest. "You know what? You just made me feel a whole lot better."

"Do my superpowers hold no limit?"

I let out a giggle, and he leans in and kisses me.

"It'll happen for us, Brady. You'll see."

"I hope you're right, Seb. I want it more than anything."

"More than some of that chewy pecan praline you got on your last trip to Houston? Because that was pretty good."

I beam at him. "Even more than chewy pecan praline."

"Yeah. Me too."

I nuzzle him, and he wraps his arm around me and pulls me in for another kiss. It's short and chaste—we're sitting at a table with our friends in a busy restaurant, and PDAs are so not my thing—but it warms my heart to know how deeply he cares for me and how much he wants this baby, too.

Kennedy waves her hand at us. "Hey, you two! It's bad enough that I'm the third wheel *again* without you two rubbing it in my face with your married people canoodling."

"Sorry, sorry," I reply. "We'll try to lessen the married people canoodling quotient."

"Thank you."

Sebastian gives my shoulder one last squeeze before he gets on with the important task of eating his dim sum.

I sit and listen to my friends chat about a bunch of things, their laughter filling the restaurant air. I might not have the baby I so want. It might be proving a whole lot more difficult to get pregnant than I ever thought, but I've got a wonderful husband and the best friends.

I've got this.

"Excuse me," a woman asks Sebastian hesitatingly. "Are you Sebastian from that show *Dating Mr. Darcy?*"

He turns and smiles up at her. "I am."

"Oh, you are!" she exclaims in obvious delight. "I adore you! Can I get a selfie?"

Gracious as ever, Sebastian rises to his feet. "Of course. It would be my pleasure."

The woman huddles up to him, holds her phone out, and snaps a few shots.

"Does this happen a lot?" Kennedy asks me out of the corner of her mouth.

"Oh, yeah. Especially now that *Saving Pemberley* is on air. Personally, I can't wait for it all to be over."

Kennedy makes a face. "They still don't like you, huh?"

I clench my jaw as I think of the latest media jibes. "Not exactly. They've moved on from saying I'm some kind of weird gardening obsessive to just plain boring now. The British media's darling I am definitely not."

"Well, that sucks." Kennedy's assessment is right on the money.

"I'm very pleased you enjoyed the show. It was lovely to meet you," Sebastian says to the woman in an obvious attempt to return to our group.

"Oh, I love it. I've watched *Dating Mr. Darcy* seven times."

Sebastian's eyes widen. "Every episode?"

She gives an emphatic nod. "Oh, yes. You see so much

more with each viewing, and I've watched all the episodes so far of *Saving Pemberley* twice already."

I raise my eyebrows at my friends. This woman is what they call a "superfan," which I've got nothing against, of course. But can't she please just leave us alone?

"Well, enjoy your day," Sebastian says as he returns to his seat.

"Oh, I will *now*." She waves her phone in the air. "I'm gonna post this ASAP. My friends are going to *die*." She seems to notice the rest of us for the first time, her wild eyes landing on each of us as she works around the table. "Oh, you're Phoebe!" she exclaims. "And you're Kennedy! And you're Mr. Bingley!" Her eyes land on me, and her face drops. "And you're Emma."

Nice.

"Is this some kind of reunion? Is Camille somewhere, too?" Her head jerks as she searches the restaurant, as though Camille might be hiding behind a table, ready to spring out and declare "Surprise!" to any random fan who happens to be in for dim sum.

"No Camille I'm afraid," Sebastian replies with the impassive smile he perfected as Mr. Darcy on the show.

"Praise the Lord for that," Kennedy murmurs to me, and I've got to agree. Camille would totally ruin our little alumni get-together with her talk about how much better she is than the rest of us. Not to forget her trying to blackmail Sebastian to get him to marry her either, of course. *That* was super special.

"If you'll excuse me, I need to go to the restroom," Phoebe announces as she stands. "I've gotta pee all the time," she explains under her breath to me. "It's so annoying."

"Oh, my! You're *pregnant!*" the woman screeches when her eyes land on Phoebe's rounded belly, and people at the neighboring tables turn and stare.

"I am," Phoebe replies, her cheeks flushing with the attention.

"Oh, my gosh, oh my gosh, oh my gosh. This is amazing news. You're having a baby. A baby Bingley. A Bingley baby!"

"That's right," Phoebe replies, her smile frozen.

"Although I do wish it was going to be a little Darcy baby instead, but of course *that* didn't happen, did it?" She trains those crazy eyes on me, and I want to shrink into my chair and disappear.

Sebastian springs to his feet once more, forming a human shield between me and her. "Isn't it funny how things work out. Now, if you don't mind, we were in the middle of a rather important discussion. I won't keep you."

"Ooh, are you talking about doing another show? Because I've got some great ideas. Bring Mr. Wickham back and give him his comeuppance for a start. He never got it in the novel, and it's about time he did."

"That's an excellent idea. Thank you. Now if you don't mind?" Sebastian gestures to the door, and Just Plain Crazy finally gets the not-so-subtle hint.

"Don't you worry. I'll keep it to myself." She taps the side of her nose conspiratorially. "We don't want those unhinged fans out there to get a whiff of this. They'd go nuts."

"You're so right," Sebastian replies. "I do very much appreciate you keeping it to yourself."

"Anything for you, Mr. Darcy," she simpers. "Bye, now." She turns and leaves, and we heave a collective sigh of relief.

CHAPTER 9

The following morning, I practice my pitch for Body Sports one last time. Now that we've had a couple of design prototypes made up, Penny and I agreed it's time to test the waters with the maternity line. It's so exciting to hold the pieces in my hands and imagine my own growing belly filling them in the not-too-distant future. Whenever that may be.

On my way to the meeting, I stop at the small local market and buy a selection of cooked meats to munch on during my drive to Birmingham. If Kennedy's sister recommended eating a lot of meat, I'll happily become a super carnivore.

By the time I reach the Body Sports offices, I've eaten the equivalent of half a pig. I'm full but positive. And nervous. Definitely nervous. Body Sports taking Timothy Maternity into their stores would be a major coup for Penny and me.

Ten minutes later, my nerves have been replaced with a sinking feeling as I sit in a windowless meeting room with Nigel Plumber and Angelina Morris from the procurement team.

"The issue I'm having, Ms. Brady, is.... Do I still call you that now that you're married to a lord?" Nigel, a portly gentleman with a broad "brummie" accent placing him firmly in Birmingham, says with a grin.

"Ms. Brady is fine."

"Good, good. What I was saying is that I'm not sure British women want to exercise while they're pregnant." Nigel turns to Alison. "Am I right?"

"That's a gross generalization, Nigel," Alison says in a clipped English accent that reminds me of Mrs. Watson from *Dating Mr. Darcy* and never fails to make me feel like I'm being told off by a grumpy teacher. "There must be British women out there who want to exercise while they're pregnant."

"Do you know any?" he questions.

"Well, no, not *personally*. But there must be some. It's not like we're a nation of sloths, are we? Don't forget, we Brits ruled the world not that long ago."

"Ah, yes. The Great British Empire, *rah rah rah*," Nigel confirms, his eyes dancing.

Actually, I think it's been quite a long time since Britain dominated the world, but I'm not going to go pulling out any unhelpful historical facts right now. They're the customer, so they're right—about pretty much anything right now.

"I'm absolutely certain there's a big market for maternity activewear in Britain, and across Europe, too," I begin. "In fact, I've—"

"Not the French, eh?" Nigel interrupts. "They're too busy eating garlic and twiddling their mustaches to exercise."

The pregnant ones?

Alison laughs. "And smoking and drinking and being horribly rude."

Again, the *pregnant* ones?

"Oh, yes. They're all so rude, the French." Nigel shakes his head. "I do not like them."

"All of them?" I ask as Alison says, "Hear, hear."

"All of them. The whole stinking lot," Nigel confirms.

As long as I live, I will never understand why the British hate the French so much. I mean, what's not to love? French food, French wine, the beautiful city of Paris, not to mention French kissing…. All in all, my point is, it's the perfect country.

"Oh, those French," I say, trying to get in on the conversation. "They're so…" I struggle for a word and eventually land on, "*French*."

"Exactly. You get it." Nigel shoots me an admiring look. "She gets it, Ali."

"She does indeed."

"So, back to the maternity line," I lead, hoping we can leave the French to the side. "We were thinking of offering a few pieces to start with, perhaps this set." I press the remote control and an image of a pregnant woman in a Timothy bra top and leggings combination appears on the screen. She looks sporty and fresh and rather pregnant. "Our research suggests pregnant women between the ages of twenty and thirty-two would like this style, particularly in a gym situation."

Nigel leans back in his chair and throws me a critical look. "Was this research done here in Old Blighty, or in the US?"

"It was in the US, but I'm sure it would apply here, too."

The look on both of their faces tell me they're not quite as sure as I am.

"Look, Emma," Alison begins as she leans her elbows in the table. "We love you and we love Timothy. Our customers love Timothy. Together, we make a lot of money."

"That's true," Nigel says.

"We're just not sure a new maternity activewear line is what Body Sports is looking for right now. We've already got the big labels in our stores, and they sell well enough, but not that well." She scrunches up her nose. "Sorry."

My heart drops to the carpet. "I understand perfectly." Which is Type A personality code for *You're saying no now, but I'm gonna get you to say yes someday soon.*

"Oh, come on, love. You've got a face like Livery Street," Nigel says.

I blink at him in confusion. "A face like what street?"

"It's Birmingham-speak for having a long face because Livery Street is awfully long," Alison explains. "I could barely understand a word when I moved up here from the South East. It was all 'black over Bill's mother's' and 'ee-yar' and 'having a benny.'" She lets out a laugh. "It was like learning a foreign language."

"I know exactly what you mean," I reply, thinking of all the English-isms I've had to learn now that I live here.

"We might not be interested in your maternity line, Emma, but we do love your other lines, of course," Alison reassures. "I've got the Lydia, the Mary, and the Jane. I wear them all the time."

Before you say it, yes, I did it. I named some of our lines after characters from *Pride and Prejudice*. It was fitting for the reality TV show contestant who married Mr. Darcy, even if I'm sure Austen devotees around the globe might not love the idea quite as much as we do.

"I'm glad to hear it," I say with a smile.

"I'd love to say I wear the Lydia crop top, but they don't come in my size," Nigel says with a laugh, his belly jiggling up and down like Santa's after too much milk and cookies.

"Can you imagine?" Alison hoots with laughter. "I have quite an image right now."

"Me too!" Nigel replies.

"Yes, very funny," I say with a forced smile. "Well, I'd like to revisit this new maternity line down the road, but we'll leave it for now."

"All right, love," Nigel says.

"Nige, we've got that next meeting," Alison says as she rises to her feet. "Thanks for coming in, Emma. How's that devilishly handsome husband of yours? Still handsome?"

"Still handsome."

"Of course he is. He's a total dish."

"But would he look good in a Lydia crop top?" Nigel asks.

"I don't think so," I reply.

"Oh, I have to disagree with you on that. I imagine your Mr. Darcy looks rather good in anything," Alison replies, and I force a smile. It's more than a little awkward to be told your husband would look good in a bra top at the best of times, let alone by a customer who's just turned down your new line. "Is there a pond scene coming up?" she asks, her eyes bright.

"Sorry to disappoint you, but no."

Her face drops. "Shame."

"Well, bye now," I say.

"Tara-a-bit," Nigel says brightly, still chuckling to himself. I've learned it's his Birmingham way of saying good-bye, so I reply, "Tara."

Once I've left the Body Sports corporate office, I wander down the street to find myself a coffee. As I wander past the stores, the disappointment that Alison and Nigel wouldn't even let me pitch our new maternity line, let alone stock it, sits heavily in my belly. I didn't even get past the first slide to do the presentation I'd practiced in the mirror. But I won't be deterred. I'll find a way to get my new designs into their stores. I've just got to work out how.

I spy a chemist and remember I'm running low on ovulation test sticks. I buy a stack of them before I find a café and treat myself to a ridiculously calorific and delicious chocolate cupcake covered in M&Ms. I need cheering up, and in my experience, chocolate never fails to do the trick.

My coffee and snack finished, I locate the restrooms at the back of the café and decide on a whim to check to see whether I'm ovulating. I've been so wrapped up in the house and pulling together this new maternity line that I've not tested myself for the past few days. I pee on the stick and as I wash my hands and run a comb through my hair, the screen changes, telling me today is a great day to try to get pregnant.

Huh. That doesn't seem right. Sure, I've been taking people's advice and trying to chill out about it all by focusing on other things, but I can't be that out of sync. Can I?

I pull up the calendar on my phone. My first week has come and gone, my second is...*uh-oh*. I'm at my most fertile right now. And what's more, if my calculations are right, I'm about to ovulate. Sebastian is due to fly to Brussels later this afternoon. I glance at the time and am hit by an instant wave of panic. If we have any hope of getting pregnant this month, I need to get my sorry butt to Sebastian in London, and I need to do it now.

Any Zen thoughts of chilling out fly out the window as I race down the M40 motorway at breakneck speed. As I zip past cars, I call Sebastian's cellphone. As it rings, I drum my fingers on the steering wheel like I'm in a band that plays frenetic dance music.

This is doing nothing for my state of mind.

My call goes straight to voicemail.

I try to keep my tone light as I say, "Hey, Seb, it's me. Just checking you're in the office like you said you would be today. I'm gonna drop by to say hello, probably in a couple hours. Call me."

I don't want to leave a message about *why* I want to drop by, of course. Even though it's his private cellphone, who knows? He might get his assistant, Susie, to check his messages, and I'm positive he doesn't want her to know that: 1. we're trying for a baby and 2. I'm on my way into the office to have my way with her boss.

Boundaries, people.

I race down the motorway toward dark, looming clouds, and before long, fat blobs of rain begin to scatter across my windshield.

"It's only rain, people!" I shout to no one in particular as the traffic slows to a third of the speed we were just doing. "This is England. It rains all the freaking time."

We're now moving at an arthritic snail's speed, which is so typical. Whenever you're in a hurry, people go slow. I'm sure they go regular speed ordinarily.

I drum my fingers on the steering wheel and chew my lip.

Finally, as the view of the countryside turns increasingly urban and the slow-moving traffic builds, I make the executive decision to ditch the car in a parking lot in favor of catching the Tube. Traffic is a nightmare at the best of times in this city of thirteen million people with many streets wide enough for a horse and carriage and not a lot more, let alone when it's begun to rain cats and dogs.

I crawl through the streets as I look for the parking building we've used before. I know it's here somewhere.... Is it this street? No. The next? Double no. Parked at the lights, I do a quick search on my phone and spot the building three streets away. Hurray! Almost there.

The lights turn green, and no one moves. *No one.* I stretch my neck to see what's going on. People around me begin to sound their horns. At least others are just as frustrated as me. It's cold comfort.

Don't they know these are precious hours? This month's solitary egg could be preparing to travel casually down one of my fallopian tubes in the hopes of meeting a nice, friendly sperm right this very minute, blissfully unaware that I'm sitting here, alone, with zero hope of fulfilling its destiny.

And then the car in front of me moves and the lights turn yellow. There's no way I'm stopping. I am making this light. I hit the accelerator and lurch forward, only for the car in front of me to come to a sudden stop in the middle of the intersection. Reacting too slowly, I crash into the car and come to a sudden, thudding halt.

Oh, wonderful. This is *exactly* what I need right now.

The woman in front of me gets out of her car, opens up an umbrella, and storms over to my window in the pelting rain. I crack my window and get splattered with rain.

"Are you freaking kidding me? You rammed my car!" she yells at me.

"You stopped in the middle of an intersection," I reply. "What was I supposed to do?"

"*Not* drive into me?" she suggests, her eyes big and round.

It's a good point.

She pulls at her dress, which is pasted on her belly with a light brown splatter. "You made me spill my hot chocolate all over my new frock. It cost me a fortune, and I only wore it for an interview today."

I eye the large wet, brown mark on her lilac dress and instantly feel bad. "Sorry about the dress. That sucks."

"Thanks," she sniffs, visibly softening.

"I'll come have a look at the damage." I steel myself for the rain. I climb out of my car and dash around to the back. I pop the trunk to grab my umbrella. Since it rains, on average, half of any given month in this country, I learned early in my time here to always have an umbrella handy. I wasn't a girl scout for no reason, people. Always be prepared.

That is until you realize you left your umbrella at your friend Phoebe's place in the country and never quite remembered to replace it in the trunk for the next rainy day.

Dang it!

I slam the trunk closed. I've got no choice here. I'm going to get wet. Very, very wet.

Inspecting both our cars shows the damage is minor and superficial, although my bumper is now hanging off my car on a slant.

Cars toot their horns around us, as though we've stopped in the middle of the road for a nice, friendly chat in the pouring rain. Someone drives through a puddle beside us, splatting dirty water over my bare legs, which drip down inside my shoes.

Come on! Where's your compassion, people?

I pull my phone out of my purse. "Give me your number, and we can talk later about insurance and all that stuff, okay? We're holding up all the traffic, it's wet, and I've so gotta go."

She sizes me up for a moment from beneath her umbrella, her mouth twisted. "Yeah, okay." She too pulls her phone out, and we exchange numbers.

"Thanks for this," I say as I wave my phone in the air. "Oh, and mix a fifty-fifty mixture of dishwashing liquid and baking soda, scrub it into that stain, and leave it for ten minutes before washing it. It works like a miracle."

"Seriously? Thanks." She beams at me, and I give her a brief wave as I plunk my soaking self back in my car and maneuver it through the traffic. I make a beeline for the parking building.

Once I find a free parking space after scouring the building for what feels like an hour, I say a prayer that the rain will ease by the time I get down the elevator and outside once more.

It has not.

It's pouring like the heavens left the faucet running in the bathtub, and I've got no choice but to dash through it on my way to the closest Tube stop and simply hope for the best.

As I spot the red circle with the horizontal blue line through it, I quicken my pace. Almost there! I dash down the steps and into the dry bowels of the city, purchase a ticket, and join the throngs of people shuffling toward the escalator going down.

My phones rings. It's my husband. "I'm on my way in. I've got to see you today, and you're leaving for Brussels soon, so I won't see you until tomorrow night, and we've got to *do it now*," I hiss into the phone. A woman darts a look at me out of the corner of my eye. "We're decorating," I say to her, and she immediately averts her eyes with a "Right."

"Well, hello to you too," Sebastian replies with a chuckle.

"Sorry, sorry. It's been a total mission to get to you today, so I'm feeling rushed. Are you still in your office?" I step onto the escalator, and we start to move down.

"I will be in about ten minutes."

"Perfect. I'm just getting on the Tube now."

"Brady, I'm not sure we ought to be…doing things in my office."

"You've got venetian blinds you can close, and we need to hit that target, dude."

"As wonderful as 'hitting a target' sounds," he replies with a note of amusement in his voice, "perhaps we need to come up with another plan?"

"Seb, I don't want to do it at some pay by the hour, seedy hotel."

The woman shoots me another look. I can't cover that one up with "decorating," so instead I focus my attention straight ahead and pretend I'm not discussing where to have sex with my husband while standing on a crowded escalator.

"I didn't mean we should go to a seedy hotel. Just I'm not sure doing it in my office with my assistant's desk right outside the door is exactly ideal."

"Look, I get it, but it's all we've got. Be ready when I get there, okay? No need for anything fancy. Just get in there and get the job done."

"You sweet talker, you."

"Seb!"

"I'll see what I can do, but I've got to leave the office at three or I'll miss my flight."

"Three o'clock. Got it. See you soon." I hang up the phone as the train's doors glide open.

I find a free seat and notice people looking at me, including the woman who overheard my conversation with Sebastian before. She's now tapping on her phone, smiling to herself and occasionally glancing my way.

No points for knowing what she's messaging about.

I glance down at my clothes, knowing I must look like a drowned rat. Sure enough, my once smart cream blazer is literally dripping water on my seat, and I click open my compact to survey the damage to my hair and face. It ain't pretty. I've got straggly, damp hair stuck to my face like Elvis's Brylcreem gone wrong. My eye makeup is smudged beneath my eyes, making me look like a close relative of a panda bear. I try to wipe it away with my fingers, which only makes me look like I've come out the worse from a bar brawl.

I apply some fresh lipstick and push my hair behind my ears. There's nothing much else I can do here. Sebastian will just have to take me as I am—which is exactly what I need him to do.

By the time I arrive at his stop, my damp clothes have got a distinctive smell, my toes are languishing in puddle water inside my shoes, and my hair has frizzed in the humid subway air to twice it's normal volume. I just know I look like 80's Diana Ross—without the glamour factor. I only hope the rain has stopped when I reach street level.

As I clamber up the steps, I spot a dash of blue sky amid

the grey clouds, the rain merely spitting down on me as I traipse down the street, my shoes making a weird sucking sound with every step I take. I sound like someone in suction pads climbing a wall.

So, so sexy.

But I'm here to see Sebastian for one reason and one reason only. And I'm not about to let a bit of rain get between me and my baby-making mission.

CHAPTER 10

I push my way through the rotating glass doors and into the foyer of Sebastian's office building. I've got to check in at the reception desk in order to get up to Sebastian's floor. With one of the security guards on the phone, I wait impatiently behind a man in a tan suit who wants to discuss the finer points of horticultural investment with the only other security guard, Tony, a guy I've seen on previous visits here. He's unsuccessfully trying to close the conversation down.

"Avocados, my man. That's where the smart money is these days. Look at all your Millennials, chowing down on their smashed avos on toast and paying huge amounts of money for the privilege, I tell you. Huge!"

"That is very true, sir," Tony the security guard says. "Who was it that you were here to see?"

The man ignores the question. "Can't stand them myself. They're all slimy, aren't they? Whatever happened to good old marmalade, I ask you? Nothing wrong with a decent slather of marmalade on toast, in my books. Avocados are utterly overrated. But if I can make some mint off of other people's stupidity? Well, do you think I would like to take that chance by the short and curlies?"

"I, ah, don't know," the security guard replies, his lip curling at the descriptive expression.

I raise my eyebrows at him as if to say "Move this guy along, now, please" as I tap my fingers with increasing ferocity against my thighs.

"Oh, I will. Mark my words, I will," Mr. Tan Suit says as his head nods up and down. "They can eat their fancy brunches in their fancy cafés. I'll be laughing all the way to Barclays Bank, I tell you."

"Yes, I'm sure you will, sir. Now, if you could please tell me who you want to visit...?" Tony says.

"The only problem I'll have is working out which property in the South of France to purchase."

"I'm sure. Now, who was it you wanted to see?"

I love the British. Heck, I'm married to one of them, that's how much I love them. But along with their many attributes they can be too polite. W*aaay* too polite. No one would have suffered this guy for so long in America. That security guard needs to send Mr. Tan Suit Avocado Head away, and he needs to do it now.

I glance at the time on my phone. 2:37.

Don't they know time is running out for me here?

"And here's the other thing about avocados," the man continues. "The profit margin on them is—"

This American girl has had enough.

"Excuse me, Tony!" I say forcefully as I sidle up to the reception desk beside Mr. Tan Suit Avocado Head, who turns and gives me an incredulous look.

"We are in the middle of something here, young lady. Please be so kind as to wait your turn," he says, his chin in the air, showcasing a thick collection of wiry hair nestled inside his nostrils.

I shoot him an apologetic smile I don't mean. "I would, sir, but I'm late for a meeting with Mr. Huntington-Ross." Turning to Tony, I instruct, "Level fourteen, please. Can you sign me in? I need to get up there now."

"Certainly, Mrs. Huntington-Ross," Tony replies pleasantly as he taps away on his computer.

"That's your urgent meeting?" Mr. Tan Suit Avocado Head's lip curls in disdain. "I hardly think wanting to see your husband is enough of a reason to interrupt my conversation with this fine fellow. Do you?"

Clearly I do.

"Sorry, not sorry," I mumble under my breath.

"Here you are Mrs. Huntington-Ross," Tony says as he hands me a label, which I promptly slap onto my damp lapel. "Shall I call ahead for you, or is he expecting you?"

"No, no," I say with a wave of my hand as I turn to dash away. "I'll head right up. Thanks, Tony!"

"What a rude woman," I hear Mr. Tan Suit Avocado Head complain as I rush across the vestibule.

I wait by the elevators, pressing the *up* button at least five times. The elevator pings and the doors sweep open and out walks a group of suited workers, their clothes dry with their hair a normal volume—unlike mine. I spy Odette who is smiling and talking with someone as she exits. She looks totally put together in a navy suit and a string of pearls around her neck, her hair swept up into an elegant French twist. Whenever I've seen her, she has always looked so effortlessly stylish. She has an air of elegance that suggests what Granny would refer to as "breeding."

"Emma!" she exclaims as her eyes clamp on me. "How lovely to see you." She presses her cheek against mine. "Are you here to see Sebastian? Oh, what am I saying? Of course you are." Her eyes glide over me and she adds, "Are you quite all right? You look a little...frazzled, I suppose. I hope nothing's happened?"

Suddenly self-conscious, I reply, "Got caught in the rain."

"Oh, shame," she declares as she begins to rummage around in her black purse. Chanel, of course, to match her elegant style. "I've got a brush in here, if you'd like it. And some face powder."

I check in my reflection to see the skin on my face is all shiny. I sweep my fingers across my cheeks and pat my nose. It's no *Dating Mr. Darcy* professional makeup job, but it'll have to do for now.

The doors begin to slide shut, and I dash past her and ram my foot against one side to stop them from doing so. "Thanks, Odette, but I've gotta go. See you later!"

"Saturday. Dinner at your house. Sebastian invited me."

"Perfect," I reply as the doors lock into place and her pretty face disappears from view.

I take a deep breath to try to calm myself. With my dash down the motorway to the car crash to the rain, this has been a major undertaking to get here today. But I know it'll all be worth it when I take that pregnancy test in a few weeks' time and we learn we're going to be a family.

The elevator reaches the fourteenth floor, and I hurry toward Sebastian's office. I've been here a bunch of times before, so I offer people quick smiles as I trudge past their desks, the water in my shoes squelching between my toes with every step.

The door to Sebastian's office is closed.

Susie leaps out of her desk as I rush toward it. "Gidday, Emma?" she says in her Humpty Doo Aussie twang.

"He's expecting me. I called ahead." I glance at the window to his office and notice the venetians are firmly shut. I smile to myself. *Good man.*

"Okay, then? Go on in?" she says. "Want me to get you a coffee?"

"No!" I protest with force. The last thing I want is for Susie to come barging in on me and her boss doing our thing. I clear my throat. "I mean, thank you but no thank you. We need to talk about something important, so if you could, err, not let anyone in, that'd be just great."

"Not let anyone in?" she says, and I'm not sure whether she means it as a question or a statement.

I shake my head vehemently. "Do not let anyone in."

"Don't let anyone in?"

"That's right."

"That's right?"

"No one."

"No one?"

Oh, this is getting ridiculous.

"Susie, I'm gonna go through this door and close it behind me, and we need to be left alone."

"Okay?"

I give a firm nod of my head. "Okay," I confirm.

I push the door open and spot Sebastian sitting at his desk. He looks up at me as I push the door closed with my butt. I lean up against it and say in a husky tone, "Impregnate me now, Mr. Huntington-Ross!"

He shakes his head at me, his lips pressed together.

"Is there someone else in the room?" a voice says, and my hand flies to cover my mouth.

He's on a call with someone?

I mouth "sorry" to him as I pad as quietly as I can across the carpeted floor to one of the chairs, which turns out not to be overly quiet thanks to the water squelching between my toes.

"That was my EA offering me coffee," Sebastian bluffs to the person on the other end of the line.

"I thought I heard someone mention impregnation," a female voice says, and I widen my eyes. There's more than one person on the end of the line?

"Are you working the agriculture sector now too, Sebastian, rather than just healthcare?" the woman asks.

"Perhaps healthcare for cows?" another voice offers, and there's enough laughter from the desk phone's loud speaker to make me realize it's more than simply a handful of people who heard my announcement. I sink into the chair as mortification crawls across my skin.

There's more discussion between the people on what's obviously a *conference* call, and as Sebastian catches my eye, I offer him an apology.

He shakes his head at me and smiles before he refocuses the group onto raising assets for some purchase the company wants to make. I listen to him speak authoritatively and knowledgeably, and my heart swells with pride for him. Pride that manages to dispel my humiliation. Well, most of it, anyway.

I slip off my shoes and remove my jacket, hanging it out to dry on the back of a chair. Eventually, after ten plus minutes in which my tension builds to the point I could bounce like a pinball around the room, he wraps the call up and disconnects.

"Well, that was fun," he says as he rounds his desk and takes me in his arms. "My wife certainly knows how to make an entrance."

"No time for niceties," I say in a rush as I reach for his belt buckle. "Drop 'em, cowboy. We've got a job to do, and we've got seven minutes to do it."

"Yes, ma'am," he replies in a mock Southern accent, a grin on his face. "You sure know how to sweet talk a guy."

"Sweet talking is for wimps," I say as I work on my own clothes. "Now, get on that sofa."

He chuckles. "I think I like it when you're all bossy."

Afterwards, Sebastian leaves for the airport, and I lie with my feet up the wall for twenty minutes, just as Kennedy's older sister said to do. I concentrate on visualizing fertilization, and other than an embarrassing moment when Susie walks into the room and stops and stares at me, I'm filled with hope that maybe, just maybe, this time we've made our child.

CHAPTER 11

It's a clear and mild evening that weekend, and Odette is due for dinner any minute. This time when I see her, I plan to look a lot more elegant and put together than the last two times—which, let's face it, won't be a significant challenge. Not being drenched and wearing my dress around the right way is a great starting point.

"How do I look?" I ask Sebastian as he fixes his tie in our floor length mirror.

He turns to regard me, and his face creases into an appreciative smile. "You look beautiful, Brady. New dress?"

"Yes, it is." I model it for him, spinning around, the full skirt of the red dress swooshing against my legs. I sit down on the end of the bed and pet a snoozing Frank as Sebastian returns his attention to his tie. "Is Odette bringing a date?" I ask.

"I don't imagine so. She's not dating at the moment."

"Why not? She's a divorced, single gal out and about on the town. And she's famous! I bet she's got men lining up around the block to date her."

"You'll have to ask her about that."

"I will do just that. Maybe I could set her up with someone? I've decided to set Kennedy up with Charles," I say, naming one of Sebastian's friends.

"You have?"

"Don't you think they'd be perfect together? She's amazing and gorgeous and smart, and he's all that plus owns half the country."

He purses his lips together. "They're both headstrong. They could clash."

"Or they could be awesome."

"We won't know until we try."

I beam at him. "Good. I'll set it up."

"Are you ready to go downstairs? You know what Granny's like when we're late."

I roll my eyes as I hop off the bed. "Don't remind me." Geraldine is not known for her tolerance of tardiness. Or of anything, now that I come to think of it.

"Speaking of which, do you think we'll need to make any hasty exits this dinner?" he asks with a twinkle in his eye.

"You know I'm not ovulating anymore."

"That's probably just as well. Imagine what it would be like if you inadvertently announced that you want me to impregnate you in front of twelve of my clients? Oh, wait. You already did that," he teases.

I laugh and blush simultaneously. "Not my finest hour, but to be fair to me, Susie didn't tell me you were on a call and you'd closed the blinds like I'd asked."

"Well, it all worked out in the end."

I beam up at him as hope leaps inside of me. "I don't know how I know this. I mean, it's too early to do a test or anything yet, but, well, I've got a feeling."

He returns my smile and pulls me in for a kiss. "It's only been three days since our office escapade."

"I know. It's not based on any hard facts or anything. It's just a feeling."

He kisses me tenderly on the lips. "I hope you're right. And if it hasn't happened yet, I'm sure it will soon enough."

I knit my brows together. How can he be so relaxed about this? We've been trying for ages and have had no success. Surely that bothers him as much as it does me?

Picking up on my change of mood, he says, "What is it?"

I shrug. "I'm one hundred percent invested in this, and I *so* want it to work."

"We're both a hundred percent invested. I just wonder if we need to relax about it a little. Let it happen naturally."

"You sound like my friends."

"Maybe they've got a point?"

I paste on a smile and feign bravado. "Are you saying you don't want me to come to your office and demand sex again?"

He laughs as he offers me his arm like the true gentleman he is. "I'm not saying that."

"We've gotta do what we've gotta do. You know how this goes."

"I'm certainly getting used to it, yes."

We arrive at the reception room, empty but for Zara. She's lounging on one of the room's antique sofas, immersed in reading something on her phone.

"My tearaway little sister," Sebastian says to her as he leans down to kiss the top of her head. "When did you arrive at the house?"

"I'm hardly a tearaway, Seb," she replies. "Just because I don't have a boring City job and actually like to have fun every now and then. The fun gene seems to have skipped you completely."

"Is that so?" he replies. He shoots me a small smile, and I feel my cheeks begin to heat.

"You do you," I say as I give her a warm hug.

"Exactly. We can't all be uptight aristocratic stiffs like you, dear brother."

"Zara Huntington-Ross! That is no way to speak to the head of our family," a voice booms across the room.

Oh, good. Geraldine has arrived with her progressive ideas of gender inequality.

"Good evening, Granny," Sebastian says as he strides over to greet her. "You're looking stunning this evening. Is that another row of pearls?"

Geraldine is known for her strings of pearls, never being seen out anywhere without at least three rows. I've never seen her without a string. For all I know, she even showers in them—but then that's definitely not an image I want filling my brain.

"One can never have too many pearls, my dear boy," she replies as she gives him an affectionate pat on the cheek.

"You are *such* a suck up, Seb," Zara says, and she receives a glare from her brother.

Jemima arrives, and everyone greets each other before they settle into their seats.

"Now, come and sit next to me and tell me all about your week, Sebastian." Geraldine pats the spot on the sofa next to her, and Sebastian brings her a drink. "Thank you, my dear boy."

"There's not a lot to tell, Granny. Now that things are running smoothly with the house, I've been in the office all week."

Her face crinkles as she smiles. "That's my boy. Working hard, just as you ought."

"I do admire you, Seb. You take it all in stride, don't you? The house, your work, the television show. Not to mention your 'project' with Emma." Jemima smiles at me and, not for the first time, a part of me wishes we'd never told them we were trying for a baby. Particularly as none have materialized yet.

"It's not all hard work, you know, Mother," he replies with a laugh.

"Sebastian, you're one of those enviable men who understand their position in life and take it seriously," Geraldine says.

"You know, Granny, it's not all work and no play for me. I did get a very pleasant distraction when Emma dropped into the office for a visit a few days ago."

As heat creeps up my cheeks, I shoot him a look that says *why did you have to go bringing that up?* and he waggles his eyebrows at me in response.

"Why were you in the City?" Zara asks. "Were you visiting a client?"

"That's right. A client," I reply as a movie reel of our office activities plays before my eyes. My blush intensifies.

Zara studies my face. "Why are you blushing?"

"I'm not. I'm just warm in here, that's all." I begin to fan myself with my hand. It doesn't help.

She narrows her gaze. "It's not warm."

"How's your love life?" I ask her to divert her attention from me. "Met any cute guys lately?"

She lets out a sigh. "I'm in a man desert. Any guy who looks like he might be a vaguely decent, normal, human being turns out to be just a mirage. Or a cactus."

I let out a giggle.

She leans in closer to me so only I can hear. "You know what I've done? I've come to an arrangement with Asher. You know, my cute American friend? You met him at the garden party last summer."

I arch my brows as I picture Asher, the classically tall, dark, and handsome guy who Zara and her friend, Tabitha

116

spend a lot of time with in London. "An arrangement? That sounds very *Lady Chatterley's Lover*."

"Oh, it's nothing like that. He's my back-up guy."

"Wait. A back-up guy? As in if you're not with someone by a certain age, you'll marry him?"

Her face is bright. "Genius, right? It means I can chill out about the whole thing and focus on my interior design business and having fun until we're both thirty-five. He's my age, so we've got stacks of time."

"But what if he meets someone before he turns thirty-five?"

"Oh, he won't. Trust me. He's not the serious relationship type."

"A playboy, huh?" I ask and she nods.

"See? It's the perfect plan."

The doorbell chimes and Sebastian springs up from his seat. "Ah, that'll be Odette."

"What's this Odette like, Emma?" Geraldine asks.

"She's nice. Super successful and smart, too," I reply. "She's one of those experts on TV who talks knowledgeably about the markets and things. Seb says she's one of the best."

"She's a career girl." Geraldine's tone implies this is not a positive attribute in a woman. "Is that why she's not married?"

"I don't think so," I reply.

"Granny, you do know women these days can have careers whether they're married or not," Zara says with a laugh.

"Just because they can doesn't mean they ought," she sniffs.

I've said it before, and I'll say it again: what century does this woman think we live in?

"We women can do anything we want. Isn't that right, Emma?" Zara looks at me.

"We do have more choices than a generation or two"—or ten—"ago," I say as diplomatically as I can.

Sebastian returns to the room with Odette, who's smiling her beautiful smile, in a chic deep purple dress that emphasizes the blue of her eyes.

"Everyone, this is Odette Rojas," Sebastian announces, and we all rise to greet her. Well, not Geraldine. She remains seated, which shows her level of enthusiasm for this "unmarried career girl" currently in her house.

"It's a pleasure to make your acquaintance," Geraldine says coolly as she proffers her hand from her seat as though expecting Odette to kiss her ring.

Newsflash: she's not the pope.

"The pleasure is all mine, Lady Martinston," she replies, flashing her a brilliant smile. "Sebastian has told me so much about you."

She arches an eyebrow. "Has he indeed?"

"Oh, yes," she replies as she takes a seat. "He's told me how much you love the opera. I'm a fan myself."

"Who do you favor?"

"I love Puccini, particularly La Bohème. For me it's the perfect opera. It's passionate, beautiful, poignant."

"Italian. I see." Geraldine's features are pinched like a molded piece of clay. "Favoring" the Italian Puccini is clearly on her extensive list of dislikes. "Personally, I favor the German composers. Mozart, Strauss, Wagner. They're much more complex than the Italians."

"Wagner composed *Tannhäuser*," I say, remembering how I'd wanted to take Geraldine to see it when I was desperately trying—and failing—to win her approval. In the end, I'd taken her to see an opera about repopulating Germany after the Second World War and had to leave in a fit of giggles when the singers let go of their giant breast balloons. It was as weird as it sounds, and it did nothing to ingratiate me to my future grandmother-in-law.

"What is your point, Emma?" Geraldine asks.

"Just that I know he composed *Tannhäuser*, that's all. Which isn't a German tanning business," I add to Odette who lets out a delicate laugh at my joke.

"Would you like a drink?" Sebastian offers, cutting the awkward conversation off. Odette requests a glass of Viogner, which Sebastian pours out and hands to her.

"Tell me what it's like to be an expert on Bloomberg TV?" Zara asks brightly. "Seb tells us you're quite the star of the financial world."

Odette flushes, making her eyes sparkle. "Oh, I wouldn't say I'm a star, but thank you so much for the compliment. All I'm doing is imparting my knowledge of the sector in a public forum. Anyone could do it, really."

"I'm pretty sure I couldn't," I reply.

"But you could talk expertly about activewear, I'm sure," Odette says.

"You are so modest, Odette," Zara says. "Seb never misses you. Do you, Seb?"

"I do try to watch, even though I know I can always bribe her with a cup of coffee at Eduardo's if needs be," he says.

"The life of an analyst," Odette replies with a shrug. "Always getting taken out for cups of coffee."

"It's probably only because she's totally gorgeous," Zara says to me under her breath.

"Odette is an unusual name," Geraldine says, changing the topic from coffee bribes. "Are you French?" I detect a curl of her lip as she asks. Like Nigel from Body Sports, Geraldine despises the French, among many, many other things. Seriously, it's hard to know what this woman actually likes.

"No, I'm not French. I'm English through and through.

My mother is a former prima ballerina with the Royal Ballet. Her favorite part to dance was Odette, hence the name."

"Oh, I do love Swan Lake," Jemima says. "It's the quintessential ballet, don't you think? How wonderful your mother was a prima ballerina. That must have been such a thrill."

"Should a life on the stage be considered a thrill?" Geraldine asks, her lip now curling so much I can see her gums.

Odette smiles at her sweetly and dodges replying. Instead she says, "My mother was a wonderful dancer. She gave up before I was born, but I've seen videos."

"Did you dance?" I ask her. Odette has the physique of a ballerina, very lithe, elegant, and slim.

"Two left feet, I'm afraid, which is why I do what I do rather than travel the world with the Royal Ballet like my mother."

"My friend Phoebe is a ballet teacher. She loves it."

Geraldine scoffs. "I hardly think you can compare a prima ballerina at the Royal Ballet with someone who teaches five-year-olds to *plie*, Emma"

That's my grandmother-in-law. Always with something positive to say. And wasn't she just looking down her nose at Odette's mom for leading a "life on the stage?"

"Oh, I don't know," Odette replies with a smile. "I take my hat off to anyone who can teach children to do absolutely anything. I love my two darlings, but I wouldn't ever want to teach them."

"You have children?" Jemima asks.

"Two. The only good thing to come from my marriage, I'm afraid."

"Oh. I see. You're a single mother."

By now, I half expect Geraldine to announce that it's time for Odette to leave before she "pollutes the shades of Pemberley" à la Lady Catherine de Burgh.

"I am a single mother these days, yes. It's not the way I would have chosen to parent, but it's for the best."

I rush to Odette's aid. I've got firsthand experience of being on the end of Geraldine's mirth. "You should see these kids, Granny. They're just gorgeous. Odette brought them here to do a house tour in the spring. They're little sweethearts."

"Thank you, Emma," Odette replies with a proud smile. "Would you like to see a photo, Lady Martinston?" She doesn't wait for a reply. Instead, she whips her phone from her purse and pulls up a shot. "Here they are at your fountain. We'd just had a simply lovely morning tea at the café, and Joaquin decided now would be a good time to go for a swim."

"Oh, they're darling," Jemima exclaims as she takes the phone from Odette and turns it to Geraldine. "Don't you think, Mummy?"

"They look like children to me," she replies with disdain she doesn't even try to throw a veil over. Then she peers closer at the screen and declares, "The fountain needs a clean. Be sure to see to that, Emma."

"Err, sure," I reply. Why the heck is that my job? "Where are your kids tonight? With a sitter?" I ask in an attempt to divert Odette's attention from Geraldine's rudeness.

"I have some family not far from here, so they're having a bit of an adventure staying there for the night. I thought it was best to bring them rather than leave them at the flat in Chelsea with a babysitter."

"Is your family in the village?" Jemima asks.

"My aunt and uncle have a home in the country only about an hour's drive from here, actually. It's a lovely place. We spent summers there when I was a child."

Geraldine's interest is suddenly piqued. "Who are your

people? I don't believe I know any Rojases from around here."

"Rojas is my married name. My family name is Jocaston. In fact, I'm going back to it soon. The final step in shaking off my marriage, I suppose."

"Good for you," I say.

"Mummy, don't you know some Jocastons?" Jemima asks Geraldine. "Algernon Jocaston, I think. Isn't that right? Oh, and Bertie and Felicia and the younger one. What was her name? They're all Jocastons, aren't they? Or are they Johnstons?"

"I'm pretty sure they're the Jocastons, Mum," Zara says. "Perdita Jocaston was a year ahead of me at school."

"That's right. Perdita is my cousin, and Algernon Jocaston is my uncle," Odette replies. "Bertie and Felicia are my second cousins, and Primrose and I went to boarding school together."

"Her brother is Montgomery, isn't it? He was at Cambridge with me. He's a good fellow," Sebastian says. "Funny to think we have this connection and didn't even know it."

Geraldine sits up straighter in her chair. "You're a Jocaston. Well. How wonderful to meet Algy's niece."

I blink at her in disbelief. This is *such* typical Geraldine behavior. In her eyes, Odette has gone from being a career-focused single mother from bad stock to someone worth knowing simply because her family is rich. She begins to fire questions at Odette, who answers them with good grace.

"Did you grow up here? Which boarding school did you go to? Are you related to Barnaby Jocaston with the estate in Gloucestershire?"

Blah blah blah blah blah. I'm sorry if that sounds harsh, but I've heard it all before. You're a nobody in Geraldine's eyes unless you're related to some aristocratic snob with piles of money.

The evening progresses well enough with Geraldine and Odette finding many people in common and the rest of us talking among ourselves. By the time we finish our dessert, Geraldine is Odette's biggest fan, and I wonder how I ever felt sorry for her.

Not that I'm jealous, of course. I love being treated like a pesky, poverty-stricken peasant who refuses to scurry back to her hole in Texas. Really, I do.

"How is your activewear business, Emma?" Odette asks when Geraldine has finally stopped salivating over her and gone upstairs to bed. Zara has made her excuses, and Jemima is sitting quietly in the corner, nursing a brandy as we chat.

"It's going great. We've got big orders coming in from the sports stores here now, and our next goal is the fashion retailers. A lot of them do their own activewear lines, but some are open to carrying our label."

"That sounds like a wonderful next step," she replies.

"Actually, we're working on a maternity line right now, too."

Odette's eyes flick to Sebastian's. "Maternity activewear, hmm?"

He smiles back at her. "Emma's trying something new."

"That's right," I reply, feeling disconcerted. Why did she shoot him a look?

"Are you interested in getting into Marie's Maternity?" she asks, naming one of the largest retail maternity fashion chains in Europe.

"Of course we are. Getting Timothy into Marie's would be insane."

"One of my closest friends works there. She runs their procurement team for Northern Europe, I believe. I could set something up, if you like?"

"Are you kidding me right now? That would be incredible." I catch Sebastian's eye and say, "Wouldn't that be incredible?"

"It certainly would," he replies. "You're very kind to do that, Odette."

"It's nothing. Henrietta is just lovely, and I'm sure she'd be happy to meet with you to discuss your new line."

"Thank you so much, Odette. You're amazing." Which she is. Super successful in her career with two gorgeous children and totally beautiful, too. The woman can do no wrong.

She lets out a delicate laugh as she shakes her head. "You're the amazing one running your own business, Emma," she says, and I glow. "It would be a pleasure to introduce you."

After we say good-bye to her, Sebastian and I make our way hand in hand up the stairs together.

"Can you believe it? I get to meet Marie Maternity's procurement manager for all of Northern Europe to talk about our new line!"

"I'm sure you'll do an incredible job," Sebastian replies.

"Oh, I will. I'm gonna get Timothy Maternity into their stores, and then Body Sports will see how well it sells and come knocking on my door."

Once ready for bed, I slip under the covers and kiss my husband goodnight. I might be pregnant with our first child, and I've got the chance of a lifetime, getting our new line into one of the biggest fashion retailers in Europe. Things are starting to look up, and I could not be happier.

CHAPTER 12

a couple of weeks later, Odette has come through on her promise, and I'm about to meet Henrietta Dixon from Marie Maternity. I flash the time up on my phone: 09:59. I've arrived with one minute to spare. I push through the door to the café and am immediately hit by the aroma of coffee and sweet treats. I scan the room and spot Odette sitting on her own at a table in the back corner, talking on her phone. Dressed as always in an elegant outfit, her long, slick hair lying against her back, she looks up and waves me over.

"All right, sweetie. Give Hippo a kiss from me. Mummy loves you so, so much. *Mwah mwah.* Bye, darling." Hanging up, she grins at me. "Joaquin, my cherub. He always gets his nanny to ring me when I'm at work. He is such a treasure."

Her face bright with love, my ovaries twang. *That's* what I want, a child who loves me so much he wants to talk to me, even when I'm not around. I place my hand over my belly. I have such a strong sense that I'm already pregnant. I know it's only been a couple of weeks since I visited Sebastian at his office, but maybe, just maybe I've got new life brewing inside of me right now. Maybe before too long I'll be sending kisses over the phone to my own "little treasure."

The thought fills me with joy.

"He always wants me to kiss his soft toys," Odette continues. "Hippo is his absolute favorite, but there's Ginger and Melby and Oscar, too. Joaquin is a big animal fan."

"He sounds like it. Do you miss him when you're at work?"

A shadow passes briefly over her face. "Of course, but I need to work to pay the bills, and he and his sister, Antonella, have a wonderful nanny who they adore. I get to spend quality time with them at the weekends doing things like visiting stately homes in the country that belong to my friends. Now," she says, placing her hands on the table. "You're not here to talk about my life. You're here to meet Henrietta Dixon. I told her about you and your line. Timothy Maternity isn't it?" she asks, and I nod. "She said she'd do some due diligence on your company before she meets us today, and she is interested."

Hope spreads down my limbs. "It would be amazing to get our label into her stores. Did you know Marie Maternity has a dozen stores in London alone? Not only that, but their online presence is also incredible."

"I did not, but it's good to see you've done your homework."

"I'm serious about this maternity line. It's a new direction for us, but it feels right to do it now. Penny, my partner, is pregnant again, due to give birth to baby number two any day, in fact. She thinks there's a real gap in the market for comfortable maternity activewear."

"I could barely move late in my pregnancies, I was so huge," she says with a laugh.

"I cannot imagine that. You're so thin."

"Thank you, but carrying the next generation certainly

takes its toll on your body." Her phone lying face down on the table vibrates, and she picks it up to look at the screen. "Oh, it's Henrietta. That's a shame. She says she's been held up and can't make it today."

My heart drops to the hardwood floor. "Oh."

"I'll message her back and suggest another time for us to get together."

"That'd be great, thank you."

As she taps out her reply, a good-looking guy in his thirties approaches the table. Odette looks up at him and offers him a smile.

"You're Odette Whatsit from Bloomberg TV, innit?" he says in what Brits refer to as a "wide boy" accent—basically a cockney, as far as I can tell.

"That's right," she replies.

"You're well famous. I watch you all the time. You've got good info, girl. You know your stuff." He taps the side of his head. "I'm a trader, see." He glances at me, and it's obvious I'm of little interest to him when he returns his gaze in a flash to Odette.

"Thank you, that's very sweet of you to say," she replies graciously, and I wonder how often she gets recognized like this.

"You're a bi' of alright, you are. You single? Do ya wanna go out with me sometime?"

I press my lips together to stop from giggling. The guy's got game!

"Thank you so much, but I'm a very happily married woman, but it was lovely to meet you."

"Oh, right." He glances at me once more. "You a lesbo or something?"

I lose the battle, and the giggle escapes my lips.

"I do appreciate you stopping by to say hello," Odette says smoothly as she dodges the totally inappropriate question about her sexuality. "Would you like a photo before you leave?"

The guy grins as he takes his phone out of his jacket pocket. "That would be mint, that would." He snaps a few shots of himself with Odette before he leaves.

"You handled that so well," I say in admiration.

She lifts her shoulders in a shrug. "It's par for the course when your main audience is stock brokers, I'm afraid."

"I still can't believe he asked you out. Does that happen a lot? No wait. It does. You look like, well, *you*."

She laughs. "It's happened before, yes," she says modestly. I bet it happens all the time. "I'll finish that text to Henrietta before I forget."

As she taps on her phone, I feel a sudden cramp low in my belly. It's sharp and unexpected and it makes me wince involuntarily.

Odette looks up at me from her phone. "Are you okay, Emma? You do look pale."

"Oh, for sure," I reply brightly. "Do you have time for a coffee before you go? My treat."

"You know what? That would be just lovely. It'll be nice to chat about something other than the results from the latest drug trial and the potential impact on the markets."

"I can promise you not to talk about any of that," I reply as I stand to make my way over to the counter. "A flat white, cappuccino, long black?" I ask.

"Long black, please."

I order our coffee and feel another twinge. Perhaps it's something I ate? I cycle through my recent meals and snacks. Although I've gotten to the point where I can barely face another slice of meat, I ate a plateful of leftover roast beef for breakfast and added a banana, blueberry, and kale smoothie, as recommended by a pregnancy site online. Maybe I've overdone it on the kale? Because let's face it, any kale is over-doing it. Horrible stuff.

I spy the restroom sign and tell the server which table to deliver the coffees to. As I close the door to the stall, I get another twinge, this time stronger than the last. I sit and pull my underwear down and blink at it in disbelieving shock.

I started my period. My *period*. Which means...I'm not pregnant.

I sit motionless for I don't know how long as my mind reels. I thought I was pregnant. In fact, I was certain I was. I had that feeling, deep inside, the feeling that I just *knew*.

And I was wrong. Completely and utterly wrong.

My throat thickens, and I let out a heavy breath.

Another month. Another chance gone.

We're back at the start once again with nothing to show for our efforts.

I finish up and look at my reflection as I wash and dry my hands. Hollow eyes gaze back at me, the corners of my mouth turned down as I work hard to contain my rising despondency.

When will it be my turn?

Someone enters the room, and I immediately avert my eyes from my reflection and rummage through my purse. I locate my lipstick and apply some more as the woman disappears behind the door of one of the stalls.

I lift my chin and paste on a smile. What is it they say? Fake it until you make it? Although I feel like curling up into a ball and sobbing my eyes out right now, I need to stay strong. I'm here with someone I don't know very well who's offered to help me with Timothy, someone who works with my husband.

I've got this.

I walk back to our table to find our coffees have already been delivered. Taking my seat, I smile at Odette and say,

"These look good. I love the way they've put a chocolate on the spoons. That's totally cute."

"They're chocolate fish," Odette says, picking hers up. "Marshmallow covered in chocolate. Apparently, they're big in New Zealand, which is where the owner is from."

"Huh." I pick mine up and pop it in my mouth, hoping the sugar will bolster my mood—and knowing nothing can even come close to doing that right now. "Yummy."

She grins at me as she chews hers. "How do you find living in England? Do you miss your family back in the US?"

At the thought of my mom, that throat thickness I thought I'd gotten under control returns full force, and I swallow furiously, trying to get my emotions back in check.

"Oh, no. I've said something wrong." She reaches across the table and places her hand on mine. "I'm sorry. You must miss them a lot?"

My breath is ragged as I fight back the tears. *Pull it together, Emma. You've got this, remember?*

It's no use.

The kindness in her voice has my misery swelling inside until it spills over in a sob. I cover my mouth with my hand as tears well in my eyes.

"Oh, Emma." Odette rubs my hand, which does nothing for my state of mind, throwing me over the edge into a sea of sobs.

She sits there patiently rubbing my hand as I fight to pull myself together. Eventually, after accepting a tissue from her and blowing my nose noisily, I manage to wrangle my emotions back into line, replacing my sadness with embarrassment.

"I'm not usually like this," I say to her as I dab my eyes and attempt a watery smile. "Thank you for being so sweet."

"Of course."

"I, ah, I just found out I'm not pregnant, and I thought I

was." I'm not sure why I'm telling Odette this. There's something about her openness and kindness that makes me feel safe.

"Oh, that's so hard. Do you need medical assistance?"

I press my lips firmly together and give a shake of my head.

"Had you done a test?"

"It's weird, but I just had a feeling, you know? Like I was definitely pregnant. I guess my radar is way off."

"I had the feeling when I fell pregnant with Antonella, before I'd had it confirmed, before my period was even late."

"But you were right about yours, weren't you? Mine was just a silly fantasy." I look down at a wood chip in the table and begin to trace its edges with my finger.

"You're right. That's a bad example," she says. "Do you know what I think? I think we need more chocolate fish."

I let out a weak laugh. "I'm not going to argue with you about that."

"I'll be right back." She hops up from her chair to go to the counter, and I check my compact to see what state my face is in once she's gone. It ain't pretty. Smudged mascara, a swollen nose, blood shot eyes. I look like one of the ugly sisters next to Odette's Cinderella. I do my best to repair my face as Odette returns to the table, a couple of plates of chocolate fish in hand.

"There. I thought this might do the trick. I don't know about you, but I find chocolate can fix absolutely anything."

"I was under the impression the Brits thought a cup of tea fixed absolutely anything."

"Would you prefer tea?" she asks with a cocked eyebrow, and I shake my head.

"Do you remember that movie *Chocolat*? The one with Juliette Binoche and Johnny Depp? Juliette's character knew what type of chocolate every customer needed. I fancy myself as a bit of Juliette, you know."

"A chocolate psychic? Is that even a thing?"

She grins at me once more, and I'm struck by how kind her eyes are. "It's a very useful skill, you know, particularly when analyzing businesses for the market."

I chortle. "Clearly." I take another bite and actually do start to feel brighter. Maybe there's something in this psychic chocolate after all? "Did you find it easy to have kids?"

She scrunches up her nose. "I did. We agreed to start trying, and we conceived Antonella very quickly."

"Oh."

"But Joaquin took a lot longer."

I perk up. If someone as perfect as Odette had trouble conceiving, perhaps there's hope for me yet? "He did?" I ask.

"Oh, yes. We tried for at least a few weeks."

A few weeks? "Right."

"Have you been trying for long?"

"You know how that saying goes, *first comes love, then comes marriage, then comes baby in a baby carriage*? Well, two of those things have proven a whole lot easier to do than one of them, that's for sure. Love? Yup. Marriage. Done. Baby in a baby carriage? Not so much." I lift my eyes to hers, suddenly worried I've said too much. "Please don't mention this to anyone at the bank. I don't want people asking Sebastian about it."

She mimes locking a key over her lips. "Mum's the word," she says before her jaw drops, her eyes wide. "Oh, gosh. Sorry. That was totally unintended."

"No worries."

She turns her wrist and glances at the time. "Emma, I do have to go. Look after yourself, will you?"

We get up to leave.

"I will, and thanks for…you know."

"Of course."

Out on the sidewalk, she presses her cheek to mine briefly before she says her good-byes and dashes off down the street, her Louboutins clicking against the sidewalk with every step.

As I wander down the street toward the Tube stop, my phone rings, and Penny's name pops up on my screen. I could do with talking to my oldest friend right now. I answer, and immediately her happy face fills my screen. "Hey, Penn."

She grins at me and says something I can't work out.

"Hold on. I'll find somewhere quieter to talk." I spot a pretty little park with a wooden seat, where I sit down and pull out my ear buds. I hold the screen up and say, "Okay, I've got you now."

Her face beams as she croaks, "How are you, Em?"

I let out a heavy sigh. "I've been better, I guess," I begin, preparing myself to share the story of my "lost" pregnancy. Because although rationally I know I haven't lost anything, someone forgot to tell my heart that.

Penny has news she cannot wait to share. "I wanted you to meet someone," she says as she moves the camera angle and an image of a tiny, pink, sleeping baby, wrapped up tight in a blanket in her mom's arms beams across the Atlantic at me.

A heavy brick fills my belly, my heart deflating like a punctured tire.

Penny's had her baby.

And I've got...nothing. Not even the vaguest hope of a child.

My throat begins to tighten.

"Meet Delilah Jane, the newest addition to my growing brood," Penny's hoarse voice says with the camera still aimed at her newborn. "Isn't she perfect?" she gushes. "Ten fingers and ten toes, just the way they ought to be."

I give myself a mental shake-up. I can't go feeling sorry for myself just because someone close to me has had a child. Women give birth every minute of every hour of every day. This isn't about me. It's about Penny, my closest friend.

The problem is my head might know one thing but my heart feels something different altogether.

I can't let my heart take charge.

So I push the rising lump in my throat down and I ignore the heat growing in my chest and I do my best to feel happy for my friend. "She's beautiful, Penn," I say, and I hope she misses the quiver in my voice. "Tell me all about it. How was the birth? How are you feeling?"

As Penny shares all the details, I work hard at maintaining my smile. I'm incredibly happy for her, of course I am. But it's so hard not to dissolve into a flood of tears here on the park bench in the warm summer sun. She has what I want, lying in her arms right now, in a hospital way across the ocean in Houston.

And I hate myself for feeling like this.

Because this isn't me. I'm happy for my friends to experience successes. I've never been spiteful or jealous. I take pride in not being a selfish person, and yet here I am thinking only of myself as my friend shares the miracle of new life. The last thing I want to do is take anything away from her right now. So instead of letting myself fall into a great cavern of sorrow, I congratulate her again and tell her Delilah Jane is the most darling child ever and promise to come visit just as soon as I can.

Once I hang up, I sit motionless, staring into space, working through a plethora of emotions. Happiness, excitement, sorrow, and a deeply held sense of my own loss.

In a sudden rush, I miss my mom with a fierce intensity

that sucks the wind from my lungs. She's the only one I want to talk to, she's the only one who'll understand.

I dial her number and wait, willing her to answer.

"Hi, honey. How wonderful to hear from you," she says, and the sound of her voice instantly has me tearing up.

"Hey, Mom," I reply with a wobbly voice as tears prick my eyes.

"Oh, sweetie. What's wrong?"

"Penny had her baby. A little girl called Delilah Jane."

"Oh, how darling." She pauses before she asks, "Is that what's bothering you?"

"I'm probably being silly."

"If it's making you cry, it's not silly at all. Tell me what's going on."

It comes out in a rush. "I'm trying not to be jealous, really I am, but I'm still not pregnant, and it's been months since the doctor advised us the best times to try, and I've been charting my cycle and using ovulation sticks and we've been trying at the right time and everything and nothing has happened." I come to a choking stop.

"Wow. That's a lot, honey. I'm so sorry. Getting pregnant can be so hard for some couples, and it's only natural you'll have feelings about Penny having her baby. She's got what you want."

She's hit the nail on the head.

"I feel terrible. I should be over the moon for her."

"And you are. It's just there are some other things going on for you right now that have taken pole position."

I exhale, my shoulders slumped. "I want it so bad, Mom."

"Have you thought about going back to the doctor to get some more tests run? It might be wise."

I twist the tassel on my purse. "Mom, what if they find there's something wrong with me or Seb?" The thought has my tummy muscles clenching.

"Then you'll know what you're dealing with. It's better to know the truth than fear the worst."

The worst. I don't like the sound of that.

"Honey?" Mom asks when I don't reply. "Are you still there?"

"Yeah, just deep in thought, I guess. I would know if I had endo though, right?"

"Not necessarily. Some women have it and don't have any symptoms, and some have totally debilitating symptoms. It all depends."

"That's not encouraging," I say with a sardonic laugh.

"I think y'all should go see the doctor."

I think of Dr. Sheffield. "When we went to see him, he told Seb he had to get his soldiers to breach my fortress."

"He sounds like an interesting character."

"'Interesting' is not the word, Mom. More like 'inappropriate.'"

"You'll need a fertility expert anyway. Do your research and find the best. Then go see that doctor."

"Maybe it'll happen naturally this month? Who knows?"

"Maybe it will, but there's no harm in getting checked out. Promise me y'all will go."

I push out a breath and say, "I promise."

"Good. Now, let me tell you what your Aunt Judy and me did last weekend. It'll make your hair stand on end."

I smile down the phone. "Sure, Mom. Tell me all about you and Aunt Judy."

As Mom regales me with a story about her and Aunt Judy getting up to no good at the local tennis club summer party, I make a decision. No more messing around with ovulation kits and inconvenient encounters with my husband. We want a child, and it's not working for us. It's time to get serious about this.

It's time to call in the big guns.

CHAPTER 13

*T*hat night while lying in bed, my head resting on Sebastian's chest, his heartbeat drumming rhythmically in my ear, I tell him about what had happened at the café.

"The thing is, I felt so sure I was pregnant, Seb. Like I just *knew*, you know?"

He strokes my hair. "It must have come as such a shock."

"I'm sorry I told Odette about it. I don't want you to have to answer people's questions at work about whether we're expecting."

"Odette is the soul of discretion, so don't worry yourself on that front."

"Seb, I so want us to have a family."

"I know you do, Brady. So do I. But all we can do is keep trying."

I trail my finger over the skin of his chest, deep in thought. Mom's advice had been ringing in my head since our conversation earlier in the day. I lift my head, and our gazes lock. "What if we went back to the doctor?" I ask tentatively.

He offers me a wry smile. "You want to hear more about soldiers breaching your fortress, do you? Lady Martinston, I didn't realize you were quite so militaristic."

I snort giggle. "I do not need to hear about any of that again. No, I wondered if we could go see a fertility specialist. Someone who can run some tests."

"That sounds serious, doesn't it?"

"But we need to get serious about this. We've been trying for ages now. We've been having sex at the right time of the month, I'm eating more meat than I ever thought I would in my life—"

"That is a peculiar one."

"It's meant to help. Something to do with our Paleolithic ancestors."

"Were they particularly fertile?"

"Well, they sure as heck didn't run around the jungle eating donuts."

His smile is sardonic. "I imagine not."

"I figure it's worth a shot. Right? And my point is, we've been doing all the right things for months and months and we're still not pregnant."

"I'm not sure we need to go getting tests run or anything like that. It all sounds so...medical. Don't you want to make a baby the old-fashioned way?"

I try to keep the agitation from my voice when I reply, "Seb, the old-fashioned way isn't working for us. You know that, and I know that. If we're going to do this, we need to do it right."

"How about we just give it some more time? You've been working so hard and stressing out about getting pregnant—"

I sit bolt upright in the bed. "Do not tell me I just need to chill out and it'll happen," I snap, interrupting him. "Look at me. I'm chill. So, *so* chill. I could be in a coma, that's how chill

I am." My voice raises an octave, and I know I sound manic. But how can I be chilled out when I'm *still* not pregnant?

Sebastian's brow furrows. "Brady, I can see this is getting to you."

I widen my eyes at him. "No it's not," I insist. After a beat, I exhale, and I scrunch my eyes shut. "Sorry. Seeing Penny's new baby today got to me, and I'm not doing so well with this. I want it so bad, I can taste it."

"You can taste a baby?" he asks, his lips quirking.

It works to lighten my mood. "You know what I mean. Anyone I know who wants to have a baby either has one or is pregnant. Look at Penny and Phoebe. Odette told me she got pregnant like that," I snap my fingers. "Why hasn't that happened for us?"

"I don't know why. What I do know is that this has been harder on you than on me and I wish I could bear the load for you some more."

My heart melts for him, and I lean in and kiss him tenderly on the lips. "You're amazing, did you know that?"

"As long as I do the pond scene for the middle-aged ladies of Southern England, that is."

I let out a giggle. "There is that."

"I'm sorry you're finding this so hard."

"The thing is, I'm constantly thinking about whether it's worked each month and that I need to avoid shellfish and wine and soft cheeses and all those things just in case I'm pregnant. And then there's the guilt when it doesn't work each month. Did I do something wrong? Is it my fault? Should I have not gone on that run? Did I stand too close to the stove while cooking dinner?"

"Stand too close to the hob?"

"You know, heating up too much."

"I see." He presses his lips together as he regards me

through soft eyes. "I'm always here for you, whenever you need me."

His kindness has a sob constricting in my throat. "I know you are."

"Come here." He opens his arms, and I cuddle up to his warm chest. He plants a kiss on my forehead and says, "I'll book us in to see Dr. Sheffield again, and we'll take it from there. I think we'll need a referral from him for a fertility clinic, like you do for any other medical specialist."

I nuzzle his neck, feeling instantly calmer. "Then we'll know what we're dealing with here."

"Or it could be that we've just missed that tiny window so far and next month it could work."

I gaze up at him, a cocktail of hope and worry washing through me. Hope that he's right. Worry that it's more than likely he's wrong. "Maybe."

* * *

A FEW DAYS LATER, we visit Dr. Sheffield once more, who in between telling us that lying with my legs up the wall and eating meat are "a load of old codswallop" and "total poppycock" gives us our referral to a top-rated fertility clinic in London.

"I don't envy you. Beastly business all this fertility what-not. Needles and hormones and being poked and prodded. The works. Petri dish babies, that's what I call them," he says as we get up to leave.

Sebastian and I share a look. Petri dish babies? Encouraging, much?

"We'll do our best to navigate it all, Dr. Sheffield," Sebastian replies in a much more polite manner than I know I could manage right now. "And perhaps next time one of us sees you, it will be with a little Huntington-Ross."

"Good-oh. Now off you go."

We leave the medical office, and I've already pulled my phone out to dial the clinic before we've even stepped onto the sidewalk. Sebastian knits his brows together as I hold the phone to my ear and hear it ringing at the other end.

"What?" I ask.

He shakes his head. "Nothing."

Someone answers at the other end. "River Clinic, Raewyn speaking. How can I help you?"

"Hello, my name is Emma Huntington-Ross, and my husband and I have been referred to you by our doctor."

"Huntington-Ross? I'll check."

"Oh, he's only just done it about three minutes ago, so I'm not sure you'll have us on your system yet."

"Oh, no. It'll take a few weeks, perhaps a month. We'll call you once we receive the referral."

"A month?" I guffaw. "But it's only a letter.'

"These things take time, I'm afraid. But I assure you, we'll be back in touch once we're ready to book an appointment for you."

"How long does it take to get an appointment once you have the letter?"

"Oh, that's not too long."

Relief floods through me. "Oh, good."

"It'll be two, maybe three months."

"What?! That's crazy. Why does it take so long?"

"I'm afraid that's how the process works. There's nothing we can do about it."

"What if we're in a hurry? What if we know there's something wrong and we need to see someone quickly because we've been trying to get pregnant for ages and we need help, like, right now?"

"Ms. Huntington-Ross, *all* of our clients are in that position. Now, we'll be back in touch once we receive your referral letter."

"But—"

"Good-bye," she says pleasantly and hangs up before I can protest any further.

I let out a defeated sigh and lift my eyes to Sebastian's. "It's gonna take some time."

"I'm not surprised."

"I thought we might have to wait a couple weeks, maybe more. Not *months*."

He slings his arm around my shoulder. "Well, in the meantime, let's keep on doing what we're doing, and who knows? Perhaps it'll work itself out and we won't need the appointment after all."

I force myself to think positively. He might be right. We might have somehow missed that small fertility window over the last six or more months. Perhaps this month it'll happen for us.

And perhaps I'm kidding myself.

CHAPTER 14

$\mathcal{I}$ run through the spreadsheet Penny sent over. Although she only gave birth a couple of weeks ago, she's already back working a couple of hours a day. Try as I might, my mind is elsewhere, and I'm finding it virtually impossible to focus on shipping volumes and distribution lines.

Why can't time speed up? What I need is a short music montage of my life for the next few months right up to the point where we're sitting in the consult room with the world's most incredible fertility expert, telling us exactly what we need to do for guaranteed baby results.

I mean, is that too much to ask?

Apparently, yes, it is. It's *way* too much to ask.

It has been thirteen days since my conversation with Raewyn at River Fertility, and I don't even know whether Dr. Sheffield has written his referral letter to them yet. I've called his receptionist and asked on several occasions, and she's assured me it's "in the works"—whatever that means.

I let out a sigh as I look out the central city café window at the people bustling by in their summer outfits. People always have a spring in their step at this time of year, enjoying the fleeting British summer after a dank and cold winter.

Not me. Without that fertility clinic appointment locked and loaded in my calendar, there's no spring getting anywhere near my step.

But I've got no time to wallow in self-pity right now because today is the day I get to meet Henrietta Dixon from Marie Maternity. With our first meeting being cancelled at the last minute, I'm excited to finally have the opportunity to pitch Timothy Maternity to her.

As I take a sip of my coffee, I look up and spot Odette walking in through the door to the café. I wave them over.

"Hi, Odette," I say as I give her a quick hug. She does the weird cheek press she favors. "And you must be Henrietta. It's wonderful to meet you. Thank you for making the time." I extend my hand, and we shake before the three of us take our seats at the table.

"It's my pleasure, Emma. Any friend of Odette's is a friend of mine. She has immaculate taste. But you already know that, don't you?" Henrietta replies with a pleasant smile, her medium-length light blonde hair curled into perfect loose waves.

"I do indeed. Odette is very kind to introduce us. Can I order you a coffee? I got here early, so I've already had mine."

"I'll get them," Odette says. "You two sit and chat. Emma has put together some great pieces for her new maternity line, Hen."

"I'm eager to hear all about it," Henrietta says as Odette leaves the table. "But first, let me tell you I loved *Saving Pemberley*."

It hadn't occurred to me that she might have seen me on TV. "I don't feature a lot, but it was fun to make."

"They do focus mainly on your husband, don't they? I think the media has been very harsh on you."

"Thank you! I read yesterday that some fans are still holding out for Phoebe to dump Johnathan and marry Sebastian. I mean, they need to just get over it, right?"

She laughs. "Right. It's sour grapes because they didn't see your blossoming romance on the show, I imagine. Now that *Saving Pemberley* is off the air, I'm sure they'll move on to their next victim."

"I rarely read their comments anymore. I decided to focus on other things."

"Good for you."

"Let me tell you about Timothy Maternity. I hope you like our prototypes," I begin as I flip my laptop open.

"We're always on the lookout for new designs for our customers."

I take her through our concepts in my presentation and show her some samples.

"Can I keep these?" she asks.

"Sure. I've got a few."

Odette returns to the table, trailed by a server carrying a couple of cups of coffee. He's so busy gazing at her, he spills the hot liquid into the saucers as he plunks them down on the table.

"Thank you, Patrick. You're so sweet," Odette coos, and Patrick looks like he might pass out from having her attention bestowed on him.

"Do you need anything else?" he asks.

Odette offers him her gorgeous smile. "I think we're good. Thank you."

"I'm right over there if you need me," he says, pointing at the counter without moving.

"Thank you," she says again.

"Anytime."

"You can go now," Henrietta says to him, and he reluctantly moves away. She rolls her eyes at me. "Odette always has the guys drooling over her, ever since university."

"I've noticed," I say.

"He wasn't drooling," Odette says with a flip of her wrist. "He was only carrying the coffee for me and being polite. It's his job."

"And spilling the coffee all over the place because he was too busy gawking at you." Henrietta starts mopping up the brown liquid from the saucers with a napkin.

"He was totally gawking," I confirm.

"Speaking of gawking, Hen is a huge fan of your Mr. Darcy," Odette says with a cheeky grin.

"Odette!" Henrietta complains, her face coloring. "Don't embarrass me."

"He gets that a lot," I say. "Every time he's spotted when the house is open, he gets hauled down to the pond by a bunch of women. Some of them can be quite insistent."

"Oh, for the pond scene?" Henrietta says, her color deepening.

I land on an idea. I'm not adverse to using my husband to get Timothy Maternity into a retailer, particularly when it comes to the new maternity line. Whatever works, right?

"Henrietta, would you like to meet Sebastian? I can totally call him and ask him to come meet us. His office is just down the road."

"Would you?" she asks excitedly. "I mean, only if it's no trouble, of course."

"Of course." I pull up his contact on my phone and press *call*. It rings a couple of times before rolling to voicemail. I hang up and try again, but the same thing happens. "He must be in a meeting," I explain.

Actually, if I'm being honest, it's becoming increasingly difficult to get a hold of Sebastian at work these days. He tells me he's super busy working with a new company to raise funds, but a small part of me wonders whether he needs a break from me and this whole baby thing.

I can't blame him, of course. It's not been easy. Sure, it started off as this wild adventure, having to have sex on demand whenever that little stick told us to. But lately…well, I can't quite put my finger on what it is exactly, but it feels like he's pulled back from me. Like he's purposefully putting some space between us.

It's not a nice feeling.

"I'll call him again later and see if I can set something up," I say, and Henrietta's face lights up.

"That would be wonderful," she gushes before she checks herself. "I mean, it's always exciting to meet someone you admire, isn't it?"

"I think Sebastian senses he's got a rabid fan here with you, Emma, just waiting to meet him, and has shied off," Odette says with a glint in her eye.

"I'm not rabid, thank you very much." Henrietta sniffs. "Let's change the subject, shall we?"

"Good idea," I say with a laugh. Although I'm very aware how hot my husband is, it's always weird to hear when other people have a crush on him.

"Let me see your designs," Odette says to me, and Henrietta hands her one of the sample tops we had made up. "Oh, this is cute. It's like the Nike top I wore that time for you, Hen. Remember?"

"We used Odette as the model for a couple of our lines when she was pregnant with Antonella," Henrietta explains. "She's a total natural in front of the camera." She scrolls through her phone until she finds what she's looking for. "See?"

I take the proffered phone and regard the image. Odette looks beautiful with her hair longer than it is currently, her pregnant belly protruding from her long, lithe body, exposed from the bottom of a bra top to just below the bellybutton. She looks sporty, healthy, beautiful, and above all, wonderfully pregnant.

The same feelings I had when Penny showed me her new baby twist inside, and I hand the phone back swiftly. "That's such a nice photo," I manage.

"It was so fun doing that shoot. Well, all the shoots," Odette says. "Maybe I'll have another baby someday and do a Timothy shoot for Marie, Emma."

Her flippant tone that she could get pregnant so easily—because past experience suggests strongly that she can, let's face it—makes me uneasy. I'm hit by a mixture of jealousy and hope and disappointment and well, probably mainly jealousy.

"That would be amazing, but you might need a new man for that," Henrietta says with a laugh.

She replies, "That would be a good place to start."

"Now, Emma, it was lovely to meet you, and thank you very much for the information. I'm going to meet with my team to discuss Timothy, and I'll be back in touch," Henrietta says to me.

I push the cocktail of emotions that photo evoked aside and beam at her. "That would be amazing."

"Now, I must dash. When home and work are both manic, you've got to at least try to keep up."

The three of us walk out of the café and onto the sidewalk.

"How are things on the home front?" Odette asks.

Henrietta beams. "Wonderful," she replies, and it makes me wonder what's got her so happy. But I've only just met the woman, so I'm not going to ask. She air kisses Odette. "So good to see you again, darling. And Emma? I'll be in touch." She lifts her phone to her ear as she waves good-bye and disappears onto the crowded street.

"I'm so glad you got to meet Hen in the end," Odette says. "Speaking of which, how are things going with your baby plans?"

I slap on an *everything's fine* smile. "No news yet."

"Well, all you can do is keep trying with that gorgeous husband of yours."

I hold my fake smile in place. "That's true."

"And you two will definitely make beautiful babies. I've got a stack of old baby things when you need them. So many Dolce and Gabbana sleepsuits, I don't know what to do with them."

"Dolce and Gabbana do sleepsuits? Who knew?"

"Oh, you are silly," she replies with a laugh, and I can't help but feel patronized. Why would I, the woman who can't get pregnant, know that Dolce and Gabbana does baby grows?

"You know, sometimes when Joaquin and Antonella are driving me crazy, I wonder if I should just give them away to you two. That would solve all our problems, wouldn't it?"

I gawp at her in total disbelief. She's fake offering me her children when they're driving her crazy? Is this woman for real right now?

I open and close my mouth as I try in vain to work out how the heck to reply.

"Oh, look at your face!" she exclaims in glee, clearly loving her joke. "Don't worry. I'll keep them to myself. Unless they're very, very naughty, that is," she adds with a nudge of her elbow.

"Right. Okay," I mutter, completely thrown.

My face must give me away because she responds with, "Oh, Emma. Don't be like that. I'm only trying to keep things light."

"Light. For sure," I mutter.

"We can't go through life taking things too seriously, can we?"

"Of course not."

She puts her delicate hands on my shoulders and presses her cheek against mine in a waft of perfume. "I'm so happy I could help your label. I do so love helping people. It makes me feel good in here, you know?" She places her hand over her heart and cocks her head to the side, regarding me as though I'm some an underprivileged charity case.

"Yes, err, thanks for that."

"Bye-bye, darling. Go get that husband of yours and make that baby!" she says too loudly as she turns to leave, and I'm left smiling awkwardly at passersby as they shoot me quizzical looks.

CHAPTER 15

"*C*an you believe she offered me her children like that?" I say, the feelings it evoked rising to the top once more. I'm regaling the story to Kennedy at a pub in the West End the following week. Sebastian is at the bar getting us some drinks, and Kennedy is sitting back and letting me pour my heart out to her like the good friend she is.

"That's insane, Em," she says with a shake of her head. "I mean, how insensitive of her."

"Right? And then when it was obvious to her that I was bothered by her comment, she told me to lighten up and find the humor in things, like there's something wrong with *me* for feeling the way I do about not being able to get pregnant. It was super awkward and humiliating."

"That's like you offering a homeless person your huge house to go live in and then telling him you were just kidding. Not that I'm saying you're like a homeless person," she adds hastily.

"No, I get it. I'm the homeless person of the fertility world," I say with a wry smile.

"But a totally nice and gorgeous one, of course."

"Of course," I say with a laugh, enjoying being able to talk about this with her. "Seb thought she probably realized she'd said the wrong thing and felt bad about it."

"Of course he'd say that. He's a guy. He doesn't get the whole female rivalry thing."

"It's not a rivalry. She put her foot in it and then made it sound like *I* was the one in the wrong. Seb thinks I'm overreacting to it and should just let it go."

"Are things okay with you guys?"

"Of course," I say quickly. "Well, not a hundred percent. Trying to get pregnant has been...difficult."

"Still nothing, I've got to assume?" she says, eyeing my glass of wine.

"We'd have to have done it at the right time this month for that to have happened."

"Why didn't you?"

"Because Seb was away working in Sweden. I can't just turn up at his meeting in Stockholm and demand sex."

"That sounds like a very Swedish thing to do to me. You could have gotten on a plane. Where there's a will there's a way, right?"

I think about how I'd said that exact thing to Sebastian at the time, and how he'd shot the idea down right away. "He didn't want to do that."

She narrows her eyes at me. "He does still want a baby, doesn't he?"

"Oh, yes. There's no doubt about that. It's just—" I chew on my lip as I try to put this feeling that's been growing lately into words. I know Sebastian wants a child just as much as I do, and I know he's finding it hard that despite doing everything we've been advised to do, we're still not pregnant. But after starting with an initial bang—pun fully intended—he's drawing back from me. It's nothing major. It's not like he's said anything or has avoided coming home to me. It's just that I feel a lot more invested in this whole process than he seems to be.

And it's started to bother me.

I look down at my hands. "I think this whole thing has started to take its toll on him. On *us*."

"Oh, babe. I'm so sorry. It's gotta be so hard on both of you."

"It's no picnic. I'm holding out for the fertility specialist appointment right now."

Sebastian arrives at the table, heavy laden with drinks. "Are you talking about me again?"

"You are all we ever talk about, honey. You know that," I say to him with a plastered-on smile.

He places the drinks on the table and plunks himself down next to me. "Well, you may need to break that habit when Charles arrives."

"I can't believe I let you talk me into a blind date with one of your 'chums,' Seb," Kennedy says.

"You're the one who said you wanted to find love, girl," I protest.

"We're simply oiling the wheels for you," Sebastian adds.

She holds out her hand. "Show me his picture again."

Sebastian scrolls through his phone until he finds it. "It was from a long time ago, remember."

She takes the phone in her hand and examines it. "I can't believe he's not on social media. *Everyone's* on social media. What's his deal?"

"He's a very private person," Sebastian replies, which I know is code for 'he's super rich and prefers to keep a low profile in case gold diggers try to latch onto him.'

"There's private, and then there's old-fashioned," Kennedy says. "He's our age, right?"

"We were in the same year at boarding school."

"Boarding school, huh?" Kennedy says as she takes a sip of

her glass of wine. "That figures. Is he a lord or something, too?"

Sebastian shakes his head. "His family owns most of Yorkshire, I believe. In fact, he runs the family business these days, since his father had a stroke some years ago. Poor chap. It's a huge responsibility for Charlie, but he takes it in his stride." He looks over our heads and says, "Ah, here he is."

Both Kennedy and I turn to watch him approach. Charles is a tall, handsome guy with dark blond hair and the bluest eyes I've ever seen. He's wearing a beautifully cut navy jacket over an open neck light blue shirt which compliments his classic heartthrob looks. Those Bradley Cooper eyes of his land on me, and his white tooth smile spreads from ear to ear. His eyes flick to Kennedy, who immediately sits up straighter in her chair, sticking her chest out.

Ha! Kennedy likes what she sees. This matchmaking expedition is off to a good start.

"Lady Martinston," Charlie announces as he leans down and kisses my hand like I'm the queen of England. "Always a pleasure. And your husband is here too, I see." He slaps Sebastian on the back.

"Good to see you, Charlie. It's been too long," Sebastian says.

He turns his attention to Kennedy. "Hello. I'm Charles Cavendish. It's a pleasure to make your acquaintance." He bows his head at her, and her smile amplifies, her cheeks flushed with pleasure.

I turn to Sebastian and mouth "she likes him," and he waggles his eyebrows at me in response. Sebastian was the one who came up with the idea of setting Kennedy and Charles up in the first place. Well, when I say he was the one who came up with the idea, what I mean is I badgered him for so long that eventually he cracked and suggested Charles as an option for her. Semantics.

"I'm Kennedy Bennet," she says, looking up at him from under her dark lashes.

"A Miss Bennet?" he questions. "With Mr. and Mrs. Darcy over here, does that mean you're all Jane Austen themed at this table?"

Kennedy lets out a girly giggle that confirms my suspicions. "It's my real name, actually. Nothing to do with the TV show. I've had it all my life."

"That's the way surnames usually work, I believe," he replies as he takes a seat at her side. "Unless you marry a lord, and then you get named after a large house in the country. Isn't that right, Emma?"

"Yup, although I prefer to be plain old Emma. Lady Martinston sounds super stuffy to me."

"Yeah. You're right," Kennedy says.

"So tell me, Kennedy, do you get set up with strange men by your friends often?"

"Oh, I wouldn't call you *strange*, exactly."

"Oh, I'm very strange, actually. You'll find that out soon enough."

"Not the run of the mill hottie then, huh?"

"You think I'm hot?"

"Oh, I, uh…it's an expression." Her cheeks turn a brighter shade of pink.

The edges of Charlie's lips tug into a half-smile. "I'm more than happy to be labelled 'hot' by beautiful women."

I happily watch their back-and-forth flirtation as they grow oblivious to anyone around them but one another. I tilt my head toward Sebastian and whisper, "They are totally into one another."

"I think you're right."

"Well done on the matchmaking, husband."

"Why, thank you."

Meanwhile, the flirtation turns to fact gathering. "Do you live here in London, Charles?" Kennedy asks.

"I do, yes. And please, call me Charlie."

Kennedy's cheeks have turned nuclear. "Sure, Charlie."

"I've got a place not far from here, in fact. It's very handy. I use it all the time."

"Charlie's got a *pied-à-terre* in Mayfair," Sebastian explains. "It's seen a few parties over the years."

"What's a *pied-à-terre*?" I ask. "It sounds like a French soccer player."

"Brady, we've talked about this before. It's *football*, not soccer," Sebastian mock scolds.

I roll my eyes good naturedly. "Three hundred and thirty million people in America say it's soccer, Seb."

"So, we're going with majority rules, are we?" he asks.

"Well, we do live in a democracy, so she does have a strong argument," Charlie says, and I grin at him. "*Pied-à-terre* is just a French expression for a small pad in the city."

"I'd hardly call your flat a small pad, Charlie," Sebastian says.

Charlie deflects the comment by saying, "Remember that time Rupert dressed up in a pair of nappies, sung 'God Save the Queen' on the balcony, and the neighbor called the police?"

Sebastian laughs at the memory. "Rupert was never much of a wallflower, was he?"

"He sounds like a total party boy," I say.

"That is an understatement," Sebastian says.

"Are you a party boy?" Kennedy asks Charlie, and I know she's holding out to hear his response. Kennedy's like me: she likes to have fun, but she's not much of a *go out and drink too much with your friends every weekend* kinda gal. Charlie being a party boy could spell a sudden end to her interest.

"I used to be a bit of one, but that was the version of me

that thought he was invincible. It turns out, I wasn't. Just a bit of a fool."

"Well, that sounds like a story," Kennedy leads.

"Perhaps for another day," he replies elusively. "Tell me all about your life here in London. I believe you moved here recently from across the pond."

As Kennedy tells him about how she left San Diego after appearing on *Dating Mr. Darcy* and falling in love with London, my phone vibrates on the table. I turn it over to read the screen. I jump out of my chair when I read the words *River Fertility*.

This is it. This is the call that I've been holding out for. I show the screen to Sebastian, who raises his eyebrows at me, and then I slip away from the table. My heart is beating in my throat as I rush through the pub and out onto the sidewalk where I answer the call. I'm positive the person on the other end of the line can hear the excited tremor in my voice.

"Is this Emma Huntington-Ross?" the voice says, and I reply a breathy affirmative.

"Would you and your partner be free to meet with Dr. White on Monday the twenty-fifth? We have a slot at 9:15."

Yes! Finally, an appointment.

"We sure can. Which month is that?" I fully expect it to be sometime in fall after what the receptionist said to me.

"Well, this month," she replies as though I'm a sandwich short of a picnic.

"This month? As in next week? Not three months away?" I squeak, barely believing our luck.

"We had a cancellation, and as you know, you were on the waitlist. Should I pencil you in, or did you want to wait for an appointment in three months?"

"No!" I say with too much force. I clear my throat. "I mean, the appointment on the twenty-fifth would be perfect. Put us in your calendar in permanent marker because we are definitely gonna be there." I do a mini air punch. That's only nine days away! I can wait nine days. No problem.

"Uh, it's all digital, actually. There are no pens, permanent or otherwise."

"What I meant was that we're excited to be there. You can count on us being there," I explain.

"Right," she replies uncertainly. "Well, thank you and good-bye."

I end the call and then clutch my phone to my chest, my tummy all fluttery with anticipation. This is really happening! We're meeting the leading fertility expert Dr. White, who I've read all about. Apparently, she is super successful in helping couples make babies.

With a renewed spring in my step, I return to the pub. Sebastian gives me a questioning look as I sit down next to him, and I give his hand a squeeze. I whisper, "We've got an appointment in nine days. *Nine* days."

"That's wonderful," he says, his eyes warm and full of love for me.

Instantly, I regret how I'd complained about him to Kennedy earlier. He loves me, he wants our baby, and he's in this with me one hundred percent.

I need to remember that.

"I love you," I murmur to him as our gazes lock.

"I love you, too."

Kennedy's voice punctures our love bubble. "All I'm saying, *Charles*, is that we don't all start out in life with a silver spoon the size of Texas in our mouths."

"That does sound awfully uncomfortable," Charles replies with a laugh. "In fact, I'd go so far as to say it's an anatomical impossibility."

"It's a metaphor," Kennedy grinds out.

I widen my eyes in surprise. How did they go from flirtation and blushes to whatever this is? I shoot Sebastian a questioning look.

"Things have gone downhill since you left," he explains under his breath.

"They're not getting along?" I ask totally unnecessarily. They're now staring at one another, their body language screaming totally *not* getting along. "But they were flirting up a storm before. I thought it was so on."

"Apparently not."

We need to do something to salvage this situation. They were so obviously into each other when I left the table, and I just know they'd be a perfect match if they could stop this weird bickering, like they're an old married couple.

"Hey, did you two know that you've got a bunch of things in common?" I ask. "Kennedy grew up in San Diego and loves the beach. Right, Kennedy?"

"The beach. Sure," she replies, her features tight.

"And Charlie, you like to race motorboats, right?" I lead, searching for common ground.

"I have been known to dabble," he replies stiffly.

Geez. This is like getting blood out of a stone.

"You see that's where we differ once more: I like to surf and paddleboard and swim, whereas you like to create noise pollution and actual pollution in a speedboat," Kennedy says to him.

Charles's eyebrows lift to his hairline. "So you're at one with nature, and I'm some ignorant petrol head, is that what you're saying?"

"I didn't say that," Kennedy replies with a shrug.

"You're impossible, did you know that? Oh, what am I saying. Of course you do."

"*I'm* impossible?" Kennedy guffaws. "I'm not the one ruining the serenity of the ocean and spilling gas onto the poor sea creatures below, destroying their delicate ecosystem."

I raise my eyebrows at her. "Hey, that's a little over the top."

They both ignore me.

"It's not like I get a tin of *petrol*," he says pointedly, "and drain it overboard every time I take a boat out."

"You'd may as well," Kennedy snaps.

Charlie downs his pint of beer, places the empty glass on the table, and says, "Well, this has been an excellent evening. Thank you, Sebastian and Emma, for the drink." He rises from the table and gives a curt head nod to Kennedy. "Such a pleasure, Kennedy. Let's *not* do this again."

"Sounds perfect to me," she retorts, her arms crossed.

I think better of trying to salvage the situation, and instead I say good-bye to Charlie, and Sebastian walks him out of the pub.

"What the heck, Kennedy?" I say to her once the guys are out of earshot.

"What? The guy's a jerk."

"You liked him. You were flirting with him."

"That was before I knew he was an overprivileged speed-boat racer who thinks he's God's gift to women."

"He's not like that," I protest. "Sure, he's wealthy, but he's a regular guy. Seb and he are great buds."

She harrumphs. "Lucky Seb."

I push out a breath and lean back against the high-backed leather booth seat. "Okay. Fair call. Charlie's not the guy for you."

"Nope."

"Got it."

"Great."

"But you *did* like him."

"He's a jerk."

"Good to know."

We sit in silence, Kennedy still fuming, until Sebastian returns.

"Well that went well," he says with a laugh. "I'm sorry it didn't work out between the two of you."

"You win some, you lose some," Kennedy replies.

"And I think that signals the end of our matchmaking career, Brady," Sebastian says.

"What about Rupert?" I suggest, and both he and Kennedy reply with a forceful "No!"

It was worth a shot.

CHAPTER 16

*K*ennedy's and Charlie's weird interaction is the last thing on my mind nine days later. Today is the day we meet with Dr. White at River Fertility. *Finally*. I barely slept a wink last night as thoughts drummed against the walls of my brain.

What if they don't find anything wrong?

What if they do?

What if it's something wrong with me?

What if it's Seb?

What if...

What if...

My nerves are still rattling like fine china in an earthquake while we're sitting side by side in the clinic's waiting room. It's dotted with other couples, all concentrating on *not* looking at anyone else, finding their footwear endlessly fascinating.

"I am so excited. Are you excited?" I say quietly to Sebastian.

"I've got mixed feelings, to be honest."

"Because we don't know what they're going to find?"

He nods and gives my hand a squeeze.

"Yeah, me too. But I'm mostly excited." I grin at him.

"I love your positive attitude."

"Sebastian and Emma?" a woman in thick-rimmed glasses and curly gray hair holding a brown folder in her hands says from across the room.

Sebastian glances at me. "Are you ready for this?"

"Heck, yes."

We follow the woman out of the modern reception area and down a hallway lined with photographs of babies on the walls to an open office door.

"Here you are," she says as she stands back for us to enter.

As we walk in, a small, slim woman with sharp features who can't be much older than me is sitting behind a glass desk, tapping on her keyboard. She's dressed reassuringly in a white lab coat, with a stethoscope around her neck, looking every inch a stereotypical doctor—and nothing like Dr. Sheffield.

Thank goodness.

She raises her index finger in the air as she continues to tap on her keyboard with her other hand. "Take a seat, and I'll be with you in one minute."

We do as we are instructed, and as we wait for her to finish, I try to curb my excitement a little. But not a lot. Let's face facts here. The person sitting across from us right now could be the one who manages to get us our baby, people! It's hard not to feel at least a little bit buzzed.

"Now," she says, removing her glasses and looking over at us, "you must be the Huntington-Rosses. I'm Dr. White." She smiles, and her lips lift right up over her teeth to show a strip of gums. With her long skinny face, she bears more than a passing resemblance to a horse.

We say hello, and she asks us to tell her why we're here today.

"We've done everything, Dr. White, and still nothing," I say in exasperation.

"How long has it been since you started trying to conceive?"

"Ten months and twelve days," I reply promptly.

"Someone's keeping track," she replies.

Sebastian places his hand on my knee. "My wife is *very* focused on this."

I keep my tone light when I reply, "You say that like it's a bad thing, honey."

He puts it simply with, "Well, you are."

I know he's right, which is actually kinda irritating right now, but does he have to make it sound like I'm obsessive over this? Because I'm not. I'm simply driven to achieve my goal. That's all. End of story.

"I think as a woman it's important to be focused. We're the ones trying to get pregnant. It's our bodies," I say, and I know I sound defensive right now, but come on! No one could fastidiously track their cycle, test continually for ovulation, schedule in sex, and avoid alcohol and certain foods for half the month and not be super aware of it. It's simply not possible.

"You are absolutely right, Emma," Dr. White replies, and I smile at her, exonerated. "Sebastian, you are also right in that there should be a balance in all things, and the pursuit of a family is no different."

I blink at her. She's agreeing with both of us?

She consults the notes on her screen. "You're coming up on thirty-one soon, Emma, and you're thirty-four, Sebastian, I see. There's no problem with your ages, but we obviously need to do some investigative work to determine what's happening and why you're not conceiving."

"That's what we want. We want tests. Lots of 'em," I say. "Don't we, Seb?"

"If that's what Dr. White thinks," he replies.

What is he saying? Of course it's what we need, and Dr. White is going to tell us that.

"Well, before we move into that territory, I have a few questions. Do either of you have any children?" she asks.

We both reply, "No."

"Have you been pregnant before, Emma? Had any miscarriages?"

"No."

"How about you, Sebastian. Have you impregnated any other mates?"

I let out a sudden nervous laugh. She makes him sound like a bull on a farm, going around getting a herd of cows pregnant.

"No, I have not," he replies firmly.

She taps on her keyboard. She reads something on her screen and then looks back at me. "Emma, I see here you've got a family history of endometriosis."

"My mom."

"Did it affect her fertility?"

"She and my dad were only able to have me. She couldn't get pregnant again after I was born."

"I see." The only sound in the room is her tapping on her keyboard, and I wonder what she's typing. "Were you an assisted pregnancy?"

"No. Did they even have that back then?" I ask with a laugh.

"Oh, yes. Modern medical fertility treatment has been in use for decades." She types something further on her keyboard, and I glance nervously at Sebastian.

He fires me an encouraging smile. We wait while she

continues to type. The incessant *tip tap tapping* is doing nothing for my nerves.

"Sebastian, did your parents have any problems conceiving?"

"Not that I know of. We're not the type of family that talks about that sort of thing, though, so I don't know. There's my sister and I."

She peers at her screen as she types. "Emma, tell me about your menses."

"My what?" I ask.

"Your menstrual cycle. Do you have any pain?"

"Well, yeah. Doesn't everyone?"

"No, they don't. How would you rate your pain level, on a scale of one to ten, one being minimal and ten being fainting with pain?"

"I'd say a one or two usually." A thought occurs to me. "Actually a while back my period was late, and I had quite a lot of pain when it came." I turn to Sebastian. "It was when I was meant to meet Henrietta that time with Odette."

"How late were you?" Dr. White asks.

"Only a few days."

"You might have had what we call a chemical pregnancy that ended in miscarriage, causing some pain and late menstruation. It's fairly common."

Stilled, I stare at her in shock. "Are you saying I might have been pregnant?"

"Perhaps. Did you do a test?" she asks, and I shake my head. "Then there's no way of knowing now. But it is a possibility."

My eyes find Sebastian's, and we share a look of hope and love and dismay, all rolled into one. He shifts his chair closer to mine and wraps his arm around my shoulder. The gesture causes a lump to rise in my throat as heat radiates across my chest.

"What does it mean if my wife had been pregnant and lost it?" he asks.

"I'd love to tell you that it's a good sign, but we simply don't know. There are multiple reasons why a woman can miscarry, and without the relevant data in this case, I cannot comment with any authority. Might I add that it's only a theory, as well."

"Sure," I manage, my mind abuzz.

I might have held a new, fragile life inside of me. And then lost it.

She weaves her fingers together as she fixes us with her gaze. "Eighty percent of women under the age of forty conceive naturally within twelve months of trying, so it could be that you're here prematurely. It hasn't yet been a full year."

"I had wondered that myself," Sebastian says, and I tighten my jaw. So what if eighty percent conceive naturally within twelve months. We could be in that twenty percent.

"With your family history, however Emma, I'd like to run some tests." She moves her gaze to Sebastian and adds, "On both of you, just to be sure."

It's music to my ears.

"Tests. Good. What are we talking here? Hormone blood tests, an ultrasound scan?" I ask.

She offers me a small smile that disappears from her long face before it's even fully formed. "You've done your home-work. I'm going to get your blood tested so we can measure your FSH hormone, Emma. That's your follicle stimulating hormone, which needs to be at a certain level in order for you to ovulate each month. I'll give you both an examination now. Considering the family infertility, I'll also order you an ultrasound, Emma, so we can have a better look at what's going on."

I tap my foot in apprehension. What does she mean

"family infertility?" I'm living proof that my parents were perfectly fertile. Aren't I?

"Sebastian. How about we start with you? Pop yourself behind that curtain, undress your bottom half, and let me know when you're ready."

"Err, all right." He pulls his lips into a line as he gets up and disappears behind the curtain. A few moments of sitting watching Dr. White write even more notes on her computer later—and yes, I'm dying to read what she's writing, but know I should stay put—he calls out that he's ready, and she too disappears around the curtain.

I sit and wait. It's got to be one of the weirder life experiences to know your husband is having his privates checked by a woman you've only just met a mere ten feet from where you're sitting. But this is the world we now find ourselves in, so it's got to be a case of go big or go home. And right now going big involves Sebastian getting manhandled—or *woman*handled—by Dr. White.

"Get yourself dressed again, and I'll examine your wife."

Sebastian appears from behind the curtain, an embarrassed look on his handsome face.

Dr. White returns to her desk and resumes her typing.

"Everything okay?" I ask Sebastian under my breath.

"No idea."

"Now, Emma. I'd like to examine you as well."

"Sure thing." I rise to my feet and hesitate. "Dr. White? Do you think I've got what my mom has?"

"The only certain way to determine whether you yourself have endometriosis is to perform what's called a laparoscopy."

"That sounds serious," I say with a light laugh that belies my anxiety.

Dr. White's face doesn't crack. "The procedure is performed under a general anesthetic, so there are risks associated with it, of course, but we'll cross that bridge when and if we come to it. Now, pop yourself behind that curtain there, remove your undergarments, and lie down for me." She pulls out a pair of rubber gloves from a box on the windowsill behind her and snaps them on. "We're going to try to find out what's going on."

CHAPTER 17

I feel like a rat in a laboratory. I've been pricked with needles, scanned in places I never thought I'd need to be scanned, and even sent off to a specialist to have ink pushed through my fallopian tubes to check for "blockages," like I'm a kitchen sink filled with coffee granules.

It's not as fun as it sounds.

Correction, it's not fun at *all.*

Meanwhile, while I've been poked and prodded and generally put through the ringer, what has Sebastian had to do? Let me tell you his role in this whole thing. He's had to go to the clinic during his lunch hour, closet himself away in a room, and produce a "specimen" for testing. Seriously, I get put through all that and all he's got to do is what he no doubt perfected as a teenage boy.

On no planet in the whole freaking *universe* is this fair.

Now, we find ourselves sitting back in Dr. White's office, waiting with bated breath for her to share the test results with us. It's like finding out whether you've got your dream job you've always wanted and you know will change your life for the better—or you've got to go back to the drawing board and start all over again.

She fixes a smile on her face and places her hands palms down on her desk. "I'll start with you, Sebastian. Your blood test is perfectly normal, in fact your testosterone levels are in the top twentieth percentile of all the men we've tested over the years. Well done, you."

"Thank you, I think?" he replies with a light laugh. "I'm not sure I have much control over my testosterone levels, though."

Dr. White regards him with alarm. "Of course you don't. That would be absurd."

My husband's eyes dart to mine for a second, and I crack a small smile, despite my nerves. "Of course. Utterly absurd," he replies.

"The other good thing is that your sperm count is stellar. Those little fellows have excellent motility and seem to know their purpose in life, thanks to your solid FSH level. So, you're good to go, as they say."

Sebastian turns to me. "That all sounds like good news, doesn't it, Emma?"

I grip my fingers tightly in my lap as I nod at him. If the problem doesn't lie with Sebastian…

"Now, Emma," Dr. White begins, turning her intense gaze on me. "Your blood test results are also normal, and it looks like you are ovulating successfully each month."

Relief washes through me. "Phew. I've been so worried."

"What we have found is that your fallopian tubes are blocked."

"Blocked?"

"Blocked," she repeats.

"Like a fixable kind of blocked? Or a fatally blocked kind of blocked?" I ask, not expecting the latter. I mean, this is the twenty-first century. Medical science has come a long way.

"That depends on several factors. Although blocked fallopian tubes can be caused by fibroids or pelvic inflammatory disease among other causes, I theorize that the blockages are in fact caused by adhesions which occur when endometrium grow outside the uterus, thickening and bleeding with each menstruation, thus causing scar tissue to form. In essence, endometriosis, endometrium being the root of the term."

I blink at her, comprehending about ten words out of that whole speech. "I'm sorry, what?"

"In English, please, Dr. White?" Sebastian says for me.

"You didn't understand that? All right, I'll take another shot." She lets out a breath as though she's now got to explain something complicated to a toddler. "When you have your period each month, Emma, the lining of your uterus sheds. Are you with me so far?" she asks, and I nod. Of course I know *that*. "Good. What happens when you have endometriosis is that some of the cells responsible for the twenty-eight-day shedding grow outside the uterus, usually throughout the pelvic area, but there have been some cases where it has been discovered in the lining of the nose. Which is quite incredible, don't you think?"

I lift my hand and touch my own nose as thoughts rush through my brain. Thoughts that range from the fact she's telling me she thinks I've got what my mom had to wondering whether nose tampons are a thing, and if they are, how would you stop the string from hanging down to brush your lip?

Random, I know.

"Anyway, once these misplaced endometrium cells have been shed, they create scar tissue, which over time, become adhesions. I believe your fallopian tubes are blocked by these adhesions."

Sebastian reaches for my hand. "Are you okay?" he asks softly.

"Sure, I…" I turn back to Dr. White. "Are you saying I've got endometriosis?"

"I'm hypothesizing that you do. I won't know until I operate."

My voice rises as I say, "Operate?"

"Yes," she replies in a matter-of-fact way that belies the smoothie of emotion blending inside of me. She regards her screen. "I can book you in for a procedure a month next Tuesday, if that suits?"

My eyes dart in alarm to Sebastian's.

He leans across and takes both my hands in his. "You knew this was a possibility."

"I guess."

"Do you want to think about it?" he asks, and I nod, thoughts crashing like waves against my skull. "Dr. White, can we take some time to talk about this and come back to you?"

"Of course. You can speak with reception when you're ready to book."

"Could it be anything else? I mean, it might not be Endo, right?" I ask.

"That's what the surgery will allow us to deduce," she replies.

"What if I don't have the surgery. What are our chances of pregnancy then?"

"Extremely low, considering your tubes are about ninety percent blocked."

"Ninety percent?" I echo breathlessly. Bees buzz in my chest.

"Can the surgery unblock them?" Sebastian asks.

"That would be the goal, although it's not a guaranteed outcome," she replies.

"So...so you might not be able to unblock them, which means I can't—" My voice catches, and I try again. "I might not be able to have a baby?" Despite trying to keep a handle on my emotions, my voice is quivering like a yodeler in full voice.

"Given your age there is every chance you can still have a successful pregnancy and live birth. It just may be the way you go about it might not be what you had originally expected, that's all."

"I thought there was only one way, Doctor," Sebastian says.

"I think she means in vitro fertilization," I mutter.

"That's right. In vitro fertilization, otherwise known as IVF around here, is our specialty, and it's a thoroughly viable option for you."

Sebastian and I share a look. This has gotten super serious super-fast.

"But first we need to determine what is causing the blockages and do our best to fix it for you. All right?" she asks, and we nod our heads. "Good. Have a good think and get back in touch. You can see yourselves out?"

"Of course," Sebastian replies.

Summarily dismissed, ten minutes later I'm sitting in a virtually empty restaurant down the street, processing it all as Sebastian gets us a couple cups of coffee.

He returns holding two glasses of brown liquid. "Brandy. I thought we could both do with it after that discussion."

"My tubes are blocked," I say dully as I gaze out of the window at the gray sky above a plain brick building across the street. "Blocked, Seb. As in no way in and no way out. My eggs can't go anywhere. They're on house detention, like tiny criminals." I gaze across the table at him. "No wonder we can't get pregnant."

"She didn't say they're completely blocked, Brady. There's still hope."

"You're going to tell me that your 'superb swimmers,'" I say as I do bunny ears with my fingers, "should be able to smash that blockage to reach their target?"

"My words exactly," he says with a smile. "Take a sip."

I lift my brandy glass to my lips and take a small sip, the liquid singeing my throat as it travels down. "Wow, that's strong."

"It's medicinal. Pretend I'm your St. Bernard."

I giggle despite myself as an image of Sebastian as a dog in the Swiss mountains with a barrel of brandy around his neck fills my mind. "You're an oversized, super fluffy dog now, are you?"

"Whatever makes my wifey smile her beautiful smile," he replies.

"Wifey, huh? That's a new one." I take another sip of the brandy, and the same thing happens. I exhale loudly as I place my drink back on the wooden table. "What do you think about me having surgery?"

"I think there's no rush to any of this. She only said ninety percent blocked. There's still a ten percent chance we can get pregnant naturally."

A small light of hope glows bright in the gloom before it's extinguished by sobering reality. Ten percent isn't a whole lot in anyone's books, least of all someone hoping for the miracle of new life. "I guess that's true."

He raises his glass. "Here's to that ten percent."

I clink my glass against his and down the rest of my brandy in a gulp. It seeps down into my belly, warming me as it dispels my sinking feeling for a good ten seconds.

And then that feeling comes right back.

* * *

WE DECIDE TO KEEP TRYING, but that sinking feeling takes up permanent residence in my belly. Although I didn't want to hear it in her office, I know in my heart of hearts that what Dr. White said is true.

But I haven't gotten where I am in life without working hard, so the moment I get on the train to head back to Martinston, I google how to unblock your tubes. There is a *lot* of info out there. From taking vitamin C, garlic, and castor oil, to massage techniques, yoga, and something called an herbal tampon—which I decided not to get within a mile of, not least because of how uncomfortable it had to be. There are a lot of options.

My eyes glide over another couple of options until they land on the words *vaginal steaming*. I skim read the article and show it to Sebastian.

"You want to hover over a steaming bowl of water and let it steam you?" he asks, the incredulous look on his face telling me exactly what he thinks of the concept.

"I don't *want* to do any of this, but it says here that Gwyneth thinks it can help with infertility among a bunch of other problems."

"Who's Gwyneth?"

"Gwyneth Paltrow of course."

"Well, if Gwyneth Paltrow thinks it can help," he replies with a laugh, and I nudge him with my elbow.

I sink back into my seat, deflated. "Do you think it's all futile? I mean, should I just have the surgery and be done with it?"

"I think we should take our time before we decide. And in the meantime, let's take a break from all this and think about something else. Perhaps we could plan a weekend away, somewhere we've not been before? I hear Barcelona is lovely this time of year."

"Maybe we could plan a trip while I'm ovulating? That

way we can do it as much as we need to without me having to do things like traipse through London to find you."

He places his hand over mine. "Brady, what I meant was let's just go away and do other things. No pressure. No agenda. Just you and me."

I knit my brows. "But don't you want to make this work?"

"I do, with all my heart, but I also want to be a person, not just a sperm donor."

"I'm not making you a sperm donor," I protest, and a couple of teenage boys sitting across from us snigger into their palms.

Sebastian frowns at them and lowers his voice. "No, of course you're not. That was a poor choice of words. It's just —" he pauses as he looks down at our entwined hands, "I don't know. I want to have a child just as much as you do, but how about we have a weekend away and come back to it with renewed vigor."

I kiss him on the cheek. "I like the sound of that."

"And no steaming of any body part, no matter what some celebrity might say online, okay?"

I giggle, and it ends in a snort. "Deal."

CHAPTER 18

*A*s planned, we go to Barcelona the following weekend, and it is blissful. We wander down Las Ramblas hand in hand, we eat paella and drink *tempronillo* at a gorgeously romantic, tucked away restaurant, we swim in the Mediterranean and bask on the golden sand of Barceloneta beach. It's like it was before we embarked on this whole baby-making mission: just me and Sebastian, together, enjoying one another.

Well, *almost* like it was.

No matter how much I love my husband and no matter how many candlelit dinners we have under the Spanish stars, it's always there, this nagging, persistent feeling that we should be focusing on making our child.

I try to push it away and focus on being in a romantic, foreign city, but it keeps creeping into my consciousness.

By the time we're back at Martinston, my mind is made up about what we've got to do, and here's a hint: it doesn't involve downing huge amounts of herbs or vitamins, and definitely not steaming any body parts.

No way. If Dr. White thinks I need surgery, then that's

what I'm going to do—and I'm a mixed bag of anxiety and excitement about it.

"I'm so sorry you've got to have an operation tomorrow," Kennedy says as we chew on our toasted sandwiches at a café overlooking a quaint tree-lined street a month later. "That sure is taking things up a notch or two."

"Actually, I feel good about it," I reply. Which is true. Mostly. I mean it *is* surgery, so I'm not exactly doing a happy dance about it, but I'm excited about the prospect of what having it could mean. "Having this surgery means we get to deal with whatever the problem is and get on with having our family."

"It sounds like a big deal."

"Oh, it won't be. It's a laparoscopy, which is keyhole surgery. No big scars and faster recovery. It'll be a cinch."

"A cinch? Babe, they put you under, right?"

"Yeah, but it'll be fine," I reply, fear twisting inside. I'd read up about the procedure and what the doctor might have to do if I do have endometriosis. All I can say is using a laser on my insides to zap away scar tissue sounds more like a sci fi movie to me than a medical procedure. "And anyway, if I've gotta do it, I've gotta do it."

"I so admire your strength. What does Seb think?"

"Oh, he's totally on board with it."

She narrows her eyes at me. "Is he?"

My stomach tenses. I lean in and say, "Actually, here's the thing. Seb didn't exactly see the urgency to all this. He felt we should give it some more time and keep trying naturally."

"What do *you* think?"

"I think giving something more time when the pathway to my eggs is almost completely blocked is as hopeless as me thinking I'll ever be as elegant and effortlessly beautiful as," I search my mind for a target until I land on, "Odette Rojas."

"Odette Rojas? Is she the one who joked about offering you her kids?"

"Yup. She might say dumb stuff sometimes, but she's beautiful and elegant and kinda an all around amazing person."

She cocks an eyebrow. "You hate her."

"Of course I don't hate her."

She leans back in her chair, examining me. "Yeah, you do. You totally hate her."

"I guess she's a little too perfect, you know? She's got this huge career, she's super gorgeous, she was married to some famous Chilean soccer star, and on top of it all, she's mom to two perfect freaking kids."

"Yeah, I know how *that* feels. She's the person you want to be. I've got some experience in that department."

"You do? I can't imagine you of all people feeling inadequate next to someone else."

She leans forward in her seat. "I went on this reality show once where the bachelor was posing as Mr. Darcy and he only had eyes for this one girl, despite the fact there were a bunch of us all vying for his attention. You might have heard of them? They're a big deal right now."

I let out a giggle. "Yeah, there is that. And we're so not a big deal."

"You're still talked about, girl."

I groan. "For sure, but not in a good way. Well, not me, anyway."

She scrunches up her nose. "The media's still not a fan?"

"Someone made a meme of me always in my rubber boots, watering the same freaking pot plant, which is all the production company would let me do on the show. It's not my fault." I pout like a child.

"The show is done and dusted. They'll forget about you and move onto the next thing."

"Women are still lining up to ask Seb to dive into the pond in his white shirt and Regency 'breeches.'"

She lets out a laugh. "Girl, you married a super-hot, rich guy—that's your problem."

"Speaking of hot guys, what happened with you and Charlie that time? When I left you were totally into each other, and then when I got back, you were bickering like an old married couple. What happened?"

"He's not my type, that's all," she replies stiffly.

"Handsome, charming, and smart isn't your type, huh?" I goad, and she makes a face at me. "I saw how y'all looked at each other. You were totally into him, and I could tell he liked you, too."

"Look, I'll admit I thought he was pretty hot, but that was before he opened his mouth and started rubbing his privilege in my face."

"He did?"

"Oh, yeah. It was all 'my yacht' this and 'my super expensive sports car' that and all that crap. I'm so not into guys who flaunt their wealth and privilege like that. That was my ex all over again."

I run through all the things I know about Charlie but come up blank. "I've never known Charlie to do that."

"Maybe I brought the jerk out in him?" she offers.

"How about you give him another try? You two are so right on paper."

She shakes her head firmly. "Next subject."

"I think you should give him another chance. Who knows? He may end up being Kennedy Bennet's Mr. Darcy."

"Emma," she begins, using my name to make her point, "I can assure you Charles Cavendish the third, or whatever number he is, will never be my Mr. Darcy."

"Never say never, girl," I tease. "I forgot to say that I'm meeting Zara here after. We're going shopping for a new dress for me." I take a bite of my sandwich and glance around the room. My eyes land on a familiar set of shoulders, and as he turns around, a smile busts out across my face. "Seb's here."

Kennedy looks up. "Who's he with?"

I watch as he turns to a woman beside him, who laughs at something he says. She's tall and slim and immaculately dressed. An emotion twists inside my stomach.

I clear my throat. "That's Odette Rojas."

"The woman who wants to give her children away." Kennedy offers me a wry smile. "I see what you mean. She's stunning. Well, her profile is, anyway."

As Odette turns around, I wave at her, and her smile broadens. She says something to Sebastian, and he too looks our way, smiling and mouthing, "We'll come over."

"I guess you're about to meet Ms. Perfect," I say under my breath to Kennedy as Sebastian and Odette move our way.

"No one's perfect, girl. Remember that."

They arrive at our table, and I greet them both before I introduce Odette to Kennedy.

"What a wonderful coincidence to bump into you here," Odette says. "Did you adore Barcelona?"

"Oh, yes. It's a beautiful city and so much warmer than here."

"That's why you need to take as many chances as you can to go to the Continent," Odette says. "I hear you loved Olivano," she adds, naming the restaurant Sebastian and I had a particularly romantic candlelit dinner at.

"We did, didn't we?" Sebastian asks me.

"Did you have the *crema Catalana*? I told Seb you had to have it there. It's the best I've ever had, and I'm a big fan of that dessert."

"You don't look like you eat dessert," Kennedy observes, and Odette laughs her pretty, tinkling laugh.

I, on the other hand, am dealing with another topic.

"You recommended the restaurant to him?" I ask. Why does the idea that we dined at Odette's suggested restaurant bother me?

"Of course," she replies, as though it's completely obvious she would have. "I think I put together quite the itinerary for a romantic weekend away," she says to Sebastian with a smile. "Olivano, Barceloneta Beach, ambling arm in arm down Las Ramblas. It's hard to beat."

I blink at her a couple of times in shocked silence. That's exactly what we did: we dined at Olivano, we swam at Barceloneta Beach, and we ambled down Las Ramblas together. We'd may as well have done everything she suggested, right down to the smallest detail.

I lift my gaze to Sebastian's. He's looking uncomfortable, which he darn well should in my opinion. "I didn't realize we had a tour operator," I say in a controlled voice.

"Odette had been there with her husband some years ago and had made some suggestions. That's all," he replies.

I pull my lips together into a tight line. "Right. Got it."

"All that matters is you had a wonderful time away, Emma," Odette purrs. "You both deserve it after everything that's been going on."

An icy coldness strikes my core.

What did she just say?

"I think that's our cue to leave you to it," Sebastian says hurriedly. "Lovely to see you again, Kennedy." He kisses her on the cheek. "And I'll see you at home tonight, Emma." He plants a chaste kiss on my lips.

"I'll get us a seat, shall I?" Odette asks him. Sebastian thanks her, and she says her good-byes and leaves.

Zara chooses that exact moment to make her entrance, arriving at our table with rosy cheeks and panting lightly. "Am I late? The traffic was impossible, and I was sure you said twelve," she says as she greets both Kennedy and me. Noticing Sebastian at a nearby table, she adds, "What's my brother doing here? Is that Odette?" She waves at them, and he offers her a stiff wave in return.

"Ms. Perfect," Kennedy says, waggling her eyebrows at me, and I shush her.

"Gawd, my brother is so blimmin' uptight," Zara says. "You're so good for him, Em, but you've still got more work to get that carrot out from up his butt."

"Charming," Kennedy says with a giggle.

I try out a laugh, but my heart's not in it. As I look over at their table, I watch my husband talking with Odette. An odd sensation spreads across my chest. She knows more about us than I've ever told her. Of course logically I know Sebastian must have told her we were planning a trip away and she suggested Barcelona.

But why does that bother me so much?

CHAPTER 19

Sebastian comes home after I've gone to sleep, so we don't even talk to one another until we're on our way to the hospital for my surgery at the break of dawn the following day.

"But Seb, we did every single thing she suggested," I complain as we speed down the motorway toward London, "right down to eating that creamy dessert."

"Look, all I did was ask her advice for things to do on a romantic getaway, and she gave me some ideas. That's all. I don't get why that's a problem."

"It's not a problem exactly. It's more that I thought the dinner and the walk and all of it was your idea, not hers."

His jaw tightens. After a beat he says, "I'm sorry it bothers you, Brady. I had no idea it would."

"Thank you," I reply, feeling odd.

"Shall we focus on what's happening today? How are you feeling about it all?"

"Hopeful, but also worried."

He rubs my leggings-clad knee—Timothy activewear, of course. "You're a total warrior. You'll take this in your stride, and then you'll be home, propped up against your pillows, with me waiting on you hand and foot as you binge watch Netflix and eat chocolate."

"That doesn't sound bad at all."

"I'd rather like the break myself."

We share a brief smile before he returns his attention to the road, and I know I've been making a mountain out of a molehill. So what if one of his colleagues suggested a bunch of things to do on our romantic weekend away? Really, it's no big deal.

To distract myself, I pull out my phone and tap out what's now become my weekly *How do you like the Timothy Maternity samples and do you want to start stocking the line soon?* message to Henrietta Dixon at Marie Maternity. I get an *out of office* reply. I pinch my lips together in frustration as I switch my phone off. Other than a message about a month ago, telling me she loves the samples and will be back in touch, it's been crickets. Loud ones.

But my head's too full of what-ifs today to deal with it.

We arrive at the hospital, and as I get checked in my nerves are jangling like loose change in a purse. We're taken to a small room, and I answer a gazillion questions about myself, from what I weigh to when I last ate. They give me the most horrendous looking nightgown to wear, which does up at the back and fits me as well as an oversized potato sack. To complete the super sexy look, I get to tuck my long hair into a paper shower cap and slip on some paper underwear.

"I don't think I've ever seen you look so sexy," Sebastian says as I sit perched on the edge of the hard bed swinging my legs.

"I'll be sure to keep this outfit for you," I joke.

"Team it with the wellies, and you've got a deal."

We wait for what feels like most of the morning, my belly announcing loudly that it would like some food, *and now.*

Eventually, the nurse who peppered me with all the questions from earlier in the day arrives at our little room, followed by an orderly, and tells us it's time to go.

I clasp Sebastian's hands in mine. "I'm nervous."

"Don't worry. Everything is going to be okay," he tells me and pulls me in for a hug.

I get up on the gurney and lie back, spikes of fear encircling me. The anesthetist arrives, a portly man in his sixties with a red nose like Rudolph. "Here's your gin and tonic," he says as he injects some white fluid into my arm.

And that's the very last thing I remember.

The next thing I know, I'm lying in a bed, my vision blurry and a strong cramp in my belly.

"There, there. You're doing just fine," a soft, kindly voice says, and I blink a few times to try to focus, my head stuffed full of clouds.

A sharp pain settles low in my stomach, and I croak, "My tummy hurts."

"How about we fix that for you?" the voice says, and the next thing I know the pain drains away and I'm floating off in a dream about the Little Mermaid who's sitting on a toadstool talking with Nelson Mandela about which school to send her kids to on Mars. Or something like that. It's super fuzzy, and I'm on the good stuff here, people.

Sometime later, after I'm in my room and have been wafting in and out of sleep as Sebastian works quietly away on his laptop, Dr. White arrives by my bedside.

"We've had mixed results," she announces without preamble, immediately grabbing my attention.

Mixed results does not sound good.

"Your ovaries looked normal for a woman of your age, and I can confirm that you have endometriosis, although by my assessment it's only Stage 2, which is good news. You may not need another surgery to address any future adhesions, but we'll cross that bridge as and when we come to it."

"Normal ovaries sounds positive," Sebastian says. "Doesn't it, Emma?"

"What's the bad news?" I ask with more than a dash of foreboding. If the good news is that I've got a disease, surely the bad news can't be good?

"The bad news is that the damage to both your fallopian tubes was extensive. I tried to unblock them, but with little success."

My drumming heartbeat pushes away any remnants of sleep.

"What does that mean exactly?" Sebastian asks.

"It means that you and Emma are unlikely to be able to conceive naturally and that instead you will need to go down an alternative path in order to achieve a live birth. I'll have our receptionist book an appointment for you to come and discuss the options."

"Options?" I croak.

"Well, I say options, but there's really only one if you both want to be the biological parents of any future child, and that's IVF."

My heart feels like it's shrinking inside my chest. "Oh." I reach for Sebastian, and he wraps a comforting arm around my shoulders.

"Thank you, Dr. White. We'll have to have a conversation about all this once my wife is back on her feet."

"It's very straightforward," she carries on in her usual brisk, matter-of-fact manner. "For Emma to carry a pregnancy to full term and achieve a live, healthy birth, there is only one option open to you now as far as I can see it. Should you decide to abandon the idea of carrying a pregnancy, Emma, you could go down the surrogacy route—"

My eyes dart to Sebastian's. Surrogacy? What the...? We jumped there in a New York minute.

He takes in the horrified look on my face and cuts her off with, "We'll need to take some time to digest this before we make any rash decisions. Thank you for all your work and advice, Dr. White. I'll see you out." He leaps to his feet and escorts her from the room.

I lean against my pillows, my mind so abuzz with thoughts I feel like a nest of mad wasps has been set free within my skull.

Sebastian returns, and I sit up straighter.

"I told you there was something wrong. I knew we needed to do tests."

He balances on the edge of the bed and offers me a glass of water. "You were right, Brady. I had no idea."

"Well," I say, feeling vindicated once I've sucked on the straw to get some much-needed liquid, but the feeling is short lived. "Although, being right about this doesn't feel that great. What do you think we should do?"

"I think you should lie here and sleep some more, maybe read that book you've been talking about, and—"

I cut him off with, "I think we should do IVF."

"I thought you might say that."

"She said it's the only way." I grip his hand as tears well in my eyes. "Seb, I want this more than anything."

"I know you do, and I do, too."

"Does that mean we're gonna go for it? Try IVF? See if we can get our baby?"

He cups my face in his hands and leans in to kiss me. "I think we should get you back up on your feet—"

"Seb!" I protest.

"Let me finish, Brady," he says, his lips lifting. "What I was going to say is I think we should get you back up on your feet and then go make ourselves a baby with Dr. White."

I throw my arms around his neck in a fit of glee, only to pull back when pain stabs me in the belly. "Ow!" I call out and instantly dissolve into a flood of tears, saturating his shoulder.

"Are you okay there, champ?" he asks me once I've begun to slow my sobs.

"I think I'm a little emotional." I wipe my eyes with the top sheet.

"Do you think?" he asks with a smile on his face. "You have every right to be." He offers me a tissue, and I blow my nose loudly into it.

"We're really doing this?" I ask him, and he grins back at me.

"We're really doing this."

* * *

WE SURGE AHEAD WITH IT. I'm on a mission here, people! There's no time to mess around.

After I've recovered from the surgery, we meet with Dr. White who puts us on a protocol that involves medicated wipes, needles, and a stack of hormones. I tell you, the word "sexy" doesn't even begin to describe our new baby making regime. But I do not care. I am positive this is how we're going to make the next generation of Huntington-Rosses, and I feel totally blessed to have this option.

Dr. White explains that there are five phases in the protocol, starting with stimulating my ovaries to increase the number of eggs I produce, then collecting those eggs, fertilizing them to make embryos, and finally transferring them so I can cook them up nicely inside to make us a baby.

See what I mean? *Totally* sexy.

Weirdly, she put me on the contraceptive pill two weeks ago, which was totally counterintuitive to me, but who am I to question the experts? Now, on day fourteen of the cycle, it's early morning, and we're in our bedroom at Martinston. I unroll all the medical bits and pieces the clinic gave me on our king-sized bed. Frank jumps up and lands elegantly beside them, gives them a cursory sniff, recoils, and then jumps back off the bed in disgust.

"I'm not sure Frank approves," I say drily.

"He's a cat." Sebastian laughs. He regards the parapher-nalia laid out on the bed. "So, you've actually got to inject yourself each morning in the stomach or thigh?" Sebastian asks.

"Yup." I hold up one of the syringes in its packaging. "A jab with one of these babies each morning and we're on our way."

Sebastian's face takes on a distinctively green hue.

"Are you okay?" I ask him.

"I'm not big on needles. Never have been."

"Mr. Darcy's kryptonite," I say with a laugh. "Or am I totally messing up my fictional heroes here?"

"I think Jane Austen would love to think of Mr. Darcy as some kind of alien superhero from Krypton."

"Mr. Darcy in a cape," I say as I stroke my chin. "I can totally see that. And you know what? You're not the one having to inject yourself, dude."

"But I have to watch you do it in bed each morning."

I grin at him. "I've got an idea. While I do the injections, you can get up and bring me back a cup of coffee in bed."

His laugh rumbles through me as he pulls me in for a hug. "I love the way you've managed to twist this to your advantage."

I brush my lips against his. "I think it's the least you can do, considering all you have to do throughout this whole process is make a quick deposit in a cup."

"That's a jolly good point you make, Brady." He leans

down and kisses me softly on the lips again before he eyes the syringe. "I'll be off then."

"A piece of toast with that coffee would be just perfect," I call out to his retreating back.

"Your wish is my command," he replies before he disappears from the room.

I load up the syringe from the little glass bottle as I've been shown and tap the air out. Wiping my thigh with the medicated cloth, I say a prayer before I plunge the needle into my flesh.

We have officially begun.

CHAPTER 20

The following morning, I snap on the light and lay the little hormone-filled bottle, the syringe, needle, and a medicated wipe out on the bed. Just as he said he would, Sebastian takes one look at it and leaps out of bed like he's been bitten by a snake.

"Toast and coffee?" He glides his head hastily through the neck of his sweatshirt and pulls it down over his muscular torso.

"Perfect," I reply as he slips out of the room.

Who knew doing a round of IVF would get me breakfast in bed each morning? A definite silver lining to this whole process.

Just as I did yesterday, I swipe the cool wipe over a spot on my thigh, pinch my flesh, and plunge the primed needle into my skin and depress the syringe.

This is so easy. I have totally got this, *and* I get a coffee in bed from my hot husband.

What's not to love?

I slot the used syringe into the yellow tub the clinic supplied me with and slide it under the bed. Sebastian and I agreed that we wouldn't tell anyone when we were doing the cycle, so the last thing I want is for anyone in the family to find a syringe or bottle of hormones. We figured there would be too many questions and expectations. Instead we're going to simply announce when it's worked and everyone can feel happy for us. A much better way to do things.

I go about my daily routine, feeling perfectly normal but for an extra spring in my step. After all this time of trying and failing to get pregnant, with IVF I know we've got a real shot at making this work.

Soon enough, it's been a couple of weeks since I started the daily injections and I've been scanned more than I ever thought I'd need to be in my life, with endless pauses in the scanning process to capture images of what look like the fuzzy dark mud pies of my insides. Sebastian had wanted to come with me to the scan appointments, but I told him that I could handle it and there was no need for him to be there.

"We're up to the stimulation phase now," I explain to him as I read the information given to us by the clinic. "This is when the eggs will start to grow until they're big enough for them to collect."

"That involves needles, too, doesn't it?" Sebastian makes a face.

"Everything involves needles, Seb. *Every*-thing."

"Well, I suppose I'm still on morning coffee then, in that case."

I reach across to cup his face in my hand and plant a kiss on his lips. "And you do it so very well, too."

He lets out a low laugh. "Thank you?"

Referring to the information booklet once more, I do a quick mental calculation. "If I've got this right, I'll be having my egg collection procedure on the twenty-third."

"The twenty-third," he repeats as he scrolls through his phone. "I'll block the day out. Oh, we've got the Henley

Regatta with Phoebe and Johnny and Kennedy the following weekend." He lifts his gaze to mine. "You might be pregnant then."

Butterflies flap their wings in my belly. "Can you imagine? Me, pregnant. Oh, Seb." I let out a sigh as I lean up against him. "It'll be our little secret, just you and me."

He kisses me on the top of my head. "What a wonderful secret that would be." After a moment of contented silence, he says, "Do you mind if I invite Odette to the regatta? Only she mentioned she'd like to go but didn't have a ticket."

I push myself up and turn to face him. "I guess," I reply in an uncertain tone.

"Why do you say it like that? I thought you were over Barcelona and her misjudged comment offering you her children. You know she feels awful about it."

I raise my brows. "She said that?"

"She did. She's a good person, and I feel for her in her current situation."

I try to keep the frustration from my voice when I repeat, "Her current situation? Seb, she's some sort of a celebrity in the financial world, she's got men leaving puddles of drool in her wake, and she's a mother to two perfect children."

"Oh, I'm certain they're not perfect."

"You know what I mean. Her life is enviably good. The last thing she needs is us inviting her along to Henley as an added extra."

"I know she'd appreciate it. We could ask Mother to take her children for the day. She'd love that."

I gawk at him. "You want your mother to look after Odette's kids?"

Isn't that crossing a line? What line exactly I don't know, but I'm pretty sure it crosses one all the same.

He studies me for a beat before he replies, "If you don't like Odette, I'll not invite her."

"It's not that I don't like her. It's—" What is it? That Sebastian so obviously likes her? That she's wormed her way into our lives? That she got pregnant precisely when she wanted to with no effort whatsoever?

That she makes me feel *inadequate*, somehow?

My tummy twists into a reef knot. I know the answer, and it sits uncomfortably.

It's all of it.

"It's what?" he questions when I don't utter another word.

I push out a breath and ignore the growing knot. "It's nothing. I'm being hormonal or something. Invite Odette. It'll be nice to see her again."

"Only if you're sure."

I give a firm nod. "I am."

"Good. I'll set it up."

The door to the living room creaks open, and I immediately shift off Sebastian's lap. Despite Martinston being our home, we do have to share it with Sebastian's mother, his uptight and frosty granny, and Zara when she's not working in London. Alone time is hard to come by, even in a house the size of Martinston.

"Oh, hello, you two," Jemima says as she enters the room, trailed by Zara. "Isn't it a glorious evening? I love late summer, don't you? The flowers, the bees, the distant haze. Bliss."

"You're in a good mood, Mother," Sebastian says as he rises to his feet and kisses both her and his sister on both cheeks. "When did you get here, Zara?"

"About an hour ago," she replies as she flops down into one of the armchairs. "I'm exhausted."

"Poor dear. You've been working too hard," Jemima says.

"I have," she replies.

"Is that what they're calling clubbing these days? 'Work'?" Sebastian says.

Zara shoots him a withering look. "Oh, very funny."

"Emma, darling. How are you?" Jemima asks me.

"I'm great. We were just talking about the Henley Regatta. Are either of you going this year?"

"Yup," Zara replies as Jemima says, "Not this year, although Sebastian's and Zara's father and I met at Henley, you know."

"You did? Tell me the story."

"Does she have to?" Sebastian asks.

"You know she loves this story," Zara says. "Although I for one am deeply disturbed by the thought my parents were anything other than just my parents."

"We are fully rounded human beings, darling," Jemima says.

Sebastian says as he moves away from us. "Gin, Mother?"

"Thank you, darling." She takes a seat opposite me, her face alight as she says, "I was with a couple of my good friends from school. Prunella's father had a marquee, and we were flitting around flirting with boys and sipping Pimm's in our pretty summer frocks and hats and generally having a lovely time, when I spied this older boy who must have been at least twenty-something. I'd just turned eighteen. I was a lot younger and quite innocent."

"Did he look dreamy?" I ask and win a good-natured eyeroll from Zara.

"Oh, he did. He was in a bowtie, braces, and a straw boater. He was a total dish. All the girls wanted to meet him, but he only had eyes for me."

"Did he come over to talk to you?"

"I wanted him to. If you could get someone to talk to you by staring at the back of their head for as long as I did, then he would have. But no, he was having fun with his friends, so I had to take things into my own hands."

"You went to talk to him?"

"Oh, no. Nothing as forward as that. I was from an era when it was usually the men who approached women, not the other way around. No, what I did was I walked past him and accidentally spilt my drink all over him."

"What?" I shriek with a laugh.

"My mother was crafty," Zara says.

"Of course I apologized profusely and grabbed a cloth napkin to pat him down, and it was then that he wrapped his fingers gently around my wrist to stop me, our eyes met, and that was that."

"It was love," I say dreamily.

"It was. Absolutely. That and I noticed what marvelous abs he had, and I thought, my goodness, I would like to see what *they* look like."

"Mother!" Sebastian exclaims with a laugh as Zara puts her fingers promptly in her ears and declares she'll need emergency therapy in the morning.

I ignore them both. I totally get wanting to see a Huntington-Ross's abs. "That is such a romantic story. Love at first sight."

Jemima's face beams. "Most certainly."

"Isn't that romantic?" I ask Sebastian and Zara.

He hands a glass to Jemima and sits back down next to me. "It is indeed."

"We all have our stories, don't we? Not that your father's and mine was anything nearly as exciting yours," Jemima continues. "No television cameras or glamorous frocks for us."

"I'm not sure falling out of a limo onto my butt on national TV should be called glamorous, exactly," I say with a wry smile.

Sebastian lets out a laugh. "It was dramatic for the television-viewing public."

"You did it in great style, Em," Zara comments.

"They told me they weren't going to use that footage," I huff. Although it's been over two years since that fateful day —the day I fell out of a limo and met the love of my life— televising me falling out of that limo set me up as "the funny one" on *Dating Mr. Darcy*, although I guess my terrible rendition of the song "Old Town Road" didn't help that much either, especially because I replaced most of the words I didn't know with "horse." I've long suspected that if I hadn't been cast in that role, the media might have accepted me as Sebastian's partner much earlier, and things might have been a lot easier for us.

"My dear girl, you were utterly charming on that show, and I for one am glad my son chose you and not that hideous Camille."

"Gosh, yes," Zara confirms.

"I was never going to choose Camille," Sebastian replies.

The door creaks open once more, and Geraldine comes hobbling in with the support of her walking cane. We immediately spring out of our seats, and Sebastian rushes across the room to help her.

"Don't get up on my account," she says without meaning it. If we didn't stand when she walked into the room, I suspect she'd turn on her heel in disgust and leave.

"Here, Granny. Take my arm," Sebastian says as he leads her at a snail's pace across the silk Persian carpet to one of the room's high-backed leather armchairs.

"Good evening, Granny," I say to her with a smile as she bends her creaking knees to sit.

She fixes me with her watery glare, and I feel the corners of my mouth drop. There's something about this woman that scares the living daylights out of me. She's got a way of looking at you that slices right through your chest, lampooning your heart in its path.

Geraldine Huntington-Ross is no warm and fuzzy mother figure, that's for sure.

"Is there something you need to share with us, Emma?" she asks without preamble.

I wrack my brain. Did I say the wrong thing again? Did I forget to do something? Did I breathe wrong? Let's face it, it could be anything. "I don't think so."

She turns her attention to Sebastian. "Do you know about your wife's new habit?"

"I'm sorry, Granny. I don't know what you're talking about." He turns to me. "Do you have a new habit I don't know about, Emma?" He lifts his eyebrows to tease me, and I suppress a giggle.

"No new habits," I reply with a shrug. "I'm just regular old me, doing my usual stuff."

"Well then, if you're not going to come clean, you leave me with no choice."

I dart a look at Sebastian, who shrugs back at me. Neither of us have a clue what's going on here.

Geraldine rummages in her pocket for an uncomfortably long moment as we wait to see what evidence she's going to produce of this alleged new "habit" of mine. She pulls something out, brandishes it in the air, and my heart drops to my shoes.

Uh-oh.

"Drugs!" she declares in a deep horror movie voice that would impress Vincent Price himself. "That's what this is used for. Taking illicit drugs. Your wife, Sebastian, is a drug addict!"

I eye the syringe in her hand. It's one of my IVF syringes. I must have left it on the bed after I injected myself and somehow, she found it.

As the initial shock begins to subside, a disturbing thought occurs to me.

She's been in our bedroom.

"Emma?" Jemima questions. "Why do you have a needle? Are you a diabetic? I didn't know she was a diabetic, Mummy. Did you?"

"Oh, diabetic be damned," Geraldine spits, and I suck in air at her cuss word. In all the time I've known Geraldine Huntington-Ross, this is the very first time I've heard any such word fall from her lips. Sure, she's mean-spirited and has an endless array of insults she sees fit to throw my way, but cussing? Never.

"It's as clear as day that your wife is a drug addict, Sebastian. And this is evidence of that most egregious habit." Geraldine brandishes the syringe in the air once more for dramatic effect.

"Seriously, could you get any more OTT, Granny?" Zara asks. "This is like an episode of *Dating Mr. Darcy*." She turns to Sebastian and me. "No offence."

"Emma isn't diabetic, and she's certainly not a drug addict either," Sebastian says sternly. "You know that as well as I do, Granny."

Geraldine's eyes widen so much, she's in danger of them rolling out of her head and landing on the priceless antique rug. "Are you trying to tell me this thing is *yours*?" she asks him, incredulous.

He shakes his head as he exhales. His eyes find mine, and we share a nonverbal communication that entails realizing we've been busted—and knowing we're now going to have to come clean to the family about trying fertility treatment.

Sebastian moves to sit next to me, and we entwine our hands, his warm thigh pressed against mine. "Although we had thought we'd keep it to ourselves for now—" he begins but is cut off by Jemima.

"You're pregnant!" she exclaims with excitement.

"Mum, why would they need needles if they're pregnant?" Zara asks. "It doesn't make sense."

"We're not pregnant, although we do hope to be soon," I say, and Sebastian gives my hand an encouraging squeeze. "We're trying assisted fertility. It's called IVF, and it involves me injecting myself with certain hormones each day. That's why I'm using syringes, Granny."

Geraldine's features go from lemon-sucked to vinegar-soaked in two seconds flat. "It's not drugs?"

"Not drugs," I confirm.

Zara springs to her feet and collects us both in a hug. "You're doing IVF? You guys! That's amazing. I so hope it works."

"We do, too," Sebastian says. "It's early days. This is our first cycle, but they're hopeful it'll work in the first few times."

"Oh, darlings, that's wonderful news," Jemima gushes. "I think," she adds.

"It *is* wonderful," Sebastian says firmly. "We're optimistic."

"Super optimistic," I confirm.

Geraldine arches one of her thin, gray eyebrows. "What's wrong with letting it happen naturally like the rest of us? It worked for your parents, it worked for me."

"We tried that, but we have some challenges on that front," Sebastian replies evasively, and I love him all the more for it. He's not blaming it on me—even if we both know we can't get pregnant naturally thanks to my blocked tubes.

"Do you indeed?" Geraldine looks me up and down, and it's no guess as to who *she's* blaming. "Well, the important thing is that you'll be producing an heir. However it's done."

"How are you coping with it?" Jemima asks. "I heard it can take quite a toll on a woman's body. Weight gain, water retention, mood swings. My friend Susannah's daughter Trixie did it. She was a terrible fright for the longest time, but she did get a baby out of it." She makes a face. "Ugly little thing."

"Mum!" Zara says.

"Sorry, sorry. But that boy was not a pretty baby."

Zara glares at her mom. "Not the point, Mum."

"What I mean to say is, are you all right with it all, Emma?" Jemima asks.

I grin at her. It's true that I've put on a few pounds, and I have noticed my tummy is bloated, but it's all part and parcel of the process. "I'm super excited about it working."

She returns my grin full force. "Well, I am too, then."

There's a big part of me that just knows this is going to work, and that the very next conversation we have with the family on the topic will be my husband and I announcing that we're going to be parents.

And the thought makes me pop with happiness.

CHAPTER 21

*I*t's official: I've become a blimp.

Where once my clothes fit me perfectly, now I'm spilling out of things and loosening buttons and notches on my belts.

On one of my many, many trips to the clinic for scans and blood tests, the doctor assures me it's just water retention. But I feel like my belly has swollen to three times its usual size, and I can only wear Timothy pants a size larger than my usual or waistbands dig uncomfortably into me, leaving an ugly pink mark.

And the mood swings! *OMG.* I'm not a moody person. Really, I'm not. I'm level-headed and calm, and I'm usually pretty upbeat. But looking back over the last few weeks, I've got to admit that I've been like a traffic light rolling through different emotions, only not in any logical sequence. Oh no. One minute I'm all loved up with Sebastian, thinking life couldn't get better, and the next I'm in floods of tears because we both forgot to buy a new tube of toothpaste to replace the empty one in the bathroom.

I know I'm not being rational, and I'm even self-aware

enough to know that it's the hormones I'm injecting every day that are making me crazy. But it's cold comfort right now.

And it's all culminating in this: thirty-six hours ago, I had what they call the "trigger shot" to make the gazillion eggs I've made mature from my overstretched ovaries. The walls of my poor belly are as taut as a fully inflated helium balloon. I'm like an overstuffed hen, ready to lay a dozen or two eggs.

And now, here I am, lying on another gurney, about to be taken into surgery for my eggs to be harvested and then— hopefully—fertilized.

"What if I haven't made any eggs for them to collect, Seb? What if the scans were wrong and there are no eggs? What if this whole thing has been a big waste of time and I'm...I'm... barren? We'll never have a family. There'll be no nursery wallpaper to pick, no soccer to have to take the kids to, no school lunches to prepare. None of it, Seb."

It's fair to say my anxiety has begun to peak into something akin to Mt. Everest by now.

"You're going to be amazing," Sebastian says as he leans down and kisses me on the forehead. "And I know that soccer and school lunches are in our future."

My heart squeezes. "I hope you're right."

"Okay, Emma, we're ready for you," Dr. White says to me. "Sebastian, it's time for you to make your deposit, please."

"Ah, yes." He looks deeply uncomfortable.

The gurney begins to move, and I try out a confident smile. "See you after."

"You've got this," he says.

The doors swing closed behind me.

A nurse places her hand on my arm. "Now, Emma. I'm putting a cannula in your hand, through which we'll administer the medication to send you off into a nice, relaxing sleep. When you wake up, it'll all be done."

"Okay," I reply with an anxiety-denying smile.

It's obvious I'm convincing no one when she adds, "And don't be nervous, love. We've done this thousands of times. You're in good hands."

A short while and a bunch of drugs later, I'm staring up at a small spider on the ceiling tiles of the clinic, saying a prayer that not only did they find a bunch of good eggs, but that they're also going to be the beginning of the new little life Sebastian and I both crave.

"Brady." Sebastian smiles down at me. "It's all done."

"Hey," I grin back at him, feeling more relaxed than I have in weeks, possibly months. "These drugs are good. We should totally get some."

"That would confirm all of Granny's suspicions."

"But I feel so *good*. Like nothing can bother me. Not even Odette."

Did I really just say that?

He cocks an eyebrow. "I thought you were good about her?"

I give a wave of my hand. "Oh, I said I was. She's fine. Fine. Just not as fine as, say, other people."

He chortles. "I see."

Dr. White appears at the end of the bed. "Good news. We retrieved eighteen mature eggs from your ovaries, Emma."

I blink at her through my chilled-out fog. "You're gonna make eighteen babies for us, Dr. White? That's more than we probably want, right, honey?"

"It simply means at fertilization we have a good chance of embryo production," she explains. "There will be natural attrition. However with your superior sperm, Sebastian, we do stand a strong chance of healthy embryo formation."

I tease Sebastian with, "Superior sperm."

"What can I say? We Huntington-Rosses come from genetic strength."

"You do indeed," Dr. White says, and I think I detect a hint of admiration in her voice. "All going to plan, we'll have you back here for embryo transfer in three days' time. Until then, rest up."

"Will do, captain," I reply with a salute.

She offers me a perplexed look before she turns and leaves the room.

"Did I just salute her?"

Sebastian laughs. "You did indeed."

A few hours later, we're back at Martinston and Sebastian has delivered me a bowl of chicken noodle soup in bed, despite me insisting I'm not ill, just tender and bloated up like a puffer fish.

"Do you think you're going to be up to going to Henley in a few days' time?" he asks as I dip my bread in my soup and take a grateful bite.

"I'm sure I'll be doing just great by then. I won't be able to drink, of course, because all of this might have worked and I could be pregnant by then." I grin at him. "Did you hear what I just said? I could be *pregnant*."

He beams back at me. "That would be truly wonderful."

"I've been thinking about names. I know you'll probably want 'Sebastian' if it's a boy, but what about Cali for a girl?"

"We don't have to call a son Sebastian."

"But I thought it was a family name? Your dad is Sebastian, his dad was Sebastian. You're Sebastian. It's a long line."

"I rather like the name Oliver. Ollie for short. It has a certain ring to it, don't you think? Ollie Huntington-Ross."

My lips curve into a smile. "Ollie Huntington-Ross. I like it. Ollie and Cali, I can see it now. I'll get nametags made up. Ollie H-R. Callie H-R. I bet they'll be little scamps, too, running around Martinston, getting into all sorts of trouble."

He leans over and kisses me on the lips. "Just like their mum."

I let out a contented laugh. "Thank you for this. For all of it. I know we wouldn't have to go through this if it wasn't for my blocked tubes."

He shushes me with a fresh kiss. "I'd do it all again if I had to."

"Let's agree not to."

"Deal."

* * *

WE GET the exciting call that they'd made seven healthy embryos, and three days later I go into the clinic to have them transferred. With work commitments, Sebastian couldn't be there with me for the brief procedure, but he sent me some flowers afterwards to show me how much he cared. I left the clinic floating on a high, secretly positive I was already pregnant with our very first child.

And now, a few days later, we're at the Henley Rowing Regatta, surrounded by men in striped blazers and women in pretty summer dresses and elaborate hats. It's a whimsical English scene with crews of rowers in their various colors on the sparkling water of the River Thames.

"There are so many cute rowers here, I can't even," Kennedy says as she flops down next to me on the grassy bank overlooking the river. She adjusts her pale blue hat, which brings out the color of her pretty eyes as she squints out at the water.

"A target rich environment?" I question.

"I wish. They're all too busy rowing or talking about rowing. There's been zero flirting."

"It *is* a rowing regatta, babe."

"I know, but they've gotta take a break from it sometime, right? I have managed to have a few good chats with a couple of blazer guys, although one of them was drunk and kept calling me Felicia. What's that about?"

"Alcohol."

She eyes the plastic water bottle in my hand "You're on the water, I see. I so hope it works for you this time."

I beam at my friend. "Me too."

"Isn't it so nice to have some sun? It reminds me of San Diego. Like, I barely knew the sun reached England."

"You moved here in winter, that's the problem. Summers here are great."

She shoots me a sideways look. "Great?"

"Okay, not *great* great, but they're okay."

"You miss Texas, huh?"

"OMG, so much! But England is my home now, and it's where I plan on spending my life."

"And bringing up a family?" she fishes.

I can't help a smile from forming on my lips. "That too." I feel a surge of hope. They transferred the maximum number of embryos allowed in this country—which is way less than I would have had in my home state of Texas. You can tell me I'm being overly optimistic, but I have a sneaking suspicion I'm pregnant with at least one baby, if not twins.

"You can tell me if you're pregnant. I won't say anything to anyone." Her eyes drop to my dress and back up again. "Your boobs look huge."

My hand flies to my chest in a fit of self-consciousness. "They do?" I squeak even though I know they do. They strained against my dress when I tried it on this morning, so much that I had to go with one with a looser top that didn't match my hat nearly so well.

"Oh, yeah. *Melons.*" She eyes me up. "You've got a glow-y thing happening, too."

I press my lips together to stop my smile.

"You *are* pregnant!" she exclaims, and passersby look in our direction.

"Well done," says one as the other says, "Congratulations," before they walk on.

I offer them a weak smile before I say to Kennedy, "I'm gonna kill you now."

"Not until you tell me I'm right."

I exhale and say, "I might be pregnant."

She raises an eyebrow. "Might be?"

"The thing is, we did our first fertility cycle, and I had the embryos transferred a couple days ago. We're waiting to go in for a pregnancy test. I've been dying to tell you, but we agreed to keep it on the downlow because of all the pressure. Then Geraldine found one of my syringes, and she thought I was taking—"

"Wait. Syringes?"

"For the hormones. You have to inject them into your thigh or belly every day." I mime a stabbing gesture, and she looks aghast.

"I feel so bad for you."

"It's fine, especially if it gives us what we want. But I want to know whether I'm pregnant now. I'm so over waiting. This whole thing has taken weeks and weeks."

"The waiting has got to be the hardest part."

"Isn't that a song?"

"Yeah. Tom Petty. That could be your fertility theme song."

"Hello, girls," a female voice says, and I look up into Odette's pretty, smiling face. She's dressed in a pretty, floaty summer dress and hat combination, like most of the women here, but she somehow manages to look more spectacular than anyone else. "This looks like a nice spot." She remembers the man she's with, hooks her arm through his, and says, "Girls, this is Charlie."

"Oh, we know Charlie," I say as I rise to my feet and greet him with a warm hug.

"Wonderful to see you again, Emma," he says, and then his eyes land on Kennedy, who hasn't bothered to get up. "Kennedy," he says in a clipped tone, despite the corners of his lips twitching as he says her name.

"Charles," she replies coolly. There's no hint of anything twitching on *her* face.

I roll my eyes. What is it with these two?

"How do you all know one another?" Odette asks.

"I went to school with Seb, so I've known Emma for some time now," Charlie explains, "and I had the great honor of meeting Miss Bennet earlier in the year."

"It's *Ms.* Bennet, actually," Kennedy grinds out. "I won't have my status defined by my relationship to a man."

"Of course you won't," he replies in a distinctively patronizing way, and I lift my brows in surprise. Charlie is usually a total gentleman, and wasn't that a little rude? "Now, if you'll excuse me, I see an old friend over there in the marquee I must say hello to."

"Oh, Charles. Leaving so soon?" Kennedy asks with mock sadness.

"I'm afraid I must," he replies. "Coming, Odette?"

"I'll just have a chat with the girls and be right over," she replies.

"Ladies." He inclines his head and then turns and leaves.

"Goodness," Odette says as she watches him walk away. "I wonder what bee flew under his bonnet. We were having such a lovely time."

"I think the bee might be about five seven with long dark hair and a bit of an attitude." I shoot Kennedy a mock accusatory look.

Kennedy harrumphs.

Odette regards her through narrowed eyes. "How can you not love Charlie?"

"With surprising ease," she replies.

"Oh, you're silly. He's divine. I wouldn't mind getting to know him better myself."

"I think that's an awesome idea. I bet you'd be so right for each other," Kennedy says, and I shoot her a look that says *behave*.

"Where is that gorgeous husband of yours?" Odette asks me.

"He's somewhere in the marquee with Johnny and Phoebe. I needed some air, so I left them to it."

Her face creases in concern. "Are you quite all right, Emma? You do look a little pink and...*puffy*."

I may be carrying a few extra pounds right now, but puffy? Seriously?

She places her hand delicately over her heart. "Gosh, is that a terrible thing to say? Sorry."

"Sorry not sorry more like," Kennedy mumbles under her breath, and I'm inclined to agree with her.

"I'm perfectly fine, thank you," I reply with a bright and probably "puffy" smile. "Just taking in the atmosphere out here on the lawn."

"That's so good to hear. Well, lovely chatting. I'm going to go and find that delectable Charlie." She clasps my hands in hers. "Take good care of yourself, darling Emma. Promise me."

"I promise," I reply, feeling like a kid being offered motherly advice on her first day of school.

After she's gone, I plunk myself back down next to Kennedy.

"Puffy, huh? I don't care what you say about her, she's *so* nice," Kennedy says with a laugh.

"I know, right? Why did I ever like her? She's perfect, but not that nice."

"She's not perfect."

"Yeah, she is. She's gorgeous, bright, successful, and has two gorgeous kids she told me she got pregnant with almost right away. She makes it all look so effortless."

"But you might be pregnant this very second, and you've got something she'll never have: your very own Mr. Darcy."

"That's true." Excitement surges inside me. "I don't want to jinx it, but I think I actually am pregnant."

She gives me a hug. "I so hope you are, babe. You totally deserve this after all you've been through, and I know you're gonna make an amazing mom."

I beam at her, my heart full at the thought of becoming a mom at last. "I wouldn't admit this to just anyone, but I have a sneaking suspicion you're right."

CHAPTER 22

*W*ith Sebastian at work, I go to the clinic to have my blood test, full to the brim with hope and expectation, knowing, just *knowing* the fertility cycle worked and I'm pregnant. Finally. After all, not only do I have all the physical signs—a swollen belly, that pregnancy glow, those "melons" Kennedy pointed out—but the only thing stopping us from getting pregnant in the first place was my blocked tubes, and the fertility treatment has neatly bypassed those.

How could this *not* have worked?

They tell me it'll be a few hours before they get the results, so I try my best to concentrate on my work. I put in a call to Henrietta at Marie Maternity to see if they're any closer to making the decision to stock Timothy Maternity, only to learn that she's been out of the office for the second week running. I leave another message for her to call me, hoping she really is out of the office and not simply avoiding me. Then I talk with Alison at Body Sports about their latest order and remind them of our new maternity line, which she says a very polite no to once more.

When the clinic calls me later in the day, while I'm sitting at my desk working on Timothy shipment numbers, I'm not even nervous when I take the call. I'm totally calm and ready.

"Mrs. Huntington-Ross?" the voice at the other end of the line asks.

"This is she."

"I have your results. Is this a good time to talk?"

"Oh, yes. This is a great time to talk."

This is it. This is the moment.

I've already decided how I'm going to play it with Sebastian. Instead of simply calling him—because let's face it, this news is w*aaaa*y too big for some boring old phone call—I'm going to turn up at his office with two baby's bottles I'll get from the Boots the Chemist near the Tube stop and ask him which one he thinks is the best, and he'll look at me all confused, and I'll grin and tell him that we need to know which bottle to get because although I plan on breastfeeding, it'd be so nice for him to get to feed our baby too, and he'll look at me in wonder before his face breaks into a huge grin and he rushes over to me and lifts me up and tells me how amazing I am and—

"I'm sorry to say the results of your test show the cycle didn't work this time."

Her words bring me crashing back down to Earth with a sickening thud.

"What now?" I ask, sure I've heard her wrong.

"You test result shows the cycle wasn't successful this time I'm afraid."

"But…but that doesn't make any sense," I reply in confusion. "Could the results be wrong? A false negative or something?"

"It's a blood test, so it's very accurate. I'm sorry to disappoint you this round."

My mind races like it's trying to outrun a sabre tooth tiger bent on getting its dinner. "But...but I *feel* pregnant. I even look pregnant."

"That's a common side effect of the hormones. I'm sure your doctor told you all about it?"

"No. No, she didn't tell me about it at all," I snap.

She ignores my attitude with a well-practiced, "Why don't I make an appointment with your doctor to discuss next steps?"

"Next steps? I don't want next steps," I huff. "I *feel* pregnant. I want to do the test again."

"You're welcome to, but I'm sorry to say it will be the same result. I know it's hard to have your expectations dashed. Now, I see your specialist is Dr. White. How does the third sound to you? We've got a slot at ten in the morning."

Like a zombie, I make the appointment and hang up. I stare out the window at Martinston's gardens, my eyes unfocused as I process the unwelcome news.

I'm not pregnant.

I thought I was, but I was wrong.

All that effort, all that hope, all that expectation. Smashed with those few words, "the cycle wasn't successful this time."

I place my hands on my swollen belly, a belly I thought moments ago contained life and now I know is only swollen from the hormones I've been pumping into myself for the last few weeks. What only moments ago felt like the beginning of something new and wonderful, now feels like...nothingness.

A cold, gaping void, where once there was hope.

I'm not pregnant.

There's a knock on my door, and Zara's head appears around the corner. "I thought you might like a coffee," she begins and then stops in her tracks when she takes in the look on my face. "Oh, my gosh, Em. What's happened?"

I try to swallow down the boulder in my throat. It's not budging. "I, ah, I just had a call," I manage before the shock hits me and the ache in my chest grows too strong. Instinctively, I place my hand over my belly, and unable to hold it together for any longer, I crumple into tears.

"Oh, Em." She rushes over to me and wraps me up in a hug. "I'm so sorry."

"It didn't work. I thought it did, but I was wrong," I manage to say between sobs.

"That sucks *so* much. I know how much you and Seb want this. Poor you. Just let it all out."

I heave another sob before I sniff and blot my eyes with my fingertips. "Not meant to be, I guess."

"Have you told Seb?"

I shake my head. "I just barely found out. I should call him. I had this whole thing worked out. I was going to get a couple of baby's bottles and…oh, it doesn't matter. It's not happening." I slump my shoulders and scrunch my eyes shut.

Zara rubs my back. "Do you want me to get you a cup of tea? We English know that tea solves just about everything."

I let out a watery laugh. "Not even this terrible news can make me drink tea."

"I'll go get you a coffee then." She gives me another hug before she leaves. I pick up my phone, call Sebastian, and tell him, my throat burning from holding in the tears that once again threaten to spill over.

"I'm cancelling the rest of the afternoon and coming home."

"You don't have to do that. I've got Zara here, and I'll be okay. It was just the initial shock."

I'm putting on a brave face, and he knows it.

"I'll get there as soon as I can. And Brady? I'm sorry. We had thought—" he breaks off, and his own loss hits me. This isn't just about my body failing me. It's failed both of us.

He does as he says and rushes home to be with me in our cavernous bedroom, and I curl up in a tight ball with cramps in my belly and let the giant well of sadness out.

Sebastian lies at my side, spooning me, his warm body providing small comfort as I sob and sob.

I cry over a loss of something we never had.

I cry for a child I'll never know.

I cry, and I cry.

After giving me the time to grieve, Sebastian tells me it's not the end of the world. He tells me our chances of getting pregnant increase with each cycle, just the way the doctor said it would. That it's normal for the first cycle not to work.

He tells me he loves me and who knows, it might just work next time.

I turn to face him, my face damp and my nose blocked from my tears. "I'm so, so sorry."

"What are you apologizing for?"

"Not being able to get pregnant. It's all my fault. We both know that."

"Brady," he says, his soft voice eliciting a fresh wave of tears, "please don't say things like that."

"But it's the truth. You've got gold medal winning swimmers, and I've got stupid blocked tubes and my uterus can't even hold on to premade embryos."

His grip tightens around me. "We're a team. We're in this together. I don't see it in terms of anyone's fault. It's just what we have to deal with. That's all."

I sniff loudly, my tears finally drying up. "Do you really?"

"Of course I do. How could you think otherwise?"

"I don't know. It's all been a lot."

"I know it has." He leans over and kisses me tenderly on the lips. "I love you with all my heart. Nothing is going to change that."

"Not even if I can't give you the family you want?" I ask, my heart thudding.

"I fell in love with *you*. I married *you*. That's all that matters to me."

"But you want a family as much as I do."

"Don't you think it's a little early to assume that after one failed fertility cycle you can't have a child?"

"It's a good point," I concede.

"How about we take some time and think about other things for a while. We can try again when we're ready."

I give him a watery smile, my heart feeling lighter. "I want to try again. I can't believe I'm saying that, but I'd go through it all again if it meant we could get our baby."

"Only when you're ready, of course. Although we're a team, you're the one who's got to do all the heavy lifting."

"I know, right?" I reply with a laugh. "Your part in this whole thing is pretty miniscule."

"Do you think you're up to the family meal this Sunday? We have Sunday lunches every weekend. People will totally understand."

"No, it's fine. It'd only make it into some huge thing if I'm not there, and I don't need a huge thing right now." A thought occurs to me, and I squeeze my eyes shut. "We've got to tell people, don't we? Your family and Kennedy."

"I can deal with them all."

"No. I can tell my friends. Maybe you could tell your mom and granny? I can totally guess what Geraldine will say. 'She's clearly broken. Send her back to America,'" I say in my best Granny impersonation.

"She'll be very sad for us and hopeful it'll work for us next time," Sebastian says firmly.

"Sure," I reply, even though I know she'll use this against me. What's the point of a granddaughter-in-law you can barely tolerate if she can't even produce the next heir? And despite feeling loved by my husband, despite knowing rationally that our chances of getting pregnant with only one IVF cycle are low, part of me thinks exactly the same.

CHAPTER 23

e meet with Dr. White, and she tells us that the likelihood of a "live birth," as she puts it in her straight up, clinical way is over fifty percent for a couple of our age, even taking into account my dysfunctional tubes. We leave the appointment feeling more optimistic than before, and within a few weeks, I start up a new program. It's back to injections and hormones, hot flashes, water retention, and weight gain.

Don't let anyone tell you that fertility treatment isn't super fun.

This time, I try to temper my expectations. I try to stop the hope. Instead, I throw myself into other things so that I'm not focusing too much on getting pregnant. I meet with customers, I discuss new designs with Penny, I meet Phoebe and Kennedy for movies and coffees and shopping.

But it's impossible not to think about it all the time, not when you wonder if you could be pregnant. So you avoid certain foods, you don't drink alcohol, you try not to overheat, you do everything you're meant to do if you're pregnant. And at the same time, you're trying not to think about it so that you don't become obsessed. So that if the cycle fails, you don't feel like your world has disintegrated around you.

It's a big ask, and I fail at it spectacularly.

This time, when I get the call from the clinic to tell me if I'm pregnant, I've made sure I'm with Sebastian.

"I'm sorry, Mrs. Huntington-Ross. Your cycle was not successful this time."

"Okay. Thanks," I reply before I press *end*. There's no arguing this time. I feel pregnant, just like I did with the first cycle, but now I know that's simply a cruel trick the treatment plays on you to lull you into thinking it worked. It means nothing.

I lift my eyes to Sebastian's and shake my head. "No banana. Or baby, for that matter."

"Come here." He reaches for me, and I give him a short, perfunctory hug before I pull away. "You're upset."

"Of course I'm upset," I reply brusquely, my spine ramrod straight. I lift my chin and push out a breath. "But I'll be fine. It's not like the first cycle. I had low expectations this time."

"Did you?"

"Of course I did. I've got stage two endometriosis and blocked tubes, remember? I'm all messed up inside." I do a circling motion in front of my belly.

"You're not messed up. We've got some challenges, that's all."

"Correction: *I've* got some challenges." I raise my hands in the *stop* sign. "But before you go giving a speech about how we're a team and we're in this together, I get all that. I just need to feel bit sorry for myself for a while. Okay?"

He collects me in another hug, only this time he doesn't let go when my body stiffens. "I get it. Truly I do."

The warmth of his body pressed against mine and the solidity of his strong arms wrapped around me, holding me close, begin to work their magic. I melt into his embrace as a wave of sadness washes over me like waves over hard, jagged rocks. Just like the first failed cycle, wracked with the painful loss, I sob into his shoulder.

I look up into his eyes and see his lightly veiled sadness. "I want to give you a child, Seb. I want to have a family so bad."

"I know you do. This is so hard. I hate seeing you like this."

He holds me, and we stay together, both of us feeling the sadness envelop us, allowing it to take hold before we get ourselves back up on our feet, dust ourselves off, and get on with living. We agree to try again. We agree that the third time may just be the charm.

But my confidence is shot. Although I know my determination will return—because that's how I'm built—there's a part of me that's stopped believing it will ever happen for us.

And the thought is utterly terrifying.

CHAPTER 24

*I*s it just me, or is Odette suddenly everywhere in my life? Don't get me wrong, other than things like offering me her kids and telling me I'm "puffy" (puffy!), I do like her—well, kinda like her, anyway. But she's everywhere. *Everywhere.* And what's more, she's always perfectly put together, with perfect hair and perfect clothes and perfectly perfect *perfectness.*

Not that I feel inadequate in any way, of course. Just because I've put on a few pounds, my breasts feel stuffed into my bra, and the waistband of the new dress I bought specifically for today's Martinston garden party only a few weeks ago, is digging painfully into my flesh, doesn't make me feel any less of a woman next to her slim, totally put together waif-ness.

Really, it doesn't.

"—and that's the thing with these sorts of companies," Odette is saying to our group of me, Sebastian, and a couple of their colleagues, two guys called James and Ravi, who hang on her every word. "You simply can't try to get away with fudging your financial results. There are too many big brains in the City, and the truth will always out itself."

"Bravo, Odette," James simpers as he applauds her like he's an audience at a show. "You do have a way of putting things."

"Oh, you do," Ravi agrees eagerly. "And you know your stuff. I loved what you had to say about Zentridon's drug trial last week on Bloomberg. It was so fascinating."

Not to be outdone, James places his hand lightly on her arm. "That guy on CNBC's got nothing on you," he says, referring to an analyst on Bloomberg's rival TV station.

"Oh, stop, you two. You're making me blush," Odette replies—without blushing.

I have to work hard not to roll my eyes. She's totally lapping the attention up. But I can't blame her. I would too if I were single and being adored by two cute guys.

"There you all are," Henrietta says as she arrives at our group, and I beam at her.

I was nothing short of ecstatic when Henrietta accepted my invitation to the garden party today. Since that time we met, she's been harder to catch than a Vaseline-dipped eel, but she's here now, and I'm determined to pull her away for a conversation. Who knows? She may have some good news for me. With all our failed fertility adventures, my life has been bereft of good news for way too long. I *need* this.

"Sebastian, this place is absolutely glorious. You must be so proud," Henrietta says.

"Thank you. It's a lot of work, but it's worth it. We were just discussing Odette's career," he says with a wry smile.

"It must be so exhausting to be as successful as you are at absolutely everything you touch," Henrietta adds as she offers her friend a wink.

"She's right," James the sycophant agrees.

Odette lets out a light laugh. "It is quite exhausting, I tell you. Might I also point out that yes, my career is very important to me and I treat it with the utmost seriousness, but I'm a mother first and foremost. That's what's most important to me: bringing up the next generation."

I shift uncomfortably in my shoes.

"So admirable," Ravi gushes.

"And such a shame you and your ex are no longer married," James adds, obviously gleeful there's no husband barrier between him and the object of his desire.

Odette lowers her eyes prettily. "It was a very difficult time, but I'm faring a lot better on that front with wonderful friends like you all." She glows at us, and I'm sure James and Ravi's hearts flutter in their chests.

One of her children, Joaquin, races past us, followed quickly by her daughter, who slams into Sebastian's legs.

"Steady there, Antonella," Sebastian says as he gets a hold of her before she topples over.

"Jo stole my bracelet and he said he was going to throw it in the pond and I need to stop him," she explains in a rush. "It's a very, very important bracelet. Isn't it, Mummy?"

"Oh, darling. I'm not sure our host needs to be bothered with such things," Odette says.

"It's fine." Sebastian squats down to her level. "Well, first of all the pond is a decent walk away, and it's also cordoned off for safety today, so unless he's got a very good throwing arm, he probably won't manage to get it in the water."

"He probably will throw it. He's such a meanie," she replies with a pout.

"In that case, I think the most important thing is to get that bracelet back safe and sound. Do you need any help?" Sebastian's face is so serious, it makes me smile.

"I do need help. Really, really badly," she replies earnestly.

"Well, I'm the man for the job."

As I watch Sebastian with her, my all too familiar sense of

abject failure strikes me hard in the chest. Sebastian would make a wonderful father. He'd be kind and loving but firm as well, the best combination in a parent.

Will I ever be able to give him the chance?

"How about we go down to the pond and find Joaquin?" Sebastian suggests.

"Okay," Antonella replies. "Do you want to come, too, Mummy?"

"Oh, you don't have to do that, Sebastian. This is your party. Surely you need to attend to your guests rather than chase after a child's plastic bracelet," Odette coos.

"But Mummy! It's my favorite," Antonella whines.

"All right," she concedes. "We can look for your brother."

"And my bracelet."

"And your bracelet."

Sebastian straightens up. "It would be my pleasure to help, Odette." Looking down at Antonella, he asks, "Shall we go?"

"Can I come with you, too?" I ask her.

"Yes," she replies with a single nod of her head. She eyes my feet. "Although you might need to take off your shoes. Mummy says she can't run in high heels. You don't want to break your ankle."

I lean down to unbuckle my heeled sandals and slip my feet out of them. "Better?"

Another serious head nod. "Much."

"I'll walk with you, Emma. I could do with stretching my legs," Henrietta offers.

"You'll have to take your shoes off, too," Antonella instructs her.

"But this is the first time I've been dressed up in months," she replies, clearly horrified at going barefoot. "And anyway, I'm only walking down with Emma to chat about boring grown up things."

"Mummy says," Antonella reminds her sternly.

"Running in heels isn't great," Odette says to Henrietta.

"Who said I'm going to run?" she replies. "Oh, all right then." She slips off her red-soled heels and holds them in her hands. "Better?"

"Much."

Antonella reaches up and takes Seb's hand in hers, and I swear my ovaries swoon at the sight of them before my heart sinks to my toes.

He'd be such a great dad.

I can't give him a child.

"Odette, I need you to tell me more about that drug trial as I get you a drink. I must pick your brain on something." James offers her his arm.

Odette glances quickly at her daughter and then back to James. "Why, thank you. I'd love a glass of champagne. Could you bring it down to me?"

"I thought we could go to the bar. Sebastian has everything in hand with the whole *Braceletgate*."

"Can I come with?" Ravi asks.

"Sorry, mate," James replies, sounding anything but sorry. "Maybe another time."

"But they're my children. I'm sure you understand," she coos, and James begrudgingly acquiesces.

"You can come with us, Ravi," Sebastian offers.

"Actually, I need to go to the loo," he says and takes off before anyone says another word.

"We have to go now!" Antonella insists, refocusing our attention.

"Of course. We have a bracelet to save," Sebastian says gravely.

We make our way through the groups of people, past the string quartet, and down through the ornamental gardens in the direction of the pond. As the manicured gardens give way to the expansive lawn, we locate Joaquin. He's forgotten his threat to throw his sister's bracelet in the pond and is instead in the process of climbing one of the large weeping willows that line the lawn.

"Where's my bracelet?" Antonella demands, her little body rigid with anger. "You'd better give it back to me or you'll be in the biggest trouble ever."

"I dunno. I dropped it somewhere," Joaquin replies from a branch.

"You *dropped* it?" Antonella's tone is so grown up I share a small smile with Sebastian.

"It's a stupid bracelet anyway."

Antonella crosses her arms, her bottom lip trembling. "No it's not."

"Jo, be kind," Odette scolds. "Do you have any idea where you might have dropped it?"

"On the grass," is his unhelpful reply. There are acres of grass at Martinston. We're facing a major needle and haystack situation here.

Antonella stamps her foot, tears welling in her eyes. "Jo!"

Odette slips her arm around her shoulders to comfort her. "It's okay, sweetie. We'll find it. Won't we, Seb?"

"We will," he confirms.

"Actually, you two, I wanted to steal Emma away for a chat," Henrietta says. "Can we leave you to it?"

I glance at Sebastian, hoping I know what the chat will be about.

"Steal her away. We'll find this bracelet together, won't we, Antonella?" Sebastian says.

"We'd better, or Jo will be in big trouble. Won't he, Mummy?"

"We'll find it, sweetie," Odette soothes.

"Be right back," I say as Henrietta and I walk along a row of trees.

We come to a stop, and she replaces her shoes on her feet. "I'm sorry. I paid a huge amount of money for this outfit, and I refuse to go a step further without my shoes."

"Are they Christian Louboutins?"

"They're my favorite. I don't get to wear them nearly as often as I'd like, what with the fact I work from home these days. You see, I became a mum just recently, which has totally changed my life."

I offer her a warm smile, that familiar hollow feeling deepening inside. "I didn't know that. Congratulations."

"Oh, it's all very new, actually. That's why I haven't been back in touch for a while."

I knit my brows together. "So you were pregnant when we met?" I cast my mind back to the slim, petite woman I met over coffee those months ago. There was definitely no sign of a baby bump.

"Oh, I wasn't pregnant."

"But then…how?"

"We adopted a child, actually. Aged two. A little girl we've called Angela, because she's like a gift from the heavens to us, our own little angel." Her face lights up as she talks about her.

"Wow. That's amazing!" That explains her radio silence. "Two years old, huh? That must have been a huge step."

"Oh, it was. Believe me. A baptism by fire. We became parents for the first time to a toddler in a hotel room in Bangkok. And before you ask, yes, it was as challenging as it sounds." Her smile stretches across her bright face. "But worth every second."

"How long ago did you adopt her?"

"It's nearly three months. It's been the hardest and the most incredible thing we've ever done. Being a parent after all this time is…well, it's nothing short of miraculous." She gets a faraway look in her eyes before she says, "But enough about me."

"No, please. I'm super interested."

"You are? Well, in that case, let me show you a picture." She takes her phone from her purse, taps on the screen and turns it to me. "This is us at a playground in Bangkok. She loves to ride on my husband's shoulders. You can see the huge grin on her face."

"Henrietta, she is gorgeous." I take in the image of a young child with the most beautiful milky coffee skin and huge dark eyes, a look of utter delight on her beautiful face as she sits astride her happy dad's shoulders. It's a picture of unadulterated joy. My longing for my own child thumps me in the chest with such strength, I'm forced to suck in air.

"Isn't she gorgeous? I can say that without boasting because I had nothing to do with her genetics." She pulls up another photo. "This is her in the back garden last weekend. She loves dirt. Just look at that face."

A pair of big, sparkling eyes in a face covered in grime peers out at the camera. "She sure does."

"I'd just bought that dress for her, too. It's pink, can you believe?"

"No. I can't," I say with an attempt at a light laugh. Because you're meant to be able to laugh at a photo of a much-loved kid covered in dirt without feeling the overwhelming urge to burst into tears or thump your chest and scream *When will it be my turn!*

So I swallow down the hurt.

I swallow down the emptiness.

I swallow down the horrible feelings of inadequacy that threaten to rise up and engulf me, like a whale swallowing a minnow.

I paste on a bright smile, look my future Timothy stockist

in the eye, and say, "She is super adorable. You must be so happy."

She gets that glowing, contented look in her eye. "Oh, yes. It was a long road for us, but we're finally parents."

"How long did it take?"

"Well, the adoption side of things took about two years, but we'd tried all sorts of things before then, so it was ten years all up."

My eyes widen in shock. "Ten years? That's so long!"

"I know, right? Going through all that fertility treatment was hell on a stick, but the way we see it, without it we wouldn't have ended up with our darling Angela."

Her words "hell" and "misery" resonate far too readily with me.

Confused, I ask, "But I thought you adopted her."

"What I mean is if we hadn't gone through all that misery, we wouldn't have got to adopt our little girl. There are children in need of loving homes all over the world, and although it was a terrible thing to have to go through, we realized there are many ways to make a family. The only thing you've got to have is love." She gets misty eyed before she gives me a smile. "We've got our little family now, and I could not be happier. Other than the early morning wakeups, that is, especially when she climbs into bed with us and elbows me in the ribs," she says.

"Why didn't you bring her today?"

"We're taking it slowly. The adoption agency advised us to focus on creating our own strong family bond first before we open her world up. This," she gestures at the people around us, "would be overstimulating for her and quite possibly overwhelming. She's only two, and she's had a lot of change in her short life."

"I can imagine." I want to ask her about what changes her little girl has seen, and I want to ask her about her fertility treatment and all of it, but I know it's not my business. It's her story and her daughter's story. Not mine. She'll share it if she wants.

"Now, enough about Angela, although I could talk about her all day if you'd let me. What I wanted to tell you is that I have some exciting news. Marie Maternal would love to stock your new line in our London stores, with a view to potentially rolling it out across the rest of England, depending on how well it sells."

The heaviness I carry around each day begins to lift, and I find myself grinning from ear to ear. "Seriously? That's amazing, thank you."

"Thank *you* for bringing it to me. We think it might be just the line we're looking for right now. It's current, it's fresh, it appeals to the young mum market, but at the same time offers comfort and support where you need it most."

I beam at her. "You sound like you've already written a sales pitch."

"Seriously, between you and me, I think you're onto something here, and I'm sorry I've been dragging the chain on it."

I wave her comment away. "You had a great excuse."

Her face glows when she replies, "I did, didn't I? Let's set up a time to talk on Monday, shall we? Get this thing rolling."

"That sounds amazing. Thank you."

"Now, perhaps we should actually help look for that bracelet?" she suggests.

I let out a laugh, considerably lighter than I was a few moments ago. This is the news I was hoping for. This is what I *need* right now. "Meeting Monday sounds just perfect."

CHAPTER 25

*H*appiness radiating through me, I turn back to see Sebastian helping Joaquin out of the tree. He tucks him under his arm like a natural dad and carries him over to Odette and Antonella. He places him down on the grass, and the boy gives Sebastian a quick hug before he runs over to Odette. She crouches down and scoops him up in his arms.

The kids chase one another around them as they talk and laugh, and the scene hits me hard, right in the chest. *They look like a family.* This young mom with her two beautiful children and their handsome dad.

My throat constricts.

I should be her.

That should be *us*.

I stand and gape until the idyllic family scene becomes too much for me. With a heavy heart, I press my lips together and push out a breath. I need to *not* be watching this right now.

I tell Henrietta I've got to check on something and make my way up the small rise toward the house. I reach the formal gardens, when I spy Jilly Fotherington—my so-called "friend" who tried to steal Sebastian from me with the help of Geraldine back when we were engaged—and quickly change course. With my emotions swirling, I'm not up to dealing with Jilly right now, even if she's apologized at least ten times for what she did to me.

Hastily, I turn away and find myself coming face-to-face with the last person I want to see. Geraldine. My heart sinks into the grass beneath my feet.

I paste on a smile, trying to push my feelings down out of sight. "Granny. Are you having a nice time?" I ask as brightly as I can manage.

"Of course I am," she replies as though I'm an idiot for asking such an obvious question. "Where are you off to?"

"Oh, I'm just gonna go get some fresh air."

"Dear girl, we're outside. We are literally *surrounded* by fresh air."

Right.

"I meant I was gonna go take a moment. There are so many people here. Sometimes you just need a bit of time out, you know?"

She quirks one of her spindly eyebrows at me, her features pulled into a sneer that tells me exactly what she thinks of me.

"Okay," I say awkwardly, desperate to get away from this woman. In my fragile state, I could burst into tears at any moment, and Geraldine isn't exactly the warm, *give a girl a hug* type. More of a *kick a girl when she's down and then stomp all over her for good measure* type, really.

I turn to leave when she says, "Sebastian is so good with children, isn't he?"

I squeeze my eyes shut as I clench my fists at my side. She's seen him with Odette and her kids. I turn back to face her, lift my chin, and reply, "He is."

"I was watching him with that divine Odette's children before. He does need to be a father, don't you think?"

My already tight throat heats up. I dig my nails into the palms of my hands. "For sure."

"It is a crying shame you haven't been able to give him a family yet, Emma. Such a crying shame. A man like my grandson needs to be a father. It's his destiny."

I grind out my reply through gritted teeth. "You know we're working on it."

"Oh yes. That's right. *The needles*."

My shoulders tighten as I struggle to contain my crushing sense of inadequacy. "I'm gonna go get that alone time right now if it's all the same to you. Enjoy the rest of your day." Once again, I turn away, and once again she gets in another dig.

"They do look quite the family, don't they? And just imagine how wonderful it would be to join our two houses together."

I take the bait. I know I shouldn't, but I do.

I know exactly what she means. She means my husband marrying Odette, the Huntington-Rosses and the Jocastons, entwined in the family tree. "Sorry to disappoint you, Granny, but Sebastian and I are solid. He won't be joining anything together with Odette, let alone his 'house.'" I use air quotes, my sweet smile belying the rising of emotions inside. But dang it! I refuse to let her superiority and sheer nastiness get the better of me. I've been there, and I'm not going back. "Now, if you'll excuse me, I'm going to go to the pond and take some air."

With a ramrod straight back, I pivot on my heel and do my best to walk steadily away. I know she'll be watching, looking down her aristocratic, judgmental nose at me and finding me wanting. It should be water off a duck's back for me by now.

But this time, her sharp, targeted arrow gets through those oily feathers, and hits me in the gut, right where she was aiming.

I dart down the rise and find myself on the stretch of grass that leads to the pond. The place is empty but for a group of birds waddling happily around the fencing on their way into the pond.

I find a spot beside one of the grand old trees and plunk myself heavily down. My heart aches, and the tears I fought and defeated rise up and spill down my cheeks.

They looked like a perfect family. My husband with another woman and her children. They looked happy and full of laughter, playing with the kids, basking in their joy.

We've been trying to have our own family for so long now. We've tried, and we've failed. No matter what I do, I can't seem to get pregnant. And it *is* me. It's all my fault.

And then there's Odette, who had her children so effortlessly. She told me herself. Jealousy twists inside. I want what she's got. I want it with all my heart.

I know what people will think about us before too long. They'll pity us. They'll whisper that they've heard a rumor that it's my fault, that I'm the broken one who can't give Sebastian a child, his family's *heir*. That if only he'd married someone else, he'd have a family by now. They'd be the Little Darcys. They'd make a reality TV show about them, all these kids and their dashing dad and perfect mom.

Did you hear poor Sebastian and Emma can't have children?

It just goes to show you can't have a handsome husband, a gorgeous house, and children. No one can have it all.

I wonder whose fault it was.

Do you think he'll leave her for a fertile woman?

I wipe my tears angrily away.

I slump further down against the tree, the bark poking into my skin. I'm so tired of all of this. I've had enough.

We've tried and we've tried and still nothing. I don't want to want something I can't have. Not like this. Not with this intensity that consumes me every day of my life. No matter how brave a face I put on to the world, I feel the pain every single day.

I'm so sick of seeing other people's kids, of watching the love between other women and their children, of not having what I so desperately want in my life. I see babies in their mother's arms, and instead of thinking how wonderful they are, how chubby their cheeks are, or how big their eyes look, I feel sadness. Loss.

Failure.

Because when it comes to having a family, that's what I am. A big, fat, undeniable failure. And I know one thing that's becoming clear, one thing that's too painful to even think, let alone say. But I know deep down inside it's the truth.

If I can't have a child, if I can't fulfil my purpose as a woman, I'm broken.

I'm not enough.

A duck quack pulls me from my thoughts, and I watch between the metal rungs of the makeshift fence as it bobs on the top of the water. It's a beautiful lone male mallard, with its blue-green head and its white collar, majestic in a sea of gray blue.

I hear a splash and look up, startled. It sounded like a log, hitting the water.

"Uh," comes a sound with more splashing, this time becoming frenzied.

I leap to my feet. Something—or someone—is in trouble.

I rush around the edge of the pond, searching for where the splashing is coming from. It's then that I see it: a dark distinctively human head, rising above the waterline and then disappearing below it as arms thrash the water.

I don't hesitate. I yank the heavy metal fence open, race to the edge of the pond, and dive in, my heart hammering in my chest. I swim as fast as I'm able over to where I saw the dark head, which has now disappeared without trace below the surface of the water. I dive frantically under, fear rising inside like loud, jangling bells. The water is foggy with dirt impairing my vision, and I feel around desperately, searching, searching.

I come up and gulp in air before I dive back down again. This time, my hands land on something warm and soft, and I feel fabric beneath my fingers. I wrap my hands around small arms and realize with a sickening thud to my chest that I'm holding a child.

With strength I didn't know I was capable of, I haul the child up out of the water and holding the child with one arm, I swim to the shore, the child's motionless body weighing heavily.

We reach the shore, and I lay the child down. It's a girl.

Oh, please, God, no.

It's Antonella.

I try to settle my nerves as I run through how to deploy the first aid training I got when I worked at summer camp all those years ago. I look around feverishly for someone —*anyone*—to help. I call out a terrified, "Help! Help!" at the top of my lungs, but no one responds.

Either I do this, or this kid will die.

There's absolutely no choice.

I push her hair back from her face and check there's nothing in her mouth as I remembered you've got to do first. I pinch her nose shut, place my mouth over hers, and blow several breaths before I clasp my hands together and press on her chest. Immediately, she sputters water out of her mouth and heaves and coughs and makes scary choking sounds. I turn her on her side to help her expel the water, and she coughs and cries. With a thudding heart, I do my best to tell her everything's okay now, that she's safe, that I'm here.

And then suddenly people are around us, and Antonella is scooped up into her mother's arms as she sobs and calls her name. I lean back on my haunches, dizzy, trying to make sense of the last few moments.

I saved a life.

I saved Antonella.

It all feels completely surreal, like it happened to someone else. Only it was me and it was her and now we're on the pond's edge, soaking wet. But alive.

"Brady, are you okay?" Sebastian says urgently, pulling me out of my haze.

I peer at him. He's crouching down at my side, his face creased in concern. "Talk to me, Brady. Please. Are you okay?"

"Antonella. She's all right?" I ask.

His face breaks into a relieved smile. "She's fine. She's fine. You saved her. We saw the whole thing."

"You did?" I ask, confused. "But...but no one was here. I called, and no one came."

"Your call alerted us to your location, and we sprinted here, knowing Antonella was missing."

"Oh."

"We'd been searching for her. That bracelet! Yes, she must have come here to look for it after her brother told her he was going to throw it in the pond. Somehow, she got through the fence. Oh, Emma, thank goodness you were here."

"Yes," is all I can manage as I nod my head.

"Do you think you can stand?"

"Of course I can," I reply and push myself up onto my feet, only to stumble and fall into his arms. "Or maybe not. I might just sit here for a bit."

I begin to shake—not because it's cold. It's a warm

summer's day—because of what nearly just happened and the shock and the exertion and the terrible, terrible fear that now slams into me like a Texas Longhorn.

Sebastian removes his blazer and places it over my shoulders then wraps his arms around me. "Brady, you're amazing. You saved her life."

"Emma!" Odette rushes over to me, Antonella still lying in her arms. "Thank you, thank you. I owe you everything for this. Everything. If you hadn't been here—" She chokes up, tears spilling down her cheeks. "Thank you."

"I did what anyone would have done."

She hugs her daughter closer. "Thank you," she repeats.

"Let's get these two checked," Sebastian says. "James, did you call an ambulance?"

I blink at James and Ravi and a host of people who have now gathered around us.

"I did. They're on their way," he replies.

"Good."

"I don't need an ambulance," I say. "Get them to take Antonella, okay? She's the one that needs the help. Not me."

"Let them check you out," Sebastian insists.

The rest happens in a dream. The ambulance. The check-up. The police. The sudden end to the garden party. I answer all the questions fired at me with Sebastian by my side. Odette thanks me again before she and Antonella are whisked away.

And then, hours later when we're alone in our room sitting on the sofa in front of the open window, gazing out at the stars, Sebastian asks, "Why were you down at the pond? I thought you were with Henrietta, and then suddenly you weren't. She said you left."

I skim my fingertips along my jawline as I work out how to respond. I'm hardly going to tell him the full truth, that I left because I found it too painful to see him playing with

Odette's kids. That I felt like an abject failure in comparison with her. It feels too…too much.

When I don't reply, he says, "Brady?"

"Henrietta told me Marie Maternity is stocking our new line," I tell him.

"That's amazing news!" He leans in and kisses me. "Why didn't you tell me?"

I lift a shoulder. "Too busy saving children?"

He lets out a gentle laugh. "My wife, the hero. I'm very proud of you, you know."

"Thanks, but you don't need to be. You'd have done the same, and people would have all swooned over Mr. Darcy's pond scene."

"Your pond scene was three hundred percent more impressive than anything Mr. Darcy did."

"How dare you," I mock. "Women the world over will crucify you for saying anything against their beloved Mr. Darcy."

"Let them," he says. He cups my face in his hands and brushes my lips with his. "Let them say what they want. I know the truth."

"Oh yeah? What's that then?"

"That you are one incredibly brave, smart, and sexy woman, and I'm lucky to have you." He pulls me onto his lap, and I let out a squeal of pleasure. "Now if you don't mind, I'd like to ravish my wife. She saved a life today, don't you know?" He begins to pepper my neck with kisses, and my body thrums.

"I've heard she's pretty amazing."

"Oh, she so is."

A while later, I'm cuddled up in the nook of his arm when he asks me again why I was by the pond earlier in the afternoon.

"I went there to think about…stuff."

I've never claimed to be smooth.

"Did someone say something to you? It was Granny, wasn't it? She raised the whole needles thing again, right?"

I let out a heavy sigh. "It wasn't the needles."

Do I want to open up and talk to Sebastian about how I feel? We've agreed to always been honest with one another, to share the truth, no matter how ugly it is. But this feels... different somehow, and I know it's because of me. Sebastian has been so supportive, right throughout this difficult ride. Sure, we've had moments when it's felt like he's pulled away from me, when it's been too much for him. The guy's not perfect, any more than I'm perfect. But he's a good man. He's got my back. He loves me.

But sharing these feelings with him right now? Well, I'm not sure I can. Not when I feel the weight of my failure, of disappointing my husband every day of my life. Because that's how this feels. Like I'm disappointing him, every time that test result comes back negative.

Instead, I change the subject. "Did you know Henrietta and her husband adopted a little girl a few months ago?" I ask him. "She's two years old and came from Thailand. She's super cute."

"I had heard about that." He pauses before he says, "Is that something that appeals to you? Adopting a child?"

I blink at him for a moment as I flip the idea over in my head. "I'd never even thought about it."

He looks down. "I have. Quite a bit, actually."

I get a heavy feeling in my chest. "You have?" I ask, my throat tight. "But we've never discussed it. We're doing all this treatment, trying to have a child ourselves."

He sits up straighter in his seat. "What if we tried another route? This has been hard for us, especially for you. Maybe adopting could be the answer. I've been thinking about it a lot lately."

My mouth goes dry, and my heart clangs against my ribs in a burst of anxiety. Does he mean he wants us to abandon our fertility treatment? To walk away from all we've been working towards? To simply give up? "But Seb, we're starting a new cycle soon. We're *trying*," I protest.

"I know we are, and I hope with all my heart that it works this time. It's just an idea to keep in our back pockets, that's all."

I struggle to stop the quiver in my voice as I say, "Sure. Back pocket sounds great."

He cocks his head, his gaze trained on me as he takes my hands in his. "I'm not saying anything negative here, Brady. I need you to hear that. I just want to tell you that it's something I've been thinking about. Odette said that she—"

"Odette?" My eyes widen in shock. "You've been talking to Odette about us adopting a child?"

"I talk to her about a lot of things. She's a decent person with a level head on her shoulders," he replies evenly. "She told me about Henrietta's child and also mentioned she has a friend who adopted several children from Eastern Europe."

The muscles in my face tighten. "Why? Why did she tell you about this friend of hers? Were you confiding in her about our problems?" As I say the last word, my voice cracks with a deep sense of betrayal. If he's talking to her about adoption, what else is he talking to her about?

My old friend jealousy turns up and tips her hat.

"I know you and she don't always see eye to eye, but she's a good person. She listens."

I suck in air as I pull my hands away from him as though they're on fire. "You *are* talking to her about us. What have you said to her? That I'm broken inside and can't give you a child?"

"No!"

"And what's this about not seeing eye to eye with her? She

can be horrible, Seb, and it's got nothing to do with disagreeing with me about anything."

"Brady, please. Don't be like this."

"Like what? Upset? Angry?"

Jealous?

I get up from the sofa and begin to pace the room, my breath coming in ragged bursts.

"What we're going through is hard on both of us. Yes, you're the one who suffers the most. It's your body on the line, but it affects me as well. Odette has let me talk about it. She's been there for me in a way my male friends haven't."

"She's *been there* for you? Are you freaking kidding me right now?"

"I needed to talk to someone about all this. I'm so sorry this bothers you. That was never my intention."

"So you chose the woman half your office is in love with." I glare at him, my arms crossed, my anger bubbling like a potion in a witch's cauldron, ready to pour over the sides and swamp the room.

"Brady, please. Don't be like this."

"Like what? I think I'm allowed to be upset when I find out that my husband has been confiding in another woman about how terrible it is that his wife can't give him a child." I pepper my words like a machine gun. *Rat a-tat tat.* I hit my target.

Sebastian recoils in his seat, his jaw tight. "You think I'd say something like that?"

"Why not?" I throw my hands in the air. "It's the truth, isn't it? You're Mr. Perfect with your perfect swimmers. You'd have no problem impregnating half the women of the English countryside if you wanted to. But not me. Oh, no. Not poor little Emma Brady. She couldn't get pregnant if she tried, and my God, has she tried."

My breath comes in bursts as I stare back at him, hot, thick tears threatening my eyes.

I stare at him, challenging him to reply, challenging him to deny what we both know beyond a whisper of a doubt.

That I'm the broken one.

That I'm the failure.

He reaches out and envelops me in his strong arms. I remain still, my body rigid as he holds me close. "Please don't ever say things like that. I love you. We're in this thing together."

"But we're not, are we? If you were married to someone else—"

"No. Don't. I'm married to you, and that's not going to change."

I pull back and look into his eyes. "If you were married to someone else, you would probably be a dad by now." My lip begins to tremble, and the hot, fat tears that had been threatening to spill over make tracks down my cheeks. "Be honest with yourself. It bothers you so much, you're talking to another woman about it."

He pushes out a breath, the sadness in his eyes like a stab to my chest. "I'm sorry," he says simply.

I lift my chin and wipe the tears from my cheeks. With my lip trembling, I give up the fight. I give up being threatened by Odette. I give up on it all.

"So am I," I whisper, my heart cracked in two.

CHAPTER 26

*M*rs. Darcy: Real Life Heroine! That's the headline that screams at me as a notification pops up on my phone. I'm rushing to meet Kennedy after my meeting with Marie Maternity in London's West End, and I stop in my tracks on the sidewalk. A man swears at me as he narrowly misses walking into me.

I quickly scan the article.

Forget Jane Austen. Forget your Empire line dresses with heaving bosoms and men in tight breeches. You can even forget your Mr. Darcy clone, Sebastian Huntington-Ross (well, not entirely). It's Mrs. Darcy to the rescue, and this writer is more than a little impressed.

What the…?

I scroll down and peer at the accompanying photo. It's blurred, but it clearly shows me dripping wet with my pretty summer dress clinging to my body. Sebastian's arm is held protectively around my shoulders, and Odette is standing beside an ambulance, cradling Antonella in her arms

"Who took this?" I murmur to myself as I scroll down further and read.

Emma Huntington-Ross is one dark horse. Here we were thinking she was simply a boring, garden-obsessed American who fell out of limos. None of us wanted our Mr. Darcy to marry her. She was clumsy and humorous, not heroine material in the least. But secretly, unbeknownst to us, she's some kind of superhero, enacting her very own pond scene at "Pemberley" at the weekend. And what's more, her version saves lives, people. Perhaps we've misjudged her? Perhaps Mrs. Darcy is our kind of lady after all?

I click my phone off and stare into space. How did they even know about this? Sure, there were loads of people there for the garden party, but who? Someone must have snapped that shot and sold the story to a media outlet.

I flick my phone back on and do a search on my name. Sure enough, a bunch of articles pop up, all of them praising my heroism and generally gushing about how amazing I am.

Huh. How the tables have turned.

A message pops up on my phone.

I'm in the back. I've ordered you a coffee. Where are you?

It's Kennedy. I look at the time and realize I'm running late, so I dash down the street, arriving at the café soon after, puffed and sweaty from the exertion.

I plunk myself down at the table and thank her for the steaming hot coffee in front of me that I'm too hot to drink right now. The British summer is a weird thing. It's grey and mild most of the time, and then out of nowhere it's suddenly ninety degrees and everyone is out in the sun turning bright red and loving life.

"Shame Phoebe couldn't make it," Kennedy says as I take my seat. "Although she does have a pretty good excuse, what with having her baby and all."

"True," I reply, feigning happiness. I heard the news last night that Phoebe had given birth to a healthy, bouncing baby boy. Of course I was happy for her, but that old feeling hit me square between the eyes just as it had when Penny had given birth.

"Have you seen this?" I show her my screen, changing the subject.

Kennedy takes the phone from me and reads. "Girl, you are on fire. Did this actually happen? You saved a kid from *drowning?*"

I give a half smile. "I just happened to be in the right place at the right time, that's all. You'd have done the same, which is what I told Odette at the time, and I only had to give Antonella a couple of puffs of breath before she spluttered to."

"Wait. It was *Odette's* kid?" Kennedy asks with her eyes wide like saucers, and I nod. "Well, there's a twist of fate for you, what with you not exactly being Odette's biggest fan."

"Not now that I know Seb's been confiding in her about us not being able to have a family."

"He's doing what?" Kennedy questions, her eyes as round as soccer balls.

I lift my shoulders in a shrug. "Of all the people he could have chosen to talk to about our problems, he chose her."

Kennedy puts it succinctly. "That sucks."

"Yup. Meanwhile, I get to go up a dress size with all the hormones I pump into myself and feel like an abject failure at the end of it." I force out a laugh. I sound bitter and manic, even to my ears.

"Oh, honey. I'm so sorry. That's so hard for you."

"I make the eggs, we get a bunch of embryos, and then... nothing." I try to keep my voice from catching when I add, "There's something wrong with me."

"No, there's not. You want this real bad, so you've just gotta keep trying, girl. Don't let it get you down."

I scoff. "Oh, sure. That's easy. I'll just smile, and it'll all be okay."

"Don't be like that, Em," Kennedy says, and I slump in my seat.

"Sorry. I'm kinda snappy today. Well, most days."

"How are things with Seb?"

I think about our argument, how desperate I felt, how we agreed to keep trying despite my lack of optimism. Since then, we've been tiptoeing on eggshells around one another, and I'm too scared to raise the subject in case he tells me he's thought about it some more and has come to the conclusion that I *am* broken and he needs to be with someone who can give him a family. Someone with proven fertility who won't put him through what I'm putting him through.

Someone like Odette.

I swallow a rising lump in my throat. "Honestly? I'm not sure."

Kennedy looks aghast. "What does *that* mean?"

I shake my head, miserable. "I guess it means I'm not sure how much more we can take. It's been so hard."

"But you're not gonna break up, are you?" Kennedy asks. "I mean, he's Mr. Darcy to your Lizzie Bennet. You're together forever. He's your penguin."

"My penguin?"

"They mate for life. That's you guys. You're in it for the long haul."

I regard my friend through hooded eyes. Her concern and love for me is written across her face as she gawks back at me, waiting for me to reassure her.

I know Sebastian is the grand love of my life. I know it better than I know anything in this world. I've never loved anyone with the fierceness with which I love him. Being without him would be, well, it would be simply unimaginable.

I sit up taller and arrange my features into what I hope is

a reassuring smile. "We'll get through this," I say, and Kennedy agrees.

But you know what? This is big. Not being able to have kids is big. Especially when it's clear the fault lies with one person.

Couples break up over this kind of thing all the time.

Will we?

"Do you know what you need?" Kennedy's eyes sparkle as she begins to count things off on her fingers. "You need to go shopping for something expensive that you absolutely don't need. You need to drink a lot of champagne somewhere fabulous, and you need to laugh until your sides ache."

"And you're the person to furnish me with these, are you?"

"Oh, I so am, girl. And I think we need to start right now."

"But I've got a meeting," I protest weakly. My heart's not in it. Shopping for something expensive, drinking champagne, and laughing sound like the perfect escape to me right now.

"Cancel it. We're hitting the town, girl. You *need* this."

My mood lightens, and I smile at my friend. She's right. I do need this. "Okay, my rubber arm has been twisted."

"Atta girl. Where should we go? You know this town."

"I say we start with a glass of champagne at the Fifth Floor Bar at Harvey Nicholls," I begin, naming a glamorous bar at the top of a swanky Knightsbridge department store, "and then work our way through the store, trying on clothes and shoes and whatever we want."

Her grin grows across her face. "I have no idea who this Harvey Nicholls is, but that all sounds amazing to me."

We spend the rest of the day together, starting out with a glass of champagne at the bar, then modelling super expensive clothes for one another, and finally indulging in pedicures. As we lean back in the nail salon's massage chairs, we get the giggles and can't stop. It's perfect girl time, and man, does it feel good to focus on simply having fun. I forget about my failure to get pregnant. I forget about Odette. I forget about all of it. For those precious few hours, I live in the moment. And I love every last second of it.

$\mathcal{I}$ go through the motions of our next fertility cycle like it's happening to a character in a book, not me. I feel disconnected from the whole thing. Just as I have before, I do all the injections, take all the hormones, and when Sebastian tells me he's sorry but he can't be there for my embryo transfer procedure again, I accept it outright without question. After all, why would he want to be at the clinic with me when he knows as well as I do that this cycle will fail, just like all the others.

It's clearly gotten to be too much for him to take.

As I'm lying in the small room following the transfer, I wait for the embryos to decide my womb isn't the place they'd like to be for the next nine or so months. My phone pings with a message from Zara.

I'm here to pick you up.

That's weird. I didn't expect Zara. I tap out a reply.

You're at the clinic?

Yes! Come out when you're ready.

Sebastian must have told her I was here today and she felt bad for me. It's cold comfort to think Sebastian might have disengaged from the whole thing, but at least he sent my sister-in-law.

Ten minutes later, I walk out of the clinic doors and am met by a grinning Zara and her friend, Asher, her "back-up guy." Dressed in a gorgeous floral silk dress that ends halfway down her thigh and showing off her enviably long legs, she pulls me in for a hug. I give her a grateful squeeze and say hello to Asher, who's dressed in a well-cut navy suit that makes him look like Taylor Lautner in *Twilight*—only with his shirt on. Clearly.

"You look amazing, you two. Have you been somewhere nice?"

"Oh, this old thing?" Zara replies with a light laugh. "Now, come on. We've got a plan for you, and it doesn't involve a pair of jeans, sneakers, and Timothy Activewear top. No offence."

I glance down at my outfit as the three of us walk through the parking lot. "I didn't think the embryos needed to see me in my designer wear."

"I think you look good," Asher says.

"Stop flirting with my sister-in-law," Zara scolds.

"I'm not flirting," he protests and Zara rolls her eyes at me in response.

"Where are you guys taking me?" I ask.

Her car beeps next to us as she unlocks it. "It's a surprise. Now get in and stop asking questions."

I salute her. "Yes, ma'am," I say before I climb into the backseat, grateful at least that I don't have to catch the train home as I'd planned.

Zara tells us about her latest interior design customers as she whisks us through the streets of London.

"You can come decorate my place, Zee," Asher says as the scenery changes from suburban into the rolling English countryside.

"Oh, you can't afford me," she replies.

"Is that so?"

"Oh, yeah."

"I tell you what. I'll save all my money in my little piggy bank and then you can come decorate."

"I'll consider it. I'm very busy, you know."

He laughs. "You do that."

"Asher's place is total bachelor pad boring," she explains. "Chunky black leather sofas, an oversize TV, and surf boards. *Surf boards*. We live in land-locked London. There's no surfing here."

"I like to look at my boards. They remind me of my home state of California," he protests.

"It sounds to me like you've got your next client, Zara," I say as she turns the car into Martinston's long, tree-lined driveway.

She parks the car, and with a heavy heart, I climb out.

"This is the surprise? You're taking me home?" I ask with an eyebrow cocked in her direction.

She ignores my question and instead instructs, "Go upstairs and change into the outfit I've put on your bed."

"Why? What outfit?"

"Just do it, okay? And stop asking so many questions."

"Look, it's nice of you to want to take me out somewhere. But right now, all I want to do is curl up in my bed and have a nap. I'm fat and bloated and exhausted and full of hormones."

"Oh, there's no time for napping," she says as she bustles me in through the front door. "I'll be up to help you with your hair soon." She grabs ahold of a clump of my limp hair in her hand. "Because believe me, Em, you need the help right now. Asher can make you a coffee. That'll perk you up."

"I might not be able to afford Zara's exorbitant fees, but I can make coffee," he says.

She pats him on the arm. "Good Asher."

I've got so little fight left in me these days, I give in. "See you up in my room, I guess," I say to Zara.

I clamber up the main staircase, my legs feeling like they're dragging sandbags through a muddy field. I enter the bedroom and spy a dress I've not seen before laid out on the bed. It's long and cream with pale pink flowers and a frill at the hem. When I slip it on, it hangs from a halter neck down to my ankles, artfully disguising my hormone-rounded belly. When I peer in the mirror, I feel pretty and lighter somehow, despite my flat mood.

"Good, you're dressed," Zara says when she enters the room, holding a cup of steaming coffee. "Take this, drink it, and let me fix that hair."

Ten minutes later, Zara has worked her magic with a brush, pins, and enough hairspray to put a new hole in the ozone layer. My hair is in a French bun with soft tendrils falling around my face.

"I feel like a Jane Austen character," I say as I gaze at my reflection and see a polished, sophisticated version of myself gazing back.

"Well, you were Miss Bennet back on the reality show, so that's only fitting. Throw on these heels and let's go." She holds out the pair of pale pink high heeled sandals I wore to the Henley Regatta last year.

"You're very bossy. Did you know that?"

"Someone's got to be right now."

"No they don't." As I sit down to buckle them up, I ask her once more where we're going.

"It won't be a surprise if I tell you."

"But I don't want it to be a surprise."

She simply shrugs. "Too bad." She offers me her outstretched hand. "Come with me to the Batmobile."

"The Batmobile?"

"According to the media you're some kind of superhero, saving kids from ponds. I figured I'd run with the theme."

A short ride later Zara, Asher, and I arrive in a small, quaint village I've never been to.

"What is this place?" I ask.

"It's our destination, that's what it is," she replies elusively.

I shake my head as I laugh. "So helpful."

She parks the car, and we get out and walk across the village green surrounded by picturesque, thatched cottages and moss-covered stone fences. I half expect to see people playing cricket and sipping cups of tea with their crumpets on the lawn. Read: it's quaint English countryside in the best possible way.

We slow to a stop outside a small stone church with a large, leafy oak tree and a vine covered archway above a path that winds its way to the front door.

"You're taking me to church?" I ask, now completely baffled.

"Doesn't it remind you of some place?"

I regard the old stone structure. I shrug. "Another church?"

She giggles. "No, silly. The chapel you got married at in Houston. That's what I think it looks like, anyway."

I take another look and am struck by the similarity. Of course this church is several hundred years older than the one in Houston, and it's made of stone, not wood, but it has the same vibe. "Okay, sure. It looks like the chapel. But what are we doing here?"

"I thought you might like to have a quick look inside this place," she says without answering my question. "It's so pretty, and I thought it might do as a wedding venue for Tabitha who's getting married next year."

"She is?" Asher asks, and receives a sharp elbow to the ribs from Zara.

I look between the two of them. "You want me to check out a possible venue for your friend? A friend who, as far as I know, is very single?" I narrow my gaze. "Tell me what's going on here."

"Nothing," she replies in a way that's convincing no one. "Right, Asher?"

"Right."

I'm more than a little dubious. "Uh-huh."

"Come on. Let's go inside. I'm dying to see this place. Don't you love the ivy on the walls?"

I follow them up the path toward the ivy-covered church. At the door, she pushes it open and says, "Age before beauty," with a wicked grin, and I walk inside. It's much darker than the bright sun outside, and my eyes take a moment to adjust to the dim light.

I think I hear a muffled deep voice say, "She's here," coming from farther into the church.

Weird.

Zara rushes around me and grins as she pulls a thick, deep red velvet curtain back to expose rows of candles, leading between the pews to the altar. The light from outside shines through the colorful stained-glass window above, and as I take a couple of steps toward it, classical violin music begins to play.

"What is this all about?"

And then I see him. My husband, standing at the end of the aisle, dressed in a tuxedo, grinning at me like he's the cat with a closet full of pajamas.

"Emma, my love," he says, taking a step toward me. He stretches out his hand, and I instinctively move closer to him, my heart beating up in my throat.

"What's going on?" I ask him as my eyes dart around the room. There are people on either side of the aisle, all standing, watching us. The light from the candles catches one face, and I blink in disbelief.

"Mom?"

"Hi, honey," she replies with a beaming smile. "I'll come hug you after. You've got something you've got to do first."

"I do?"

"You do," Sebastian confirms.

I glance around the church, recognition dawning on me as my eyes land on each person's face. Kennedy, Geraldine, Johnathan, Phoebe, Penny—*Penny*?!—Jemima, Aunt Judy. All the people I love, all here in this very church with me.

My eyes land on the pleasant face of a man I don't know. I glance at the woman at his side, and I instantly recognize her. Henrietta. She's holding a beautiful toddler dressed in a deep red velvet dress in her arms, her contentedness obvious to anyone who cares to look at her. The little girl—Angela, her angel—is looking around the church in wonderment as her small fist grips onto Henrietta's top. I grin at them, and she beams back at me.

Sebastian grabs my attention. He takes my hand in his and leads me to the altar like the dulled, blinking, confused human I am right now.

"What is everyone doing here?" I ask him before I turn and say, "Hi, everyone."

They all reply with their greetings, and I turn back to look up into Sebastian's eyes.

"Emma," he begins, "I've got a few things I need to say."

"Okay." My eyes dart around the room once more before I lean closer to him and say, "But what's going on here? I mean, we're in a church and you're in a tux and I'm in this new dress, which is gorgeous and all, but I'm totally confused. It feels like a wedding."

He squeezes my hands in his palms. "Do you think I could say my piece?" he asks with a light laugh, and his laughter is echoed by the guests around the church. "I've got this whole thing planned out."

"Sure. Go for it."

He beams at me, and my heart flutters. "Emma Huntington-Ross, aka Brady Bunch, aka my darling wife. You and I have been on quite a journey. From falling in love on a reality TV show and keeping our romance a secret, to getting married two years ago today."

"It's our two-year anniversary?" I ask in astonishment.

How had I missed that?

"I'm glad you've been paying such close attention," Sebastian replies, and a fresh wave of laughter rolls around the church.

"We've had a lot going on," I explain, ashamed.

"We have. And it's not been easy for us. It's not been easy for *you*. That's why I wanted to bring you here today, to show you how much you mean to me. Brady, what you've been willingly going through with such an open, eager heart in the last year has been nothing short of incredible to me. Brady, *you* are incredible."

My bottom lip quivers as my face creases into a smile. "Thank you," I murmur, my eyes trained on him.

"Two years ago today in a church a lot like this in your home state of Texas, I pledged to always love you, for better or for worse. The past year has tested us in a way I never saw coming. But we are strong, you and I, and our love has prevailed. So today, in the presence of God and our family and friends, I renew my vows to you, and I pledge you my eternal love."

"Hear, hear!" Jemima calls out, and there's a ripple of agreement among the guests.

"Brady, what we have is so precious. I know it's been hard, and I know neither of us have been perfect, but you are it for me. End of story. I'm content with you, and only you."

My mouth drops open as my emotions churn. Is he saying...? Does he mean...?

"But I've not been able to give you what we both want," I protest in a small voice, barely above a whisper.

"You are more important to me than anything. The last thing I want is for you to put yourself through any more pain, because you are enough, Brady. You are enough."

As I gaze at his tear-filled eyes, my heart grows with such love for this man before me I feel like it could burst. "I haven't felt like I am enough," I say in a small voice, my hands trembling in his. "Not for the longest time."

"I know you haven't, and I've hated that you've felt that way." He wraps his big, strong arms around me, pulls me against him, and squeezes tight. I melt into our embrace, and all the horrible feelings I've been carrying around for so long, the feelings of inadequacy, of guilt, of not ever being enough for him, flow out of me in a rush.

"I love you so much," I say.

He fixes me with his soft, warm eyes. "I love you, too." He leans down and collects me in a kiss. It's strong and it's powerful and it shows me the depth of his love for me.

We pull apart to cheers from the congregation and calls for me to respond.

"I didn't know this thing was happening today," I protest with a laugh as I wipe my eyes. "Give a girl a moment or two to collect her thoughts."

"Aw, just tell him you love him, and we can all get to the party," Zara says.

"There's a party?" I ask Sebastian.

"I had to do something for all these people. They've come from all over the world to be here, you know."

I beam at him, happiness filling my every pore. "Thank you for this. It's beyond amazing. I know what I want to say."

"You do?"

I nod. "I want to say that on our wedding day, I stood before you and vowed to always love you, no matter what." Tears prick my eyes, but I press on. I've got things to say to this man before me, and I'm not letting some pesky tears get in the way. I clear my throat and continue. "I've never doubted my love for you, not even in my darkest moments, and I've had a few of those lately. But even though I've felt like I haven't been able to fulfill my end of the bargain, I've never doubted that you are everything to me. So, today, in front of God and our friends and family, I vow to love you forever, no matter what."

His face creases into a smile, and I wrap my arms around his neck, pull him in to me, and kiss him long and hard. Our friends and family cheer, and the violinist begins to play once more, and then we're swept out of the little church and into cars that take us back to Martinston, where Sebastian has had the ballroom decorated with hearts and balloons.

Holding his hand, I stand and gaze at the room with its row of chandeliers hanging from the ceiling and its walls lined with paintings of Huntington-Rosses going back generations. "You did all of this?"

"I had some help." He nods at Zara who waves back at me before she returns her attention to instructing the servers hired for tonight.

"And this dress?"

"She helped me with that, too."

I kiss him on the cheek. "Seb, you're amazing. Thank you."

"I'm serious about what I said. If you want to stop this whole fertility merry-go-round, then I'll fully support you."

"Can I take some time to think about it? I only had an embryo transfer today, after all. It might have worked."

"Of course." He kisses me on the forehead. "Take all the

time you need. Just please promise me you won't ever forget your worth again."

"I won't."

"I love you, Brady."

"Ditto, Mr. Darcy."

Sometime later, when I'm two orange juices and a few pregnancy-approved mini-appetizers (because you never know, even though I probably do) into the night, Odette waltzes into the room in a stunning, form-hugging sequin dress that shimmers in the ballroom light.

"What is *she* doing here?" I hiss to Kennedy as I watch her greet an ecstatic looking Geraldine with a double air kiss.

"It's your night, babe. Go ask her."

"I think I will."

I make my way across the room to where she's now chatting with Sebastian. Her hand is on his arm as she coos, "You are a true gentleman, Sebastian."

"Hi, Odette," I say brightly.

"Emma, darling." She places her hands lightly on my shoulders and air kisses me. "Wasn't this all such a wonderful surprise?"

"It was." I share a small smile with Sebastian.

"You've got the absolute best husband. You're a very lucky girl."

I suggest she comes to get a drink, and we move away from the others.

Before I get the chance to say anything to her, she says, "I wanted to say something to you."

I notice with a small sense of satisfaction that she looks nervous.

"This is hard for me to say, but I feel I need to say it after what you did for Antonella."

I brace myself for the worst.

"I've been so horribly jealous of you, Emma," she states blandly.

I splutter and my drink shoots out of my mouth. "You have?" I ask in genuine surprise as I dab at my mouth. This is the wildly beautiful and successful Odette with the famous ex, the gorgeous children she had so easily, the illustrious career, not to mention the large following of men. What do I have that she could possibly be jealous of?

"Are you kidding me?" she says. "You're beautiful and successful and you have this rock-solid marriage to a truly great guy. *Of course* I'm jealous of you."

"But...but you're *you*."

Her laughter tinkles like glass. "Looks can be deceiving," she replies mysteriously. "I'd love to have what you have with Seb."

"You've had it before, and I'm sure you'll have it again."

"Emma, my husband cheated on me with a string of women, almost from the day we got married."

"Oh, that's awful."

"He left me for a woman ten years younger than me who makes me feel like a dried-up old hag."

I'm glad I haven't taken another sip of my juice because I might have accidentally spat it back in her face. "You? A dried-up old hag? Have you not noticed the way men hang on your every word? How they vie for your attention? Odette, they adore you."

"Well, yes," she concedes, "but they don't *know* me."

It's a good point.

"They like the idea of me, I think. All I want is a good, kind man who'll love me for me."

She has a look of such earnestness in her eyes, I find myself softening. "There's someone out there for you, Odette. I know there is. You've just got to find him."

"I so hope you're right."

I roll thoughts around my head. After a moment of deliberation, I decide to come clean. After all, she's fessed up to me, it's only fair I return the favor. "You know what, Odette? You're not the only one suffering at the hands of the green-eyed monster. I was jealous of the way you seemed to have it all, especially with being the perfect mom of the perfect children."

"Perfect?" she guffaws. "Let me tell you something about me. I feel guilty all the time. Guilty that I divorced their dad even after what he put me through, guilty that I work full time, guilty that I don't feed them one hundred percent organic food and that sometimes I'm too exhausted to cook so we have cereal for dinner in front of The Wiggles."

"The Wiggles?"

"Oh, you'll learn about them when you become a mum and their songs will get stuck in your head and you'll want to shake that darn Wiggle awake so they'll stop singing about him being asleep." She pauses for breath and clamps her mouth shut when she takes in the look on my face. She scrunches up her nose. "Sorry. I said the wrong thing, didn't I? Just like I did when I joked about offering you my kids. I'm a terrible person."

"No, you're not. You just say what comes into your head, and that's just who you are. You're one hundred percent Odette."

A smile spreads across her face. "You're right." She hooks her arm through mine. "I've got an idea, Emma. How about we become friends. *Real* friends. If I say something that sits badly with you, tell me."

"And I'll remember that you're human, just like the rest of us."

She nods, and we share a smile. "Deal."

Sebastian's laugh from nearby catches my attention, and my heart squeezes in my chest as I watch him with Zara,

Asher, and Jemima.

"You know he's devoted to you, no matter what," Odette says.

Happiness radiates through me. I do know. He's my husband, the man I've chosen to spend my life with. The man who loves me, who knows that I am enough. "I do know that. And I'm devoted to him. No matter what."

EPILOGUE

The unrelenting sun beats down on my head, and I take another much-needed gulp of water from my bottle. Where once I managed it like a pro back in Texas, the intense humidity here has sapped me of energy. If it weren't for my pinging nerves keeping me on edge, I could quite happily flop down on a recliner by the pool and take a much-needed nap.

But there's no time for that today.

I peer through the metal gate into the courtyard, hoping for a glimpse of what lies beyond. I can hear muffled voices from behind a wall, but all I see is a plain concrete pad with an old car that's seen better days parked on an angle at one side.

"Are you ready?" Sebastian's features show the mixture of emotions we're both feeling. Excitement, trepidation, joy, fear. But mostly joy. We've waited so very long for this. I can barely believe it's happening.

I exhale and shake out my hands. "Let's do this."

His face morphs into a grin. He presses the button, and I hear a distant bell tone. Immediately, the door swings open, and an elderly woman who must reach up only as far as my armpit comes hobbling out on bowlegs.

"*Sawasdee kha*," she says with an incline of her head, her hands pressed together. "You are the Huntington-Rosses?"

"We are," Sebastian replies. "I'm Sebastian, and this is my wife, Emma."

"*Sawasdee kha*," I reply as we both place our palms together and give a brief bow in what the Thais call the *wai*.

"*Sawasdee khrap*," Sebastian says.

She pulls the heavy metal gate open with strength that doesn't fit her size. "I am Khun Lamai. Welcome. We are all ready for you. Close the gate behind you." She turns and walks into the building, and we share one final look before we follow her.

Entering the building, I'm hit by a combination of sights and sounds and smells. There's incense burning on a small shrine, with beautiful Thai silks adorning the walls along with a photo of the country's beloved former king. Someone is eating a garlic-filled meal on their haunches in one corner, and she looks up and smiles at us.

"*Sawasdee kha*," I say, pressing my palms together before Khun Lamai holds another door open for us and gestures for us to walk through. "You sit here. You wait," she instructs.

We take our seats on a wooden bench.

Sebastian reaches for my hand and gives it a squeeze. "This is it. This is our moment."

My heart swells in my chest. "I can barely believe it's finally happening."

"Well, you'd better believe it, because I think I can see her now." He nods at a door with a glass panel, allowing a view of the room beyond.

"You can?" My belly does a flip as I crane my neck to see. There's a young woman in jeans and flip-flops walking towards the door, holding a small black-headed child in her arms. The child is wearing a pretty floral dress that's clearly a size or two too big for her, with bare feet and cropped hair that makes her look like Dora the Explorer.

As the door is pulled open and the woman walks into the room, we rise slowly to our feet.

"That's our baby," I say to Sebastian, my throat tight. "That's our girl."

He wraps his arm around my waist as my emotions swirl.

It's been a long, long road to get us here. But you know what? *Everything* has led to this moment, just as Henrietta had said it would the day I saved Antonella from Martinston's pond. The year of failed attempts. The highs and lows of fertility treatment. The negative pregnancy tests that broke my heart each and every time.

We did a couple more IVF cycles after our vow renewal at that sweet church. With each negative pregnancy test I found myself thinking about what Henrietta had told me about creating a family through adoption. Even though I came to the decision in my own time, Sebastian was with me every step of the way. Agreeing to leave the hormones and scans and needles behind was so freeing. We celebrated with a trip to the most romantic city on Earth, Paris. And what's more, we planned it all *together*—no input from Odette required.

Soon after, we met with Henrietta and her husband, Phil, the man at her side in the church the day we renewed our vows, and their gorgeous Angela. After Henrietta shared the exciting news that her company wanted to stock Timothy Maternity in all of their United Kingdom and Ireland stores —which literally had me jumping for joy right there in her kitchen—they told us all about the ins and the outs of the adoption process. As we left their home, we both knew it was what we wanted before we even got to their gate.

It felt so right. So *us*.

We told our families, and everyone was so supportive. Well,

everyone with one rather obvious exception. Geraldine made her thoughts on the matter obvious from the get-go, carrying on about bloodlines and all that archaic crap she thinks is so important. We sat her down and told her in as polite a way as we could that this decision had nothing to do with her, that this was our decision, our little family, Sebastian's and mine. She's been doing her best impersonation of Grumpy Cat ever since.

With excitement and more than a dollop of trepidation, we embarked on a new journey, jumping through endless hoops in the adoption process. We did parenting courses, got assessed by social workers and psychologists, answered personal questions, and hoped and hoped.

Absolutely all of it has been worth it because we're here, in this small room on the wrong side of a city thousands of miles from our home.

This is our moment, the moment we finally, *finally* become parents.

The woman holding our child comes to a stop in front of us, trailed by Khun Lamai. "Meet your baby," she says in her heavily accented English.

With my heart beating like a bongo drum, I gaze down at her, my beautiful new daughter with her big brown eyes, her black hair, and her adorable chubby cheeks. Where once she was a single photo we treasured in the year of waiting it took to get us here, now she's a fully formed, three-dimensional person, gazing back at us with questioning, wary eyes.

"Hi there, little one," I say softly with a smile.

"*Sawasdee khrap,*" Sebastian says, and I remember we were told she wouldn't know much English, and even our pale complexions might be unsettling for her.

She looks from me to Sebastian and back again and then instantly buries her head in the woman's T-shirt.

"Darcy very shy," the woman explains.

I still myself. "What did you call her?"

"Her name is Darcy," she replies simply.

"But—" I dart a look at Sebastian as panic grips me. Has there been a mistake?

"We were told her name is Malee, not Darcy," Sebastian says.

"In Thailand, everyone is given two names at birth, a formal name and a nickname. Darcy is her nickname," Khun Lamai explains.

I flick my eyes to Sebastian's. "Her name is Darcy," I say, my voice quivering.

"She was meant to be our girl," he replies, and his eyes fill with unshed tears.

"Our destiny."

"Here. You take her." Khun Lamai isn't wasting any time. She plucks our almost-two-year-old from the woman's arms and hands her to me.

Instinctively, I cradle her in my arms, and for the first time in my life, I hold the warm, little body of my daughter. "*Sawasdee kha,* little darling," I coo. "I'm your mommy. Not that you know that yet, but you and me? We are going to be so tight."

Darcy gazes back at me, her beautiful dark brown eyes taking in this new, strange person smiling down at her and speaking unfamiliar words. Her lip begins to tremble, and then she bursts into tears, and my heart breaks for this scared little child in my arms.

"She'll get used to you. Give her time," Khun Lamai says with a knowing nod. Because she *does* know. She's been doing this for over two decades, matching would-be parents with their babies and sending those precious little beings out to their new families. I cannot begin to imagine the enormity of what she does, but as I stand here, cradling my own little being in my arms for the very first time, I am deeply grateful to her for everything.

Meanwhile, our little girl has found her lungs. I do my best to comfort her, but I know I'm the one freaking her out right now.

Khun Lamai offers advice, but after a while of high-decibel wails, I place little Darcy on the floor, and she toddles back to her caregiver who scoops her up and quiets her tears.

"We'll get the hang of it," Sebastian says to me.

"You're very new to her. She will love you soon enough," Khun Lamai tells us wisely.

I know she's right. Darcy is my baby. She doesn't know it yet, but I'm going to love her *so hard*. And she's going to love me right back, too.

Once we've gone through all the formalities and said our good-byes to Khun Lamai and the wonderful women who work at the orphanage, we reach our hotel where we scurry up the elevator to the sanctity of our suite.

We do what we can to settle her—from playing with finger puppets to blowing bubbles and finally outright bribery in the form of a lollipop—and eventually she runs out of energy to protest and falls asleep.

As she lies in the huge bed with her little mouth gaping, her breath coming in slow, light snores that melt my heart, she looks so peaceful and content. We stand together, side by side, our arms around one another, simply gazing at the sheer miracle of her.

"I've fallen in love with another Darcy," I murmur to Sebastian, my heart full.

He squeezes my shoulders, not taking his eyes from our little girl. "I already love her, too."

Darcy stirs, and I wonder whether she's waking up. But all she does is slide her little arms above her head as she lets out a deep exhalation and resumes her snoring.

"Can you believe she's ours, Seb? Really, truly ours?" I lift my eyes, and my gaze locks with Sebastian's.

"After everything we went through, here we are, parents to this beautiful little girl."

"Isn't it funny how it all worked out?"

His smile reaches deep into my soul, warming me with a deep sense of peace, love, and contentedness. "It's all been worth it, Brady. Every last minute of it."

"All of it?"

"Okay, maybe not all those needles."

"You mean the evidence of my drug addiction."

His soft laugh rumbles through me.

I shake my head as I think about Geraldine's reaction to our decision to adopt. "Do you think she'll accept her?"

"I think she'll look into those dark brown eyes and fall for her, just as we both have."

We both turn to gaze at our little child once more.

"I know it'll take some time for her to love us. I know we've got our work cut out for us. But this feels so right. Like she was always meant to be ours."

"She was," he states simply. "She's our new little Darcy." He presses a kiss to my forehead. "Do you know I love you for your bravery, your determination, and your heart?"

"Ditto." I beam up at him, my heart full to the brim with love—love for my husband and love for the little girl asleep on the bed.

After everything we've been through, all paths have led us to her, our new little Darcy. Henrietta's words on that fateful day at Martinston ring in my ear. She was right. There are so many ways to make a family. But the most important way, the only way that matters, is with love.

THE END

ACKNOWLEDGMENTS

This book is like no other book I've written before, but it's one I always knew I would write, from the moment I started my first novel. It's a book that has deep personal meaning for me, and writing it brought back so many memories—good and not so good.

When I married my wonderful husband twenty years ago, we embarked on our journey to have a family. Little did we know that journey would take a grand total of ten years, involve more heartache than we thought we could ever handle, and finally, *finally* bring us such joy. Our journey meandered through so many of the things Emma and Sebastian went through, from fertility treatment to the adoption process. Ultimately, it took us to a modest home in Thailand, where we met our child for the first time, a happy boy with the most beautiful smile we'd ever seen, so full of life and wonder and love. I often tell people we became parents to a toddler in a hotel room in Bangkok, and then I smile to myself as I watch their eyes widen in surprise. But that's exactly how it happened for us, and I wouldn't change a thing.

As with any book, I have a few people to thank. Jackie Rutherford has been my invaluable critique partner for many books now. She's not only an astute and talented writer, but she's an amazing friend as well. Thanks for everything, Jackie.

Wendi Baker is an amazing editor, always getting me to think deeper, keeping my writing on the right track, and keeping me honest. Wendi, I think we're a great team, and I look forward to our next project together.

Thanks to my wonderful brother, Pete McLennan who advised me on the world of banking in London, and to my sweet friend, Fiona, who kindly shared her own fertility journey with me. Thanks also to my proof reader, Kim McCann for her eye for detail and for Americanizing this Kiwi girl's language.

Once again, Sue Traynor designed this cover for me, as she has done with all the covers in this series. Sue takes my vision and brings it to life, right down to that little hand holding a rattle that melts my heart on this cover.

Last but certainly not least, thank you to you, my readers, for taking the time to read this book. I know it's a departure from my usual "boy meets girl "stories. I truly hope you enjoyed it—and perhaps it even touched your hearts.

ABOUT THE AUTHOR

Kate O'Keeffe is a *USA TODAY* bestselling and award-winning author who writes exactly what she loves to read: laugh-out-loud romantic comedies with swoon-worthy heroes and gorgeous feel-good happily ever afters. She lives and loves in beautiful Hawke's Bay, New Zealand with her family and two scruffy but loveable dogs.

When she's not penning her latest story, Kate can be found hiking up hills (slowly), traveling to different countries around the globe (back when we used to be able to do that), and eating chocolate. A lot of it.

Made in the USA
Monee, IL
29 June 2022